CROWN

30 WIFE-CHANGING LESSONS

nancy kaser

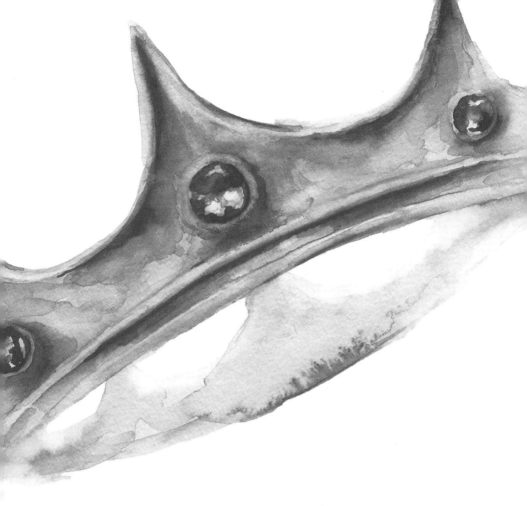

CROWN

30 WIFE-CHANGING LESSONS

nancy kaser

 ROMANS 8:28
BOOKS
AN IMPRINT OF REDEMPTION
PRESS

Published by Redemption Press, PO Box 427, Enumclaw, WA 98022

Toll-Free (844) 2REDEEM (273-3336)

Redemption Press is honored to present this title in partnership with the author. The views expressed or implied in this work are those of the author. Redemption Press provides our imprint seal representing design excellence, creative content, and high-quality production.

Dictionary citations listed are compilations of online dictionary sources, including Merriam-Webster Dictionary, the English Oxford Dictionary, and the Cambridge English Dictionary.

All quotes by Maureen Schaffer used with permission.
Quote by Sher Pai used with permission.

All quotes of women listed with first names only are used with permission or have been changed.

Unless otherwise noted, all Scripture quotations are taken from the ESV® Bible (The Holy Bible, English Standard Version®), copyright © 2001 by Crossway, a publishing ministry of Good News Publishers. Used by permission. All rights reserved.

Scripture quotations marked NIV are from THE HOLY BIBLE, NEW INTERNATIONAL VERSION®, NIV® Copyright © 1973, 1978, 1984, 2011 by Biblica, Inc.® Used by permission. All rights reserved worldwide.

Scripture quotations marked NKJV are from the New King James Version®. Copyright © 1982 by Thomas Nelson. Used by permission. All rights reserved.

Scripture quotations marked NASB are from the NEW AMERICAN STANDARD BIBLE®, Copyright © 1960, 1962, 1963, 1968, 1971, 1972, 1973, 1975, 1977, 1995 by The Lockman Foundation. Used by permission.

Scripture quotations marked ISV are taken from the The Holy Bible: International Standard Version. Release 2.0, Build 2015.02.09. Copyright © 1995-2014 by ISV Foundation. ALL RIGHTS RESERVED INTERNATIONALLY. Used by permission of Davidson Press, LLC.

Scripture quotations marked AMP are taken from the Amplified Bible, Copyright © 1954, 1958, 1962, 1964, 1965, 1987 by The Lockman Foundation. Used by permission.

Pronouns for God are capitalized in the ESV verses listed.

All artwork by Jessica Chapman.

ISBN: 978-1-64645-000-8 (Paperback)
      978-1-64645-001-5 (ePub)
      978-1-64645-002-2 (Mobi)

Library of Congress Catalog Card Number: 2019907767

For all His daughters and for mine

TABLE OF CONTENTS

INTRODUCTION

Whether you just returned from your honeymoon or recently celebrated your fiftieth wedding anniversary, you have never been in *this* season of marriage before. Your family dynamics, finances, health, emotional state, location, ministry, employment status—all the factors that equal your life—are in a perpetual state of transition. As a married woman, you are constantly *wife-changing.*

The marriage you are in today is not the one you will be in six years from now or even six months from now. You will be married to the same man under the same covenant you made on your wedding day, but he won't *be* exactly the same man, and you won't be the same wife either. You are both growing and changing, improving and regressing.

Brent and Nancy Kaser are not quite the same couple we were on our wedding day. Lovely holidays and vacations, joyous celebrations, and new babies and grandbabies have occurred between small and great trials, disasters, crises, and deaths of family and friends. We have been blessed with periods of perfect health, as well as medical emergencies, critical illnesses, and chronic pain. Great personal victories and deep failures, financial blessings and economic trials, ministry successes and failures, career advances and job changes—they have added up to the life we have built together.

Through it all, God's Word has been an unfailing, all-sufficient guide. But it took me a long time to learn this. I was once a discouraged, bitter, defeated wife married to a selfish, prideful man. My first several years as a wife were spent in tears, self-pity, and self-righteousness. But God did something miraculous and beautiful through His Word and by His Spirit, and it changed both of us. I believe He can do the same in any marriage—especially yours.

The Sections Explained

This book is designed as a six-week Bible study that can be completed alone or in a group setting. It is structured so that you can read one day's worth of material, five days a week, for six weeks.

CROWN

Crown combines Bible teaching, humorous and humbling tales of my own marriage journey, and dozens of personal stories from real wives I have counseled over the years. Some of the names have been changed, but the testimonies are true and are written as practical examples for you to relate to and to learn from. In addition, I have quoted writers and speakers who have explained ideas more articulately than I can.

As a pastor's wife, I am often invited into the lives of women who are either struggling in their marriages or just wanting all of God's blessings in their families. Though these church ladies may be well versed in the Scriptures, many are unaware of how to practically transfer biblical principles and doctrines of being a godly wife into their everyday lives and marriages.

In this practical discipleship guide, the aim is to offer this hope to every Christian woman: in every season, a glorious and God-honoring marriage—to the same man she is married to right now—is absolutely possible through obedience to God's Word.

Build Like a Wise Woman

Proverbs 14:1 says, "A wise woman builds her house, but the foolish woman tears her house down with her own hands." As wives, we have tremendous power to build up our families or tear them down. Of course, we all want to say we are wise women building our houses, but is that really the case? Good marriages are built upon something sturdier than romance and attraction and are fortified by more than shared interests and hobbies. The following six chapters in this book examine the structural essentials of being a godly wife, and you will be challenged to examine and identify what is strong in your marriage and where you may need to do some repairing or fortifying:

YIELD–Laying a foundation built on the Word of God
HELP–Understanding and occupying your role as the helper in your marriage
SMILE–Choosing to live in joy, forgiveness, and friendship with your husband
ORDER–Managing your life according to God's priorities for a wife
GIFT–Pursuing and guarding God's plan for sexuality in your marriage
INCREASE–Being married with your eyes fixed on your heavenly Groom

Jesus said in Matthew 7:24–27:

> Everyone then who hears these words of Mine and does them will be like a wise man who built his house on the rock. And the rain fell, and the floods came, and the winds blew and beat on that house, but it did not fall, because it had been founded on the rock. And everyone who hears these words of Mine and does not do them will be like a foolish man who built his house on the sand. And the rain fell, and the floods came, and the winds blew and beat against that house, and it fell, and great was the fall of it.

A life built upon the unchanging Word of God is on a solid foundation. The Word of God is powerful, alive, and active. The truths and meaning of the Scriptures *never change*, but people and seasons of life do change. Life-changing seasons call for wife-changing scriptural knowledge.

Read with Expectation

Like sunscreen needs to be reapplied to prevent overexposure and damage from the sun, the unchanging Word of God needs to be reapplied again and again as our marriages are exposed to new seasons. The same verse you read as a young bride may minister to you quite differently on your fifth, twenty-fifth, or fiftieth anniversary. I invite you to read these Scriptures and principles with fresh, expectant eyes, asking the Lord how He wants you to apply the truth in this season of your marriage.

Take Selfies

You know the little button on your phone camera that flips the image around so you can see yourself? I urge you to set your reading of this book on Selfie Mode. Self-examination is critical to becoming an excellent wife.

We are often very aware of what our husbands need to change, but we can often put a flattering filter over our own shortcomings and flaws. If we do this, we will miss the wife-changing work of genuine transformation God wants to do in us.

In Luke, Jesus told a parable about two men who stood before God in prayer, and only one was granted his request:

> Two men went up into the temple to pray, one a Pharisee and the other a tax collector. The Pharisee, standing by himself, prayed thus: "God, I thank you that I am not like other men, extortioners, unjust, adulterers, or even like this tax collector. I fast twice a week; I give tithes of all that I get." But the tax collector, standing far off, would not even lift up his eyes to heaven, but beat his breast, saying, "God, be merciful to me, a sinner!" I tell you, this man went down to his house justified, rather than the other. For everyone who exalts himself will be humbled, but the one who humbles himself will be exalted. (Luke 18:10–14)

Be like the tax collector: vulnerable and willing to admit your own sin.

In the New Testament, when we sometimes read the phrase "He who has ears to hear, let him hear," Jesus didn't assume that all who heard His words would receive them. Only those who had "ears to hear" would accept the message and heed the words. Decide right now to have ears to hear what Jesus is speaking to you and determine to respond with a willingness to obey Him. Within the next thirty days, *plan* to do some wife-changing. For the Lord declares through Paul that He does "not desire . . . that you should be ignorant . . . lest you should be wise in your own opinion" (Rom. 11:25). Maureen Schaffer, my dear friend and women's Bible-study teacher said:

> When we are people who know we need instruction, we will not be as critical or high-minded. No matter how much we know of any subject, it pales in comparison to the enormity of understanding available in that area. Being wise in our own opinion is often rooted in a misguided

confidence that we know all we can know about a situation or person. Sometimes arrogance is a symptom of ignorance.

Crown

Proverbs 12:4 says that "an excellent wife is the crown of her husband," and as I struggled with how to title this book, I worried you wouldn't want to read my book simply because of what the name implies. I pictured your spirit scoffing at the whole idea of being a crown to your husband. Many women may say (although not out loud in Christian circles), "I don't want to be the crown—I want to be the one wearing it!" Because we *don't* like what being a crown implies, I wrote **Crown**.

Real Crowns Are Rare

Consider how many people you have seen in your life legitimately wearing a crown. You can likely only think of a handful of foreign royals or beauty queens. Real crown wearers are rare, and so are excellent wives. Proverbs 31:10 declares, "An excellent wife who can find? She is far more precious than jewels." An excellent wife is a precious, hard-to-find treasure, and a man who has a wife like this is as honored as a king wearing a crown.

The word *crown* is both a noun and a verb:

> crown—*noun*. A circular headdress worn as a symbol of authority or for one to whom respect or esteem is due by reason of authority or rank.
> *The king wore a gold crown on his head.*
> crown—*verb*. To bestow honor or to give a reward; to make complete by adding success.
> *They will crown the winner with rewards and honor.*

As your husband's wife, your goal is to *be* a crown to your husband. But *crowning* is also something you *do*; you can add to his success by bestowing respect and honor on him. *Crown* is designed to be an instruction manual for those who want to practically learn how to be the excellent wives they are created to be.

"What do you want me to do for you?"

In three of the gospels, we read the account of a blind man who cried out to Jesus, and Jesus turned to the man and said to him, "What do you want Me to do for you?" The blind man said, "Lord, let me recover my sight." So Jesus gave the man exactly what he asked for (Luke 18:35–43).

Quite often, we cry out to the Lord, but we don't ask Him to do anything specific. Jesus asked this man for a direct request, and the man requested something impossible—and miraculously Jesus gave him what he asked for!

So, friend, let me ask you, in regard to your marriage, what specifically do you want Jesus to do for you? Are there some impossible, miraculous things you want to see happen in your marriage? Ask Him! What about ordinary, simple things? If He can do the impossible and miraculous, then how much more should you ask Him for the simple and ordinary?

If you could ask Jesus for three specific things in your marriage, what would they be?

11-2022

1. _honesty + devotion_

2. _to know goals + "bucket list"_

3. _Itimacy_

May you expect the same God who opened blind eyes to give you the desires of your heart.

YIELD

LESSON 1

First Things First

Before we devote ourselves to the focus of being an excellent wife, there is one essential factor we must address. Second Corinthians 13:5 says to "examine yourselves, to see whether you are in the faith." This means each of us should test ourselves to make absolutely certain we are in Christ. A woman who attends church, knows a lot about the Bible, or raises her hand during a salvation invitation isn't automatically a real Jesus follower. Without the foundation of genuine salvation, the instructions in this book will not be applicable, as only a woman who is truly born again will be able to live them out. Read this testimony from Deanna:

> I'd been in church my whole life. I was raised in Sunday school and knew all the Bible stories. Outwardly, I was a good girl. I followed the rules, sang the songs, and did the memory verses. But I didn't follow Jesus inwardly. Christianity was my culture, but Jesus wasn't actually my Savior. It wasn't until I was already married with my own tribe of church kids that I sincerely admitted I needed a Savior. After twenty-eight years in church, I cried out to God with a genuine awareness of my own sin and my own need for His forgiveness in my life. After a lifetime in church, I had to come to Jesus like every sinner before me.

Charles Spurgeon said:

> We should be very diligent to take heed that we really are "born again," for there are many who fancy they are, who are not. Be assured that the name of a Christian is not the nature of a Christian; and that being born in a Christian land, and being recognized as professing the Christian religion is of no avail whatever, unless there be something more added to it—the being "born again" by the power of the Holy Spirit.[1]

Lies and False Security

There is an attractive lie being spread from the pulpits of America today that is being used in Sunday schools and in prayer meetings and broadcasted on much of Christian radio and TV. It's the false teaching that proclaims, "You prayed the sinner's prayer; therefore, you are saved."

While it is often the catalyst to a true conversion, the "sinner's prayer," where a person "asks Jesus into his heart," has also been a very effective tool of Satan. It can be a false doctrine that promises, "All you have to do is say the magic words, and you get a free ticket to heaven!" Tragically, the sinner's prayer has given many people an unfounded assurance of eternal security.

I once counseled a woman whose thirty-year-old brother had been in a terrible accident and was on life support. She was sharing how he had been in trouble with the law, had been involved in several illicit sexual relationships, and had been using and dealing drugs. He hadn't been to church since he was in junior high school and had scoffed at her Christianity for years. Through tears, the woman said, "But I know he's saved because he prayed the sinner's prayer with me when he was eleven." There was nothing in this man's adult life that would lead anyone to the conclusion he was saved, and yet his sister clung to the hope that the words he had said as a child secured him for eternity.

I am not against encouraging people to pray for salvation, nor am I opposed to altar calls, hand raising, or other forms of answering an invitation to come to Christ. But what I *am* totally against is the notion that just because people "pray the magic prayer," they have a free pass to heaven, along with God's favor until they get there.

Jesus warned us there would be many people who would do things, even miraculous things, in His name, but that wouldn't mean they were saved:

> On that day many will say to me, "Lord, Lord, did we not prophesy in Your name, and cast out demons in Your name, and do many mighty works in Your name?" And then will I declare to them, "I never knew you; depart from Me, you workers of lawlessness." (Matt. 7:22–23)

There will be many souls in hell who will cry out to Jesus, "But we prayed the sinner's prayer in Your name!" And Jesus will say to them, "Depart from Me. I never knew you."

What Is the Gospel?

Sadly, many faithful church attendees can't answer this question clearly, but it is simply unacceptable for those who claim to know Christ not to know how to answer this question.

If a woman told you she had five minutes until she would be dead and wanted you to share the gospel with her so that she could be sure she was saved, what would you tell her? Could you share with that dying woman the essential truths for her soul to be saved?

Just to be sure, I want to provide you with a very clear explanation of the gospel. Here is an acronym for GOSPEL to help you remember the key aspects of the good news and to make sure you have claimed them for yourself.

G–God

- There is only one God, Who created all things. (1 Cor. 8:6)
- God is perfectly good, perfectly holy, and perfectly loving. (1 John 4)

O–Our Sin

- God has given us His Word (the Bible), which provides us clear direction on how to live. When we disobey His Word, it is sin. (Eph. 5:1–21)
- Sin separates us from God because He is holy and must punish sin. (Isa. 59:2)
- Every single person on earth has sinned, and has therefore offended God. (Rom. 3:23)
- The Bible says hell is a place of eternal torment where unsaved sinners will spend eternity apart from God. (2 Thess. 1:9)

S–Savior/Son

- Jesus, God in the flesh, came to earth as a man. (Phil. 2:5–8)
- He demonstrated His great love for mankind in coming to the earth and living a perfect, holy, and sinless life. (2 Pet. 2:22)
- He performed many miracles to prove He was God. (John 21:25)

P–Paid for by Jesus on the Cross

- The greatest act of love ever performed was when Jesus was brutally beaten and nailed to a cross for sins He did not commit. (Rom. 5:8)
- He died on the cross to pay for the sins of every person on earth. (2 Cor. 5:15)
- He did this willingly, to make a way for us to be restored to Him. (John 10:18)

E–Empty Tomb

- Jesus proved that He is God by rising from the dead three days after He died on the cross. (Rom. 1:4)
- He was seen alive many times, by over five hundred people after the resurrection. (1 Cor. 15:6)

CROWN

L–Life Eternal

> • By putting our faith in Jesus and following Him, we can be forgiven for our sin. (Rom. 10:9–10)
> • Only those who turn from their sin and believe in Jesus will go to heaven when they die and live with God for eternity. (Acts 4:12; 20:21)

Essentially, an understanding of who God is, what Jesus did, and what man must do are the key components of salvation. If you are a professing follower of Jesus, you should be able to share the gospel message clearly and confidently.

The Test of a True Conversion

Salvation is an absolutely free gift, but being a Christian is not just about knowing the right information and agreeing with it intellectually.

I have known women who have come to our church and attended our women's Bible study. Who posted things on social media about being Christians and said they are followers of Jesus, but they also posted raunchy jokes and photos of themselves scantily dressed, and commented about being married to "the idiot." I have sat next to women in church who lifted their hands in worship, but later told me they have their tarot cards read in order to make decisions about their lives. There is a contradiction between what these women said they believed and how they actually lived. I have also known wonderfully moral women who had a vast knowledge of the Bible, did charitable deeds, used Christian lingo, and outwardly "looked" like Christians, and yet they did not sincerely follow Jesus.

There are surely women sitting in our churches who listen to the messages every week and piously perform ministry tasks, but are not yet truly converted. Remember, Judas Iscariot played the part of a disciple so well, and no one suspected he would be the one to betray Jesus. It is quite possible to be a moral person and still go to hell.

Genuine Salvation = Changed Life

Make no mistake—we do not do good works to earn our own salvation; however, if we are saved, then we will demonstrate our salvation by our good works. James declared, "Faith without works is dead" (James 2:20). A dead faith—one void of obedience and service to Christ—is not a faith that reflects the life of a disciple.

Being born again is not merely a name change, but a nature change. If we are truly born again, we will no longer be the women we used to be. Some changes are immediate, while others take time to develop, but we can't be born again and remain the same. Charles Spurgeon said, "The grace that does not change my life will not save my soul."[2]

True conversion produces true change. Jesus doesn't save us and then leave us where we are. No. He transforms us and conforms us into His image. If the Holy Spirit has taken up residence in a heart, the fruit of the Spirit will be evident in that person's life.

If I told you I believed there was a bomb in the room that would detonate in three minutes, you would expect me to bolt for the door. But if I told you there was a bomb in the room and then sat sipping a latte and chatting with my friends, you would decide I really didn't believe there was a bomb. My words weren't backed up by my actions; therefore, my words were meaningless.

And so it is with Christianity. Only God knows what is in a person's heart, but the following Scriptures give us clear standards that we can use to measure a profession of faith:

> And by this we know that we have come to know Him, if we keep His commandments. Whoever says "I know Him" but does not keep His commandments is a liar, and the truth is not in Him. (1 John 2:3–4)

> Everyone who believes that Jesus is the Christ has been born of God, and everyone who loves the Father loves whoever has been born of Him. By this we know that we love the children of God, when we love God and obey His commandments. For this is the love of God, that we keep His commandments. And His commandments are not burdensome. (1 John 5:1–3)

> For you may be sure of this, that everyone who is sexually immoral or impure, or who is covetous (that is, an idolater), has no inheritance in the kingdom of Christ and God. Let no one deceive you with empty words, for because of these things the wrath of God comes upon the sons of disobedience. Therefore do not become partners with them; for at one time you were darkness, but now you are light in the Lord. Walk as children of light (for the fruit of light is found in all that is good and right and true), and try to discern what is pleasing to the Lord. Take no part in the unfruitful works of darkness, but instead expose them. For it is shameful even to speak of the things that they do in secret. (Eph. 5:5–12)

True salvation will be evidenced by a life that reflects a sincere love for Jesus. Jesus Himself said, "If you love Me, you will obey My commands" (John 14:15).

CROWN

Real Christians will be easy to spot by their obedience to Jesus. There will be an ever-increasing pursuit of holiness and a deepening love for the Savior, as well as a decreasing desire for the pleasures of this world and an increasing desire for the things of God. These are the standard by-products of salvation. Before we can be the excellent wives we are created to be, we must first examine ourselves to be certain we are in the faith.

LESSON 1 WIFE-CHANGING QUESTIONS

1. What is the gospel? How would you explain it to someone else? Write it out here.

Who God is: Creator of all things Good Perfect Holy.

Who Jesus is: God in flesh - Sinless + holy

What Jesus did: Paid the Price by death on the cross.

What must man do: repent, turn + obey.

2. Are you certain you are saved? How do you know?

Yes, heart change, life change, growing each day in obedience.

3. Since professing to know Jesus as your Savior, how have you changed?

Outward man - diminishing - language thoughts, actions, behavior and focus each day

4. Would others easily identify you as a Christian, or would they be surprised if you identified yourself as one?

I believe there would be NO surprize.

If you examine yourself and realize you may not be saved, take courage! You're still breathing! You can still repent of your sin and surrender yourself to Jesus right now.

Salvation is available to you through repentance and faith. In your own heart (or out loud if you prefer), confess to God you are a sinner in need of salvation, and acknowledge that Jesus is the only way that you can be saved. Ask Jesus to be the Lord of your life, and then begin walking in obedience to Him.

LESSON 2

Marriages are fixed vertically before they are ever fixed horizontally.
—Paul David Tripp

Yield

Like the word "crown," the word "yield" is both a noun and a verb that can offer us wife-changing insights.

> yield—*verb*. To surrender or give in; to give up control.
> *The sign warns us to yield to the oncoming traffic.*
> yield—*noun*. An amount produced or a total harvest; a profit.
> *The yield of oranges this spring was the best in ten years.*

If you approach a yield sign at an intersection, you understand to let the other drivers go before you. As a Christian, yielding in verb form means letting go of our own ideas of how things should be, and, instead, choosing to embrace what God says is best for us. When we come to Him for salvation, we acknowledge our need, and we give way to His authority in our lives. But salvation is just the beginning of what should be a lifelong yielding.

The noun form of *yield* refers to "an amount produced or a total harvest." When you bake cookies, the recipe will tell you that it will yield a certain amount. The farmer will speak of the annual yield of his crops. Spiritually speaking, surrendering our own ways for God's ways will result in a yield of blessings in our marriages and in our overall lives.

The Word Is Truth

We cannot know everything God says about marriage if we study only the handful of Scriptures that directly address marriage. Instead, we must study the entire Bible.

> To the degree that every portion of the Bible tells us things about God, about ourselves, about life in this present world, and about the nature of the human struggle and the divine solution, to that degree every passage in the Bible is a marriage passage. Every passage imparts to us insight that is vital for a proper understanding of the passages that directly address marriage, and every passage tells us what we should expect as we deal with the comprehensive relationship of marriage.[3] —Paul David Tripp

I did not realize this!

Many things in the Scriptures are absolutely contrary to what the world says about being a wife. There are things your mother may disagree with, principles some girlfriends will scoff at, and ideas your own heart may want to rebel against. It is imperative that you believe the Bible is totally true and the counsel given in it is the final authority in your marriage. Otherwise, you are building your marriage on a shaky foundation of your own preferences.

As a woman seeking God's will for her marriage and for all the other areas of her life, you are called to yield to His Word above all other opinions. The rest of what will be discussed in these pages is built upon the understanding that the Scriptures are your ultimate authority.

> All Scripture is breathed out by God and profitable for teaching, for reproof, for correction, and for training in righteousness, that the man of God may be complete, equipped for every good work. (2 Tim. 3:16–17)

All Scripture is inspired by God. Every. Single. Word. Nothing can be discarded, discredited, or dismissed. The Bible is the authority for all of life, and obedience to the Scriptures is not optional for a woman who truly wants to walk with Christ.

> The Bible is God's ultimate measuring instrument. It is meant to function in each of our lives as a spiritual tape measure. We can place ourselves and our marriages next to it and see if we measure up to God's standard. God's Word is one of His sweetest gifts of grace, and open eyes to see it clearly and an open heart to receive it willingly are sure signs of God's grace.[4]
> —Paul David Tripp

The Bible uniquely transcends culture and time. The verses that applied to Eve in the Garden of Eden apply to modern women all over the globe, regardless of their geography, social status, culture, or education. Every one of us is held accountable to obey it. Yielding to the Word of God is proof of a genuine faith in Christ. If you call yourself a Christian—a believer in and a follower of Christ—but you don't obey His Word, then you need to examine whether you are truly a Christian.

> And by this we know that we have come to know Him, if we keep His commandments. Whoever says "I know Him" but does not keep His commandments is a liar, and the truth is not in him. (1 John 2:3–4)

Perhaps you have never fully put your faith in His Word, and this is something you are willing to test. Be honest before the Lord. A sincere desire to trust Him and obey Him, even if your desire is mixed with fear of being disappointed, is a great delight to God because He is able to work with a willing heart.

A man once said to Jesus, "Lord, I believe, help my unbelief!" (Mark 9:24). This is a sincere, honest prayer that God loves to answer. I am often conflicted between what I believe in my head and what my feelings tell me. So I cry out, "Lord, I believe; help my unbelief!" He has never failed to answer this prayer. God knows just what help to send my way to transform my "unbelief" into "all belief."

Please let me be perfectly clear—I am in no way saying you must agree with the words of Nancy Kaser. That would be ridiculous. It's the Word of God you must believe and agree with, not my words. Actually, I ask that every example given, every principle addressed, and every prescription written be examined in light of the Word of God. Don't take my word for it. It is the Word of God that is the supreme Truth.

Shielding or Yielding?

You have two options when it comes to the Word of God and His calling on your life: *you can shield yourself from it* or *yield yourself to it.*

Sometimes we end up shielding ourselves from fully trusting in the claims of the Bible. We have it in the back of our minds, *What if the Bible is not true? What if I bank my whole life on it, and then it all falls apart? I'd better have a backup plan to protect myself just in case.* It feels risky to be completely abandoned in matters of faith.

However, if you shield yourself or give yourself to your faith only halfheartedly, you will have all kinds of excuses as to why you can't possibly obey God. You will convince yourself that His expectations are antiquated, too restrictive, or not applicable to your situation. *Shield* is a verb meaning *to block out or repel.* You will block yourself from having to obey, but you will also repel His blessings and help. *Shield* is also a noun. You can actually be the shield used to block God out of your family and your own life. Lay down your shield, Friend. Yield yourself to Him.

> I knew what the Bible said about how my family was supposed to work, but I thought I was smarter and more spiritual than my husband. I was sure that if I let him make decisions, we would suffer. We went to church and told our kids to obey God, but there was always conflict in our house. My husband and I fought over everything we ever tried to discuss, so we eventually did all we could to not talk to each other.
>
> God seriously got my attention one day when my son told his youth pastor that he didn't really live in a Christian home because we only listened to the Bible at church, but it wasn't something we followed at home. All the church attendance in the world couldn't make up for the fact that I was disobedient to God at home where it really mattered. I spent days crying over my sin. I started meeting with a group of godly women from my church who

encouraged me to be the best wife and mother I could be. I had to choose to surrender my pride and my fear and trust God.

I can honestly say the last two years of our marriage have been so beautiful. I have gotten back so much more than what I expected. God has blessed my efforts with way more love and peace in our home than I ever thought we would have. My son has seen the change too; everyone has! My full surrender to the Lord changed everything. —Renee

Yielding for a Yield

Yield is a farming term. When a farmer puts a seed in the ground, he doesn't just get one seed back. He doesn't get ten seeds back. When a farmer puts a seed in the ground, no matter what type of seed it is, he plants with an expectation of a yield that far surpasses what he has sown. A simple apple seed will eventually produce an entire tree of apples every season for decades. Each apple contains seeds that can be planted to bear even more fruit on more trees.

One little seed can eventually produce an entire orchard and bring in an enormous annual yield.

As with farming, each small seed yield has the potential to bear an enormous yield of fruit, both in your earthly relationships and in your relationship with God. When you choose to surrender to God, you will likewise produce a *yield*—an abundant harvest of joy, peace, and delight in your home, and an intimacy with God that cannot be measured.

Choosing to lay aside your own will isn't easy. Fear and doubt can rise in your heart and cause you to want to dig in your heels and demand your own way. But surrender will bring about an abundant reward.

> Those who sow in tears shall reap with shouts of joy! He who goes out weeping, bearing the seed for sowing, shall come home with shouts of joy, bringing his sheaves with him. (Ps. 126:5–6)

There is a direct relationship between the seeds you sow and the harvest you yield. The fruit growing in your marriage next year will be a direct result of the seeds you plant today.

The seeds of kindness and forgiveness will yield a harvest of blessings if you are willing to keep planting, watering, cultivating, weeding, and tending them. Likewise, seeds of anger, bitterness, and unforgiveness will yield a harvest of anguish and frustration, without you doing anything but tending to yourself.

Fruit comes as a tree matures—it never comes instantaneously. Fruit-bearing requires constant nurturing and care, and the sweetness of the fruit is often reflective of the months of labor it took before the first bud was evident on the tree.

Do not be deceived: God is not mocked. For whatever one sows, that will he also reap. For the one who sows to his own flesh will from the flesh reap corruption. But the one who sows to the Spirit will from the Spirit reap eternal life. And let us not grow weary of doing good, for in due season we will reap if we do not give up. (Gal. 6:7–9)

Your life is going to produce a yield no matter what. Either you are sowing seeds of obedience to God or you are sowing seeds of rebellion. Each seed you plant will produce fruit in your life. Your own obedience to God will be the determining factor. You reap what you sow.

LESSON 2 WIFE-CHANGING QUESTIONS

1. Do you truly believe God's Word is the final authority on every issue in your life?

   I'm beginning to believe it!

2. Are there things you think God is wrong about? Is there any area where you think you have a better understanding than He does? Be honest!

   No, in theory but my actions speak differently at times

3. Is there any area in your marriage (or the rest of your life) where you are not yielded to the Lord? What do you need to do in order to yield?

   Lord, show me! TBD.

4. Have you ever prayed, "Lord, I believe; help my unbelief"? How did God answer this prayer? Is there a need to pray this prayer now?

Yes and yes.

5. Are you tempted to shield yourself from God or from certain things you know are in His Word?

Yes.

6. Will you yield to God's authority in regard to your marriage? Will you surrender your own plans and give Him the "right of way" in your life?

YES and YES

7. Write a prayer of yielding to God.

Lord God, I lift my hands, give you my heart & life to do as You have planned. You have begun this "renewing" of my mind. I yield to Your commands & obey. Amen.

LESSON 3

The next three lessons focus on foundational Scriptures for your marriage that will be referred back to several times. The better you understand these Scriptures, the stronger your foundation will be.

In the Beginning

God is the One who thought of marriage in the first place, so let's visit the biblical account of the first marriage and how God set the whole thing up in Genesis 2:

> The Lord God took the man and put him in the garden of Eden to work it and keep it. And the Lord God commanded the man, saying, "You may surely eat of every tree of the garden, but of the tree of the knowledge of good and evil you shall not eat, for in the day that you eat of it you shall surely die. (Gen. 2:15–17)

There are several things we learn from this passage. First, Adam was alone when he received his occupation as a gardener. Adam did not have to first consult and agree with Eve on what he would do with his life because his wife hadn't been created when he received his instructions. After receiving his job description, Adam was given the rules of the garden; namely, he could not eat from the tree of the knowledge of good and evil. He was warned that if he ate of the fruit of this tree, he would surely die.

After Adam was given his occupation and restrictions, *it was God who recognized that Adam needed help*:

> Then the Lord God said, "It is not good that the man should be alone; I will make him a helper fit for him." (Gen. 2:18)

After everything else God created, He declared, "It is good." But upon seeing Adam's solitary state, God declared, "It is not good that the man should be alone." There was a void in Adam. His lack of a mate was a hindrance and a handicap. So God created the solution. Eve was the perfect counterpart to Adam, suiting him perfectly and completing him exactly.

> Now out of the ground the Lord God had formed every beast of the field and every bird of the heavens and brought them to the man to see what he would call them. And whatever the man called every living creature, that was its name. The man gave names to all livestock and to the birds of the heavens

and to every beast of the field. But for Adam there was not found a helper
fit for him. So the Lord God caused a deep sleep to fall upon the man, and
while he slept took one of his ribs and closed up its place with flesh. And the
rib that the Lord God had taken from the man he made into a woman and
brought her to the man. (Gen. 2:19–22)

God caused Adam to become aware of his need for a mate by putting on an
animal parade. Adam noticed each male had a female counterpart. In the process
of naming the animals, Adam saw there was no counterpart for himself. But he
didn't try to find a mate for himself or raise his fist at God for this lack of provision.
Remember, God already knew Adam had a need. The animal parade was set up by
God so Adam would be made aware of it.

God then put Adam down for a supernatural nap, and while he was sleeping,
God used material from Adam's body and made a woman. God then presented
Eve as a gift to Adam.

Then the man said, "This at last is bone of my bones and flesh of my flesh;
she shall be called Woman, because she was taken out of Man." (Gen. 2:23)

Adam was impressed and excited over Eve's arrival in the garden, and he
fully understood that *she was part* of him. He named her "Woman"—*isha* in the
Hebrew—which is translated "the feminine man." Adam had just named Mr. and
Mrs. Lizard, Mr. and Mrs. Dog, and Mr. and Mrs. Bird. Here he realized this was
the female version of man—Eve was Mrs. Man.

The Reason for the Leaving

Therefore a man shall leave his father and his mother and hold fast to his
wife, and they shall become one flesh. And the man and his wife were both
naked and were not ashamed. (Gen. 2:24–25)

God declared it is for this reason—because woman was taken out of man and
created as a helper for her husband—that a man shall leave his father and mother
and be joined to his wife.

Even though Adam and Eve didn't have biological parents, God set down a
mandate here as the foundation of the family: a man shall leave his parents and
be joined and cling to his wife instead. Thus, God was saying that when a couple
gets married, they form a new family, separate from the one they came from, and
the two become one flesh. The two become one in body (sexually united), soul
(emotionally united), and spirit (spiritually united before God).

We see the first marriage was not conditional. There was no "out clause." The
idea that the marriage could be dissolved or that the family could be undone did

not exist. When He founded the first family, <u>God set up a lasting establishment.</u> The *two* become *one*. Divorce was not an idea God had at the beginning.

Jesus commented on the foundation of marriage:

> And Pharisees came up to Him and tested Him by asking, "Is it lawful to divorce one's wife for any cause?" He answered, "Have you not read that He who created them from the beginning made them male and female, and said, "Therefore a man shall leave his father and his mother and hold fast to his wife, and the two shall become one flesh"? So they are no longer two but one flesh. What therefore God has joined together, let not man separate. (Matt. 19:3–6)

According to Jesus, marriage is not an experiment, but an irrevocable commitment. Yet the statistics on divorce among Christian marriages today is staggering. There is a 50 percent chance that every Christian marriage will end in divorce. Fifty percent!

How can this be? How can the people of God be so quick to dissolve a covenant they make before Him? It is because the world around them sings Satan's anthem: "You deserve better! You don't need to obey God! Divorce the loser and find someone better!" And the church is humming right along with this tune.

Marissa and Edgar fight all the time—the kids, the house, finances, in-laws, sex—every subject is fuel for the war. After being married for eight years, the constant bickering is downright exhausting. Marissa has started to feel like things would be better for everyone if they just got divorced. After one particularly nasty fight, her thoughts went something like this:

> *I can't live like this anymore. He is just a complete jerk. He shows me no respect. He treats me like I'm stupid. He wants to control everything I do. He doesn't listen to a word I say. The kids and I would be better off without him. At least if we divorced, there would be peace for a change! Wouldn't that be better for the kids? And besides, don't I deserve to be happy? Shouldn't I be allowed to have my own opinion without a big jerk jumping down my throat every time I disagree with him? I'm still attractive! Men look at me all the time. I'm sure I could find someone better, someone who treats me like I deserve, someone who makes more money and will spend more time with my parents.*

Many women in difficult marriages comfort themselves by fantasizing about divorce whenever things are hard. They soothe their wounded hearts by thoughts of how they'll be better off without Mr. Jerkface and how they will make him suffer ten times as much pain when they leave him. *This is a lie birthed out of the heart of Satan himself.*

Sisters, stop listening to the lies being spouted by the enemy of marriage. God *hates* divorce (Mal. 2:16). He *hates* it, and His people should hate it too.

Determine in your heart that you are going to stay married to your husband (the one you have right now!) until one of you dies. This is God's will for you. Hate divorce like God does, and don't let it be an option for you to even think about, let alone threaten with.

The enemy would have us believe there is no other choice, that divorce is the only way to make things better. Satan is a liar. The same God who created Adam and Eve and ordained that marriage would be a woman and a man coming together as one for their entire lives is the same God who is able to do miracles in *any* marriage.

There are very few exceptions to this. Very, very, very few. Unless you fall into one of these rare exceptions, it must be established in your own heart that God is right in making marriage a binding covenant that can only be undone by death.

When Is It Okay for a Christian to Divorce?

Every Christian marriage begins with a vow before God to stay together "till death do us part," yet over half of all Christian marriages end in divorce. Obviously there are more reasons than death dividing husbands and wives in the church. Here are just a few:

- I fell out of love with my husband.
- We just don't have anything in common anymore.
- My husband doesn't love me the way he should, and I deserve better.
- This can't be God's will for my life; God wants me to be happy.
- We are incompatible.
- I met my soul mate after I had already married the wrong guy.
- I don't find him attractive anymore.
- He lied to me before we got married. I can't stay married to a liar.
- It wasn't really a marriage in "God's eyes."
- We got married too young, and we're different people now.
- Our kids shouldn't have to grow up in a war zone. Divorce is better for them than this.

As convincing as these arguments may sound, none of them are biblical. The Bible only gives two reasons divorce can be considered—sexual immorality and abandonment.

1. Biblical reason for divorce—sexual immorality

> And I say to you: whoever divorces his wife, except for sexual immorality, and marries another, commits adultery. (Matt. 19:9)

> It was also said, "Whoever divorces his wife, let him give her a certificate of divorce." But I say to you that everyone who divorces his wife, except on the ground of sexual immorality, makes her commit adultery, and whoever marries a divorced woman commits adultery. (Matt. 5:31–32)

When a husband and wife commit themselves to one another on their wedding day, they are vowing to belong to one another sexually, excluding all others. When this vow is broken, the trust the marriage was built on is shattered. It takes years to rebuild broken trust. If a spouse is not repentant or is repeatedly unfaithful, there is no possibility of that trust ever being rebuilt. That is why Jesus said that divorce in the case of sexual immorality is permissible.

However, that does not mean that if there is sexual unfaithfulness in a marriage, the couple *must* divorce. There is *so* much hope for trust being restored if the couple is willing to rebuild their marriage.

Greg called us in tears late one night, asking if he and his wife, Marnie, could please come over. He had just confessed to her that he had been in a sexual relationship with a woman from work. The pain in Marnie's sweet face was awful. I held her, and we sobbed together in silence. In the course of the next two hours, Greg described the slow descent into depravity that had gone on in his life in the previous months. Marnie sat in numbed silence till she simply said, "I never suspected. How could I have been so stupid?"

We counseled Marnie to not make any decisions about the future of their marriage until she saw if Greg was truly repentant and she had time to heal. For the sake of their kids, they stayed in the house together, but in separate rooms. After several weeks, it was evident Greg was deeply repentant and determined to do everything he could to secure his wife's trust.

She was deeply wounded and fought bitterness, anger, and fear. But Marnie saw genuine, lasting change in Greg. He was sincerely walking with Christ, genuinely loving his wife, and aiming to heal his family. She invited him back into their bedroom. They regularly saw a Christian counselor for over a year. It has been several years since the adultery, and Marnie has shared with me that sometimes the pain is still there and the fear that she could be hurt again rears up in her heart. "But I am choosing to trust God," she said. "I'm choosing to stay and keep our family together. Honestly, Greg is a different man. He's closer to Jesus than he ever was before, which has made my relationship with God stronger too. We are going to make it."

Our God is absolutely able to heal and restore a marriage after adultery. Greg and Marnie's story is one of many victories we have seen over the years. Restoration is possible if the adulterer is completely repentant and the betrayed is committed to forgive.

We met Jeanie when she and Norm had been married for seven years. In that time, Norm had had three sexual relationships with other women. Jeanie and Norm came to the church for help as a final resort to save their marriage. Norm said he was truly sorry and wanted to save their marriage, and Jeanie wanted to forgive him.

After counseling with us for several months, Jeanie discovered yet another sexual relationship Norm was carrying on with a woman from the gym. It was incredibly painful for Jeanie to realize she had been tricked into thinking he had changed.

We counseled her to separate from him, and she and their two young children moved into a small apartment. Norm was determined to get his family back and agreed to go to weekly sessions with a trained Christian counselor. Jeanie slowly started to think that perhaps her family could be saved. She started attending counseling herself and worked toward forgiving her husband. After nine months, Norm and Jeanie moved back in together, and we all rejoiced that God had restored their marriage.

After six months, however, Jeanie discovered that Norm was still texting the woman he had been seeing from the gym. He confessed to "still having feelings for her." Devastated and totally embarrassed, Jeanie called us to say she was completely done with her marriage, and she was taking Jesus up on His offer to divorce for reasons of sexual immorality.

I cried hard and often over Norm and Jeanie. I so badly wanted theirs to be a miraculous work of redemption, and I am convinced restoration was God's will for them. However, Norm decided to satisfy his lust rather than keep his vow to be faithful to his wife. We walked through the divorce process with Jeanie and her kids, and saw God do incredible, miraculous things that proved that regardless of Norm's unfaithfulness, God would remain faithful to her.

Trust in a marriage is like an expensive vase. It's meant to be cherished and to hold beauty and life. If a vase gets thrown to the floor and shatters, it's possible that with lots of patience and care, it can be glued back together and can contain what it was intended for again. However, it is possible that a vase can be shattered to the point that it is impossible to put back together.

If trust is shattered again and again, there comes a point when it can't be restored. Divorce can actually reflect the truth that marriage is to be held in high regard, and those who do not revere the holy covenant of marriage are consequently deprived of its blessings.

This is why Jesus said divorce is permissible for reasons of sexual immorality. God does not hate divorce more than He hates sexual immorality. In instances where the marriage covenant is shattered by sin, divorce can be a biblically valid option.

So what exactly is sexual immorality?

Jesus used a broader context of immorality, knowing marital trust can be broken in a variety of ways that don't necessarily fit into the more narrowly defined terms of "intercourse" or "adultery." Intercourse, oral sex, manual sex, verbal sex—it all counts. If a husband or wife has any type of sexual experience with someone else, he or she is committing sexual immorality.

2. Biblical reason for divorce—Abandonment

In some cases, a woman who becomes a believer is abandoned by her nonbelieving husband. In this case, according to the Scriptures, the believer is not enslaved to their marriage vows, the divorce is permitted, and the believer is free to marry another believer.

> But if the unbelieving partner separates, let it be so. In such cases the brother
> or sister is not enslaved. God has called you to peace. (1 Cor. 7:15)

There is a clear distinction that it must be the unbelieving spouse who decides to divorce. A believer should do all they can to stay in the marriage and keep their family together.

> To the rest I say (I, not the Lord) that if any brother has a wife who is an
> unbeliever, and she consents to live with him, he should not divorce her. If
> any woman has a husband who is an unbeliever, and he consents to live with
> her, she should not divorce him. For the unbelieving husband is made holy
> because of his wife, and the unbelieving wife is made holy because of her
> husband. Otherwise your children would be unclean, but as it is, they are
> holy. (1 Cor. 7:12–14)

What If a Woman Is Being Abused?

Unfortunately, we live in a fallen world where men physically abuse their wives, or they are emotionally or verbally abusive. The Bible does not address this specific scenario as a viable cause for divorce, so therefore, abuse is not a reason to justify divorce.

However, a woman should not stay in a situation where her life or her physical or emotional health is in danger. In those cases, she should separate from her husband. There is a difference between divorce and separation. An abused wife should go somewhere safe, with the full support and help of her church. The reason for her separation, apart from her primary need for safety, is so that her husband has a consequence to his sin and is given a chance to repent and be reconciled to his family. Separation should always be with the hope of repentance and restoration.

Ideally, here is what should happen: A woman is being abused, so she goes to her church, where they may help her find a safe place to stay, away from her husband. The husband is confronted with his sin by the men in the church, and the church offers to help him do whatever is necessary to be restored to his family. If the husband is repentant and does what is necessary to make the wife sure he has changed and she will be safe (this should take several months at least, and possibly much longer), then the family is restored, and the man is held accountable by his church.

If the man is not willing to repent or to get any type of counseling, then the wife is to remain separated from him for her own safety and file whatever legal papers are necessary to ensure her protection (restraining orders, legal separation to protect herself financially, etc.). She should not date anyone during this time, because she is still married. Her focus should be to pray fervently for her husband's true repentance.

Women in this situation typically have one of three things happen:

1. Ideally, the man repents and gets right with God and his wife.

2. The man gets a girlfriend, and as soon as it is verified that he is in a sexual relationship and isn't planning on being restored to his family, the wife then has biblical grounds for divorce.

3. The man dies. Seriously. I saw an unrepentant man who continually tormented his wife emotionally and verbally die of a heart attack during

the time when she was separated from him. She ended up getting a huge life insurance settlement and was happily remarried a few years later.

A wife is bound to her husband as long as he lives. But if her husband dies, she is free to be married to whom she wishes, only in the Lord. (1 Cor. 7:39)

There is *always* a way to obey God's Word, and He will honor those who choose to follow His commands.

You Promised God

On your wedding day, you made a vow, a covenant, a lasting promise that God expects you to uphold. In our society, vows, covenants, and promises are not revered the way they should be, but that doesn't mean God takes them any less seriously.

I love what author Elisabeth Elliot wrote to her daughter about marriage vows:

> Your feelings cannot help but be affected by riches and poverty, health and sickness, and all the other circumstances which make up a lifetime. Your feelings will come and go, rise and fall, but you make no vows about them. When you find yourself, like the unstable man in the Epistle of James, "driven with wind and tossed," it is a great thing then to know that you have an anchor. You have made a promise before God to love. You promise to love, comfort, honor, and keep this man. You vow to take him as your wedded husband, to have and to hold from this day forward, for better or for worse, for richer, for poorer, in sickness and in health, in love and to cherish, "according to God's holy ordinance," till death parts you.
>
> Not one of us can fully face up to all the details of the possibilities at the time we make these staggering promises. We make them in faith. Faith that the God who ordained that a man and woman should cleave together for a lifetime is the God who alone can make such faithful cleaving possible.[5]

Wedding vows are necessary because of the certainty that bad times will come. You didn't really have to promise to stay for the good stuff. Friend, when you got married, you *vowed* to stay. You *promised* "for better or worse." There will be seasons of worse, seasons of sickness, seasons of poverty. Hardship may actually be what makes up the bulk of your marriage. But because you married a sinner who is going to sin, and so did your husband, you both made a promise to stay married when the difficult seasons come.

You *vowed* to stay. You *promised.* You. Promised. God.

God will supply all you need for you to keep your promise.

LESSON 3 WIFE-CHANGING QUESTIONS

1. What is your favorite part of this creation account?

   God saw that Adam had a need.

2. Do you agree that God means for marriage to be a lifelong commitment?

   Yes.

3. Why do you think so many Christian couples end up divorcing?

   Distance from God, priorities mixed up. Forgiveness, repentance not evident

4. Are you ever guilty of considering or threatening divorce as an option to deal with your marital problems?

yes

5. In your heart before the Lord, yield to His mandate that marriage is until either you or your husband dies. Choose to never believe the lie that divorce is an option for you outside the boundaries God has given in His Word. Write a prayer of yielding to His plan for you to stay married.

Lord, God I yield all thoughts of ending what you have established. I am in a covenant marriage that I lay down to You. Amen.

LESSON 4

Let's continue with our examination of the first marriage in Genesis 3:

> Now the serpent was more crafty than any other beast of the field that the
> Lord God had made. He said to the woman, "Did God actually say, 'You
> shall not eat of any tree in the garden'?" And the woman said to the serpent,
> "We may eat of the fruit of the trees in the garden, but God said, 'You shall
> not eat of the fruit of the tree that is in the midst of the garden, neither shall
> you touch it, lest you die.'" But the serpent said to the woman, "You will not
> surely die. For God knows that when you eat of it your eyes will be opened,
> and you will be like God, knowing good and evil." (Gen. 3:1–5)

We don't know how much time passed between Adam and Eve's creation
and this fatal conversation with Satan. Some commentators say it was years, and
some say that it was much shorter. Whatever the time frame, Eve and her husband
were there long enough to have discussed the rules of the garden. Eve knew the
restrictions on the tree in the midst of the garden, that God was her authority, and
that she was expected to obey Him.

Chapter 3 begins with Eve having a conversation with Satan. Perhaps she
didn't know who he was because she was used to speaking to animals in the garden
and the serpent was Satan's disguise. It is possible she had no idea there was an
enemy with them in the garden, yet her disobedience is without excuse.

Satan's opening line is to question God's Word and authority: "Did God
actually say . . . ?" His goal was to cause Eve to not take God's Word as her final,
trusted authority. He knew that if he could get Eve to believe God was not good
and fair and trustworthy, she would easily be led into sin. His method of deception
was quite effective. Satan persuaded Eve into believing that God's way of doing
things was really His way of putting her into bondage and keeping her from what
she rightly deserved.

Satan's method of deception hasn't changed since the garden. It worked well
on Eve, and it works equally well on women today. Instead of a serpent, he takes
the form of celebrities, movies, novels, websites, advertising, social media, music,
or whatever trend might catch our eye. Even the church, pastors, and Christian
authors and speakers can be his tools.

As it was with Eve in the garden, if the father of lies can convince us that we
are foolish to obey God's plan, then our own fall is soon to follow. Just as Eve was
given a choice to disobey, God has given us a free will, which enables us to make a

choice to disobey Him as well. Once our enemy can convince us that God's Word is not our trusted authority, then we feel justified in making our own decisions about whether to obey Him or not.

> So when the woman saw that the tree was good for food, and that it was a delight to the eyes, and that the tree was to be desired to make one wise, she took of its fruit and ate, and she also gave some to her husband who was with her, and he ate. (Gen. 3:6)

Eve saw three things she liked about this particular tree. The food looked appetizing, it was visually appealing, and it had the capability of making her wise. There is a really enlightening application here in regard to any type of sin.

> For all that is in the world—the lust of the flesh, the lust of the eyes, and the pride of life—is not of the Father but is of the world. (1 John 2:16)

This verse is essentially Satan's playbook! It shows us the three ways our enemy attacks. Every sin falls into one of these three categories. It will either feel good, look good, or make us feel important. These are his classic moves. If we want to beat our opponent, we are wise to identify his strategies.

We can see Satan used these three plays on Eve. She saw the tree was good for food (the lust of the flesh), that it was pleasing to the eyes (the lust of the eyes), and it was desirable to make one wise (the pride of life).

Satan even tried these moves on Jesus! In Luke 4 we read the account of Jesus being tempted in the desert. First, Satan wanted Jesus to turn stone into bread (the lust of the flesh). Then the devil showed Him all the kingdoms of the world (the lust of the eyes), and finally he tempted Jesus to throw Himself down from the pinnacle of the temple in order to easily declare Himself the Messiah and prove that God was working for Him (the pride of life).

The word "lust" means wanting what is forbidden rather than what is allowed. The enemy is a master at getting us to satisfy our God-given drives in ungodly ways. We satisfy our physical need for food with things that are not good for us, or we eat entirely too much. Our God-given sex drives can be satisfied in perverse, selfish, or unholy ways. The need for companionship and emotional intimacy can drive us to ungodly relationships. The desires of our flesh are not evil in themselves, but the enemy uses them to convince us to disobey God.

The Lust of the Flesh

"It'll feel good. It'll satisfy your appetite You need it and deserve it."—Satan

Eve saw that the forbidden fruit was "desirable for food." It looked delicious. She may have been genuinely hungry and was in the garden looking for something to satisfy her appetite. There was nothing sinful about Eve wanting to appease her hunger. Her appetite was given to her by God, and He had told her how to satisfy it: "From every tree of the garden you may freely eat." The problem wasn't with her appetite, but with where she was looking to satisfy it. Eve's first mistake was hanging around the forbidden fruit.

Satan will convince us we need something, deserve something, and that the consequences we might incur will be worth the satisfaction we will gain from getting what we want. Satan is a liar. It is never worth it!

The Lust of the Eyes

Eve saw that the forbidden fruit was pleasant to the eyes. It was a pretty tree, and the fruit was beautiful. The lust of the eyes refers to wanting the things we see. Eve had a whole garden full of things to eat, and certainly there was other pretty fruit nearby, but she had her eyes set on this particular fruit, and she was determined to have it.

The lust of the eyes refers to wanting more than what we actually have and to looking longingly at things we think we deserve.

All around us there is a constant swirl of things we can gaze at and say, "Ooh! I want that!" Some of these things are beneficial to us, and desiring them is not wrong. It is when our eyes look at what we can't have and we start coveting—*that* house, *that* body, *her* schedule, *her* husband—that our looking gives way to sinful lust.

The lust of the eyes—those longing looks for what we can't have—can bring us down and cause us to believe we aren't getting what we deserve. This can prompt us to do things we never thought we would do, much like Eve in the garden.

Terri had a very comfortable life with Chris. She got to stay home with their kids, who went to a top Christian school; had a cozy home; attended a great church; and she would say she had a happy marriage. When Terri met Nicole at the gym, they hit it off immediately. Their daily chats on the treadmill turned into meeting for coffee, and eventually they decided to meet one another's families. When Terri and Chris pulled up to Nicole's house, Terri instantly felt out of place. Nicole's home was three times the size of hers. Nicole introduced her husband, Jim, who reminded Terri of a marble statue in a museum. He was one of the most handsome men she had ever seen. Suddenly, Chris looked old and out of shape, and her life looked pale in comparison to Nicole's. That night, lying in bed, Terri started thinking about how much better Nicole's life was than hers: *Jim probably makes five times as much as Chris. How else could they afford that incredible house? I should have married a rich guy. Nicole has probably had plastic surgery—that's why she looks so amazing. I bet she and Jim have an incredible sex life. I wish Chris would work out more. He just doesn't care about being attractive to me. He never will . . .*

A few days later, Terri happened to see Jim from a distance at a coffee shop. *He is so incredible. He makes lots of money, and he's surely great in bed. I wonder if he finds me attractive.* Jim caught Terri's eye and came over to say hello. Without a second thought, Terri sucked in her stomach, put on her most dazzling smile, and turned on the charm.

Six months later, Nicole found out about the adultery.

Chris divorced Terri, and Jim and Nicole moved to a different state to rebuild their family. Terri later said, "I never would have dreamed I could do something so horrible. I ruined two families with my sinful choices. I shut off the voice of God and all I knew to be right because I thought I deserved a better life. Now I've lost the happy life I had, and I destroyed another family's happiness with it."

The Pride of Life

The tree in the garden promised to make Eve wise. She would be smarter if she ate from it. That *had* to be a good thing, right? Eve bought this lie and chose to feed her pride with disobedience. If our enemy can entice us to value the esteem of men over the esteem of God, then he will get us to sin every time.

The pride of life refers to anything that promises to make us more important, smarter, more admirable, or more highly esteemed. The fact that the Creator of the universe has reached His own nail-scarred hand to us and offered us His fellowship should be enough, but still we want more.

People go to great lengths to fuel their pride. They lie to get ahead in business, surgically alter their bodies to fit a particular image, and compromise their convictions and self-respect to gain popularity. Our sinful natures are bent toward wanting to be respected, admired, and desired. Even after salvation, we are continually battling the sinful pride of life.

Sin Is a Big Deal

Eve decided that God's instructions about what she could and couldn't eat didn't need to be obeyed. She determined that her own desires—the lust of her flesh, the lust of her eyes, and the pride of her life—needed to be satisfied over what God had commanded.

Friends, isn't that what we do so often? We *know* what the Scriptures say. We can recite the verses about how we are to live as Christians. Yet when we have to live them out, we search for the loophole. We make ourselves the exception. And just like Eve, we eat the fruit of our own ideas.

It would be easy for us to minimize Eve's sin. C'mon! It was just a piece of fruit! She didn't even eat the whole thing! And she *shared* with Adam—isn't sharing godly? It's not like she did something really horrible. She was probably sick of the other food in the garden and wanted some variety in her diet. In comparison to things people do today, it wasn't a big deal at all, right? It's not like she murdered somebody!

But Eve's sin wasn't horrible because of what she did. Her sin was horrible because of who she sinned against. Eve's (and Adam's) sin didn't murder anyone at the time. That came sixty generations later when their sin, combined with the rest of ours, became the cross of Jesus Christ. In her book *Lies Women Believe,* Nancy Leigh DeMoss writes:

> If only we could see that every single sin is a big deal, that every sin is an act of rebellion and cosmic treason, that every time we choose our way instead of God's way, we are revolting against the God and King of the universe.[6]

Satan is brilliant at making us believe God is not that good and sin is not that bad. Just like Adam and Eve sewed fig leaves to try to cover their shame, the enemy of our souls convinces us that our sins are not big deals—we easily minimize them by calling them "weaknesses," "cravings," "hormonal imbalances," "character flaws," and "struggles."

> We must reject any attempt to cover up our sin with culturally acceptable fig leaves. We need the blood of Jesus to cleanse and clothe us. We are not to sew together the fig leaves of socially accepted labels and sin-justifying rhetoric.
> Our only hope for our sin is being clothed with His righteousness, that which is given to us and put on us by belief in Jesus Christ.
> —Maureen Schaffer

Sin needs to be called what it is—rebellion against God. Cosmic treason. The magnitude of the sin is not important, as any sin is an offense against a magnificent and holy God.

We can be guilty of sitting in church and hoping for a message to make us *feel* better. We want to park on the subjects that affirm us and tell us we are loved, cherished, and accepted. But often, the message we really need to hear is the one that tells us we are sinners who have offended a holy God, and we must repent.

When we call sin what it is—treason against a holy God—then we have great hope! There is hope for sinners because God has made a way for sin to be eradicated. Through the cross of Christ, we can be not only forgiven of our sin, but we have the power to cease from it. We have a choice about sin.

It is the truth that sets us free.

Suzanne was a screamer. When she was frustrated with her children or her husband was annoying her, she made sure they knew how she felt. Screaming horrible insults, calling them demeaning names, slamming doors, and throwing things sent the clear message that they couldn't get away with whatever had set her off. At times, Suzanne felt like she became an entirely different person in these fits of rage. After years of this, her husband barely spoke to her. The children often jumped when she came into the room, expecting a verbal assault. Rather than feeling remorse for her behavior, Suzanne congratulated herself for being in control and showing her family "who's boss."

One day, Suzanne heard a sermon in church about anger that pricked her conscience. The pastor called outbursts of anger sin. The Scriptures that were shared exposed her behavior as rebellion against God. But Suzanne easily justified it. "My mother did the same thing, and I turned out okay. If I stopped screaming, then my family would take advantage of me. I have to act this way to keep them in line. Besides, I'm Italian—that's just how we are."

A few weeks later, Suzanne's four-year-old daughter got upset with her seven-year-old brother over a toy. Her daughter screamed as she threw a toy at his head, "You're the stupidest person alive! I hate you!" Suzanne watched this scene in horror, seeing her own behavior mirrored by her tiny daughter. The words of the sermon came flooding back to her. That night, she confessed her sin to the Lord. In genuine repentance, she agreed with God that her angry outbursts were sinful and could not continue. Suzanne also confessed her sin to her family, asked for their forgiveness, and shared how she desperately wanted to change.

As Suzanne chose God's ways above her own, she eventually gained victory over her anger. She still lost control sometimes, but instead of justifying it, she confessed it as sin to God and her family, and she repented. The anger that held her captive for years no longer had control over her. The truth had set her free.

The Power in Admitting Sin

The ability to confess our sin and to repent from it is a beautiful gift from God. There is no other belief system in the world that offers forgiveness of sin and the ability to sin no more.

But thanks be to God, that you who were once slaves of sin have become obedient from the heart to the standard of teaching to which you were committed, and, having been set free from sin, have become slaves of righteousness. (Rom. 6:17–18)

As you examine the Scriptures for yourself, determine you will not minimize your own sin. If some area of rebellion is exposed to you, confess it as sin and repent—turn from your sin and turn toward God.

Repentance is a powerful thing. It takes us from a place of being opposed to God to agreeing with Him. So repent quickly when you are confronted with your sin—no excuses, no justifying, just speedy repentance! The sooner you repent, the sooner you will have a right relationship with God and will be able to experience the beauty of His redeeming work in your life.

Yielded for Life

If we don't agree God is good and right and worthy of total obedience, then we can justify making our own decisions about what is right or wrong for our own lives, depending on the mood of the day. This may seem rigid and confining to some, like some sort of moral prison. But the opposite is actually true. Having an absolute standard, one that is non-negotiable and unchanging, is actually very freeing. Maureen Schaffer says:

> Boundaries are blessings.
> Restraint is refreshing.
> Commands are comforting.
> Guidelines are guarding.
> Submission is safe.
> Purity is pleasurable.
> Discipline is delightful.

The world around us is continually changing its ideas about what is right and wrong or what is good or bad. Fifty years ago, the moral climate of the world was very different than it is today. Fifty years from now, it will be different than it is today. But the Word of God is unchanging. Like a compass that always points true north, the Word of God always points to truth, and we can depend on that to safely guide us to the best possible outcome.

LESSON 4 WIFE-CHANGING QUESTIONS

Define the following terms:
1. Lust of the flesh:

   taste good, feel good, satisfying an appetite

2. Lust of the eyes:

   looks good, appealing beautiful & desireable

3. Pride of life:

   elevate, make important wise, Knowledgeable

4. How have you specifically been tempted in each of these areas?

   #1 I did what made me feel good. #2 I went after what would make me look good #3 I wanted to satisfy my control.

5. Can you identify a tactic (lust of the flesh, lust of the eyes, or the pride of life) the enemy is currently using to cause you to sin?

   Discontentment can be all 3

6. Commit to calling sin what it really is—rebellion against a holy God. Is there any particular sin in your life you know you need to confess and repent from right now?

Lord, I have realized & confessed of my discontment - where I live, how I am living - without that which I think I need.

7. What are you going to do differently about this area of your life? Write a wife-changing prayer of recommitment here.

Lord, realizing You have given placed, called, planned, ahead of time. I surrender & yield to You my disobedience & sin of - not enough - When I look to You first realize Your power and authority in my life, - Romans 12 has been such an eye opening chapter for me. Thank You Jesus!

LESSON 5

Eve exercised her free will in choosing to disobey God. We have the same option. We can choose to disobey God and sin. But we don't have the freedom to choose the consequences of our disobedience.

There were immediate consequences as soon as she and Adam ate the forbidden fruit, and there were also delayed consequences. Eve chose the sin, but God chose the consequences of her sin that were far worse than she could have ever imagined. Genesis recounts the following:

> Then the eyes of both were opened, and they knew that they were naked. And they sewed fig leaves together and made themselves loincloths. And they heard the sound of the Lord God walking in the garden in the cool of the day, and the man and his wife hid themselves from the presence of the Lord God among the trees of the garden. But the Lord God called to the man and said to him, "Where are you?" And he said, "I heard the sound of you in the garden, and I was afraid, because I was naked, and I hid myself." He said, "Who told you that you were naked? Have you eaten of the tree of which I commanded you not to eat?" The man said, "The woman whom you gave to be with me, she gave me fruit of the tree, and I ate." Then the Lord God said to the woman, "What is this that you have done?" The woman said, "The serpent deceived me, and I ate."

> The Lord God said to the serpent, "Because you have done this, cursed are you above all livestock and above all beasts of the field; on your belly you shall go, and dust you shall eat all the days of your life. I will put enmity between you and the woman, and between your offspring and her offspring; he shall bruise your head, and you shall bruise his heel."

> To the woman He said, "I will surely multiply your pain in childbearing; in pain you shall bring forth children. Your desire shall be contrary to your husband, but he shall rule over you."

> And to Adam He said, "Because you have listened to the voice of your wife and have eaten of the tree of which I commanded you, 'You shall not eat of it,' cursed is the ground because of you; in pain you shall eat of it all the days of your life; thorns and thistles it shall bring forth for you; and you shall eat the plants of the field. By the sweat of your face you shall eat bread, till you return to the ground, for out of it you were taken; for you are dust, and to dust you shall return."

The man called his wife's name Eve, because she was the mother of all living. And the Lord God made for Adam and for his wife garments of skins and clothed them. Then the Lord God said, "Behold, the man has become like one of us in knowing good and evil. Now, lest he reach out his hand and take also of the tree of life and eat, and live forever—" therefore the Lord God sent him out from the garden of Eden to work the ground from which he was taken. He drove out the man, and at the east of the garden of Eden He placed the cherubim and a flaming sword that turned every way to guard the way to the tree of life. (Gen. 3:7–24)

Adam and Eve's rebellion had enormous consequences, and those consequences didn't just affect the ones who committed the offense. All of humanity was affected by the choice of one woman. Look at this list of the consequences of Eve's choice to disobey God:

- Adam and Eve felt ashamed for the first time.
- Their fellowship with God was broken.
- Women experience pain in childbirth.
- Women desire to rule over their husbands.
- The soil began to produce weeds and thorns.
- Men have to work very hard to gain very little.
- Death began its process in all living things.
- Animals had to die to cover the shame of Adam and Eve.
- Adam and Eve were removed from their garden home, never to return.
- The sinful state of Adam and Eve was passed on to their offspring, and to every other human ever to be born.

It seems a bit harsh for just eating a piece of pretty fruit, doesn't it? Yet those are the consequences God delivered for their offense.

And so it is with our own sin. We can make brazen claims of independence and throw off the restrains of God's mandates. However, there are far-reaching ramifications for our sin we cannot foresee—consequences that affect not only us, but our loved ones and possibly generations to come. A choice to disobey God in a seemingly insignificant matter can have vastly significant consequences.

Grace from the Start

Even though God knew Adam and Eve had rebelled against Him, He *called* to them, "Where are you?" (Gen. 3:9). This wasn't the angry cry of an outraged master, but the heartbroken cry of a father. He *wanted* to be with Adam and Eve.

He *sought* their fellowship and instantly set a plan into motion for that fellowship to be restored. Oh, such beautiful mercy!

Notice something astonishing as God curses the serpent: He lays out His plan of redemption! Read the statement God makes to the serpent again:

> I will put enmity between you and the woman, and between your offspring and her offspring; he shall bruise your head, and you shall bruise his heel. (Gen. 3:15)

God immediately announced that one of Eve's descendants will be the Messiah. The offspring promised here is a reference to Jesus, who will one day crush the head of Satan. Right after the first sin was ever committed on earth, God had a plan to restore fellowship with Adam and Eve—and with you.

God eventually gave the laws of animal sacrifices to Moses as a means for men to atone for their sin and have a right standing with God. However, this atonement only covered the sin of man and did not erase it. It was only the perfect sacrifice of Jesus on the cross that completely removed man's sin and restored true fellowship with God. The separation that Eve caused in the garden has now been restored through Jesus, granting complete access to Almighty God.

Do you understand how incredible that is? Through the blood of Jesus, we can now approach a holy God. We can have a real relationship with God—like the one Adam and Eve had in the garden before the fall—all because of what Jesus did on the cross.

Your Friendship with God

> A marriage of love, unity, and understanding is not rooted in romance; it is rooted in worship.[7] —Paul David Tripp

In the Ten Commandments, God addresses a person's relationship with Himself before He addresses relationships with other people. The first four commandments address a person worshipping God, and the last six focus on loving other people. There is a premise here we can't ignore. To accurately love other people, we must first have our relationship with God in order.

This book is about becoming the excellent wife God has called you to be. But your role as a wife is ultimately all about your relationship with God. Everything you do as a follower of Jesus first runs through the filter of your faith. If a wife is truly seeking to walk in obedience to God's design for her as a wife, and she yields herself to His way above her own, that is an act of worship.

Most unhappy wives today do not really have a marriage problem. They have a God problem. Your marriage is not so much about *what* you do as a wife, but *who* you do it all for.

As wives, our focus must be that we do all *as unto the Lord.* There will be many days when our husbands won't deserve our kindness, or our submission, or our help. Yet those responses still must be ours. Loving the unlovely, gently responding to unkindness, serving the unworthy—these responses are only possible if we are doing them for the One who is always lovely, kind, and worthy.

The sooner you decide to surrender your own ideas and expectations of what your life is about and, instead, yield your life to God's will and agree His way is best, the sooner you will start to see real changes in your marriage. Therefore, *the single most important thing you can do to improve your marriage is to develop a consistent devotional life.*

If you do nothing else but determine to *daily* spend time in the Word of God and prayer, I can promise you your marriage will improve. That's not to say that your husband will start treating you like a princess or that his laundry will magically find itself in the hamper. But *you,* YOU will change. *You* will improve. You cannot spend time in the presence of God and remain the same.

Let me point out that much of what American Christianity has called "devotions" or "quiet times" is a cheap imitation of actually spending time in the presence of God. Typical "devotional" books are full of pages containing one Bible verse, or part of one verse, and then a page of the author's thoughts on that verse. There is absolutely nothing wrong with reading devotionals like this. I read them myself; however, many Christians read one page of these books over their coffee in the morning and say that they have "daily devotions." Oh, they are missing out on so much! Reading one line of Scripture and a paragraph of someone else's thoughts on it is not enough to have a deep relationship with Jesus!

Each day, your enemy will be throwing the lusts of the flesh, the lusts of the eyes, and the boastful pride of life at you from every angle. One verse a day and a paragraph of someone else's thoughts is not going to adequately equip you for the battle you face.

Imagine if you and I wanted to develop a friendship with one another. If I only spoke one sentence a day to you, and then you read someone else's opinion of that sentence, at the end of a year, how well would you know me? How close would we actually be?

There is a whole thick book full of the thoughts of God. *The thoughts of God!* The Bible is God's means of communication with humanity. He wants to communicate with you about how He thinks and feels and works. We are privileged to be literate women who can read His book for ourselves.

I am not trying to put a guilt trip on anyone or set up any legalistic rules. But I do want to plead with you to take reading the Word of God seriously. There is no discipline I can encourage you to develop more than consistent time in the Word and in prayer.

If you already have a consistent devotional life, let me encourage you to examine your time with the Lord and see if perhaps there is something you can add or change or expand. Like any relationship, your relationship with God grows and changes, and your devotional time will grow and change as you walk through the different seasons of life.

Keeping It Real

Keeping a daily appointment with God has been the single most impacting discipline in my entire life. But let me also say this: sometimes it's boring. Most days I get up, get my coffee, read my Bible, pray, work on memorizing Scripture—and then I move into the rest of my day without having any super impacting, life-altering insight. Honestly, only about two or three times a month do I come away from my devotional time feeling like I had some incredible spiritual encounter. But those two or three encounters are only made possible because I show up the other twenty-eight days of the month.

It's like eating—if I think about the last month, there are only two or three meals I can remember being spectacular (and I assure you, they were not cooked by me!). But I know I was nourished every day for the entire month, and if I hadn't eaten anything but those few spectacular meals, then I would be very weak and sickly today. I don't always perceive the effects of nourishment until I am without it.

No matter what you *feel*, spending time seeking after God nourishes your soul. Don't expect goosebumps and life-changing interactions every day. Expect nourishment. Expect to be reminded and guided and grounded. There will certainly be spectacular times, but they will be peppered throughout a life of daily seeking.

Seek His Face

When You said, "Seek My face," my heart said to You, "Your face, O Lord, I shall seek." (Ps. 27:8)

So here's where it all begins. Your first big assignment in becoming an excellent wife is to make a daily appointment with God, or perhaps to make some wife-changing adjustments to your current devotional practices. There is not necessarily a "right" way to seek the Lord on a daily basis. However, there are some practical recommended guidelines.

1. Set a time.

There are some who would say the "right" or the "best" time to spend with God is first thing in the morning. This is a great goal, but it's not always practical, depending on what season of life you are in. The "best" time is whenever you're most likely to show up!

When I was getting up with babies in the middle of the night, early morning devotions were worthless for me. I would close my eyes to pray and start nodding off. I found that using the children's nap time was more practical in that season. That lasted for a few years, and then I switched to the early morning again.

I have a friend whose husband works the night shift as a police officer. She has most evenings to herself, and she chooses to spend time with the Lord before she goes to bed. If her husband gets a different work schedule, she will change this routine, but it works in this season of her life. Other friends have shared with me they are just not morning people, and they have found their best time to spend with Jesus is in the afternoons or evenings when their minds are more alert.

The psalmist said, "Evening, and morning, and at noon, will I pray, and cry aloud: and He shall hear my voice." God is listening at all times of the day. Spend some time before the Lord examining your schedule and ask Him to show you the best time for an appointment with Him.

There is no "right" amount of time to allot for a devotional life. Set aside enough time to actually develop a relationship. If you have never had devotions before, I suggest starting by scheduling thirty minutes. That's sufficient time to spend reading a chapter of Scripture, time to pray, time to memorize Scripture, and time to listen.

2. Read the Word.

Devotional books certainly have their place. However, there is no substitute for the Bible! Be sure to read the Word of God for yourself—just the straight Bible, with nothing else.

Aim for around a chapter a day. Start in one book of the Bible, and read the whole book through to the end. If you are new at this and aren't sure   where to start, I suggest beginning in the New Testament, starting with the book of Matthew and reading straight through.

There are several great reading programs out there that provide schedules so you can read the whole Bible in a year or the whole New Testament in a few months. These are great tools to help you along. The best reading plan is the one you will actually follow!

Realize you may not understand everything you read. God will give you understanding of what you need to know at this season of your life. The next time you read the same passage, you will grasp more, and ten years from now, grasp far more. The Word of God is alive and always applicable, always speaking, always teaching and correcting. It contains everything you need for life and godliness.

If reading is a challenge for you, then find an app that will read the Bible to you! My favorite app for this is Bible.is. Adriane says,

> I had never really understood the Bible when I read it. When I started listening to it on Bible.is, though, I started to finally get it. I guess my brain just works better when I hear it out loud. I listen to at least two chapters of Scripture a day in my car on my way to and from work. My walk with God has been stronger in the last three years because I am constantly in the Scriptures now, and I understand it now that I can hear it.

We are so fortunate to have ready access to the Bible in so many platforms. We have no excuse to not be feasting on a steady diet of Scripture one way or another.

3. Use a prayer list.

Prayer is not a luxury—like donuts or coffee creamer. Prayer is like water—absolutely essential to your survival as a Christian.

Having a list to lift in prayer to the Lord can be an anchor for your prayer life. A list helps to keep things focused and specific. Rather than praying, "God bless my husband, God bless my kids, God bless my church," having a detailed list allows you to pray direct, specific prayers and look for direct, specific answers.

There are dozens of ways to make a prayer list. There are journals in Christian bookstores. There are even smartphone apps for prayer. The best list is the one you use! If you have never made a prayer list before, you can use the tools provided on the Free Resources page at www.nancykaser.com.

The additional benefit to a prayer list is seeing God's specific answers. When you've written prayers out and you are able to see how God has answered those prayers directly, it is incredible motivation to pray even more.

4. Minimize distractions.

I am so easily distracted. I will start reading my Bible and notice the windows are dirty. This will remind me I am out of paper towels, which will remind me that I need to go to the store. I'll then grab my phone to see what time the store opens and read a text from someone asking to meet with me that day, which will cause me to check my calendar and see what else is scheduled for the day—and before I know it, I'm planning my day instead of seeking God.

Here are a few suggestions about how to guard your time with God against distractions:

- Choose a location where you will be the least distracted.
- Keep all of your devotional tools (Bible, highlighters and pens, note cards, journal, etc.) all in one bin or basket to save time looking for these things every day.
- Leave your cell phone in another room.
- Set a timer to avoid the distraction of checking the time.
- If you are distracted by clutter, tidy up the area where you will meet with Jesus before you start—but don't get sidetracked by reorganizing the bookshelves!
- Get up before young children to ensure you're able to have some undivided time. If your children occasionally get up too soon, invite them to join you and let them hear you pour out your heart to the Lord.

Be careful to not make the location of your devotional time the focus of this exercise. The priority is to actually seek the Lord, no matter what chaos is going on around you. You need Jesus, whether your environment is distraction-free or not!

Susanna Wesley is one of my heroes. She was mother to John and Charles Wesley, founders of the Methodist church in eighteenth-century England. She birthed nineteen children in twenty-one years. Only ten of them survived past the age of two. This homeschooling mom took the responsibility of raising her children to know Jesus seriously. I am sure Susanna didn't have the luxury of lots of personal space and "me time," yet she was known for her fierce prayer life and spiritual vitality. One thing her children remembered about her was she would often throw her apron over her head—a signal to her children that she was praying and was not to be disturbed. Desperate prayers, uttered beneath her apron, bore fruit in the lives of her children and multiplied to impact the world for generations.

We can be bombarded by multitudes of responsibilities and relationships. Jesus patterned the appropriate response to those times we are confronted with demands that might drain us. It is healthy to go to a physical place where it is difficult for the multitudes to reach us and pray.

Yes. Pray. Spending time in the Father's presence, casting our cares on Him, admiring Him, drawing renewed strength and perspective from

Him, and valuing our access to Him above being someone He is using to reach others.

Turn off the phone or turn it over. Don't make it easy to be reached. Find your wilderness and go there to meet with your God. You will be able to face the multitudes with His power and His love.—Maureen Schaffer

Great multitudes came . . . so He Himself often withdrew into the wilderness and prayed. (Luke 5:15–16)

5. Memorize Scripture.

The discipline of memorizing Scripture is largely ignored in our culture, and yet it is one of the greatest weapons in the Christian arsenal. The psalmist said in Psalm 119:11, "Your word I have hidden in my heart, that I might not sin against you." Memorizing Scripture is a powerful weapon against sin. It is what Jesus Himself used when He was tempted by Satan, and we are wise to follow His example.

Each of us memorizes things differently, but we all can memorize Scripture. Write a verse on a card and put it on your bathroom mirror and practice it while you do your hair. Keep a verse on your dashboard and read it at red lights. I have a friend who sets an alarm on her phone to remind her to practice her memory verse. There are great songs available that are Scripture set to good music—learn the song, and you've hidden the Word in your heart. The method is not important, as long as the memorization happens.

Work on a verse until you can say it perfectly. When you have it memorized, it is then part of your own personal anti-sin arsenal. It is wisdom that you have stored up for yourself to use when a need arises. Charles Spurgeon says,

> Should you not, besides reading the Bible, store your memories richly with the promises of God? You can recollect the sayings of great men; you treasure up the verses of renowned poets; ought you not to be profound in your knowledge of the words of God, so that you may be able to quote them readily when you would solve a difficulty, or overthrow a doubt?[8]

Camels and Hummingbirds

Camels can survive for long periods with no food or water. God created them with the ability to store a huge amount of fat—up to eighty pounds—in their humps, and up to twenty gallons of water in their bloodstreams. When a camel is traveling through a desert and food and water are scarce, their bodies can live off their stored supplies for up to two weeks.

A hummingbird however, must eat continually—sometimes as often as fourteen times in one hour. This tiny bird can only store enough fat to keep it from dying while it sleeps. As soon as a hummingbird wakes, it must seek nourishment or it will die.

Dear Sister, you are a hummingbird, not a camel! You are not meant to go to church on Sunday and store up spiritual nourishment for the week. You are meant to seek God for daily, sometimes hourly, spiritual sustenance. Jesus taught His disciples to pray, "Give us this day our daily bread" (Matt. 6:11). He wasn't merely talking about physical food. Every believer must go to God daily, seeking Him to meet all their needs.

Yielding is the whole goal of this chapter. In the last five sections, there are five truths to which you have been called to yield:

1. The truth is that you are a sinner in need of a Savior.
2. The truth is that God's Word is right about everything.
3. The truth is that God says marriage is for life.
4. The truth is sin is evil and needs to be eradicated from your life.
5. The truth is that you need to invest in your relationship with God on a daily basis.

Yield to these truths—agree with God that these things are true for *you*, and you are on your way to being the excellent wife who is a crown for her husband.

God 1st !

LESSON 5 WIFE-CHANGING QUESTIONS

1. Which of the five truths above is the hardest for you to yield to?

   _4 + 5_

2. What are your common reasons for not being committed to daily times of seeking God?

   selfishness, wallowing in self pity.

3. When and where are you going to set your daily appointment with God?

   Mon - early 7 am   Fri early
   Tues - early   Sat early
   Wed - mid morning   Sun - Dickson
   Thurs   "   8:30

4. Spend some time putting together your prayer list. Keep it somewhere you will be most likely to use it.

Planner - Monday - work + community
Tues - specific people
Want. I won't stick with this -
Lord show me daily - Nourish me hourly.

5. Are there any wife-changing adjustments you can make to facilitate freshness in your current devotional life?

?

HELP

LESSON 6

Play Your Part

I love going to the theater and watching talented actors bring a story to life. At the end of a performance, the cast typically lines up on the stage and takes one final bow together. With applause and sometimes a standing ovation, the audience recognizes the hours of memorization, choreography, and rehearsals that went into the show they just enjoyed. Each member of the cast and crew worked together in their assigned roles to make the show a success.

What would happen, though, if the leading lady of the production decided to suddenly abandon the role she had been given, and instead put on the costume of the leading man and proceed to try to play both parts? The production would be total chaos. A play only works when everyone performs their assigned roles that have been given by the director.

God is our marriage director and has given us assigned roles. If we perform these roles as He has directed, then our families will operate as they should. However, if we start assuming roles we haven't been given, our homes will be in chaos and we will not be applauded. In this section, we will examine the biblical role of a wife and learn how this role is to be lived out.

Remember the diagram of the house in the introduction? The foundation of that house is a willingness to yield to God's will for your life. The next four sections are the pillars of your house—the four essential elements to being a godly wife that bring structure and stability to your home.

The first pillar is the role God has given you as your husband's wife. You are designed to be his *helper.*

> help—*verb.* To give assistance; to supply aid; to make a task easier by giving assistance.
> *The kids help with the dishes after dinner.*
> help—*noun.* Someone or something that gives aid or assistance.
> *Our son is a huge help to us with the yard work.*

It should be our aim not only *to* help our husbands, but to *be* their help.

Many women know this principle in theory, but perhaps they have never had someone practically show them how to live it out. As we move through these next lessons, may the potentially blurred image of God's design for your role in marriage become very clear.

Back to Genesis

As God moved through the first five days of creation, after everything He made, He declared, "It is good." But that was not the case when He sent Adam to his first task, to his work.

> Then the Lord God said, "It is *not good* that the man should be alone; I will make him a helper fit for him." (Gen. 2:18, emphasis added)

God had created the perfect specimen of manliness, yet there was something not good about Adam's condition. He was alone. God identified and solved this problem by taking a piece of Adam to make Eve. The word for what God used to make Eve is often translated "rib." A more accurate translation of the Hebrew text is the word "side." It could have been a rib that was taken from Adam, or it could have been a lot more—it could have been half his entire body—and Eve was quite literally his other half. This perspective gives more insight to Adam's exclamation of "bone of my bones and flesh of my flesh" (Gen. 2:23).

Regardless of how much of the original Adam was used, God made Eve directly out of Adam. They were identical in value and equally made in God's image because they were made from the same stuff.

A Glorious Helper before the Fall

Adam was given an occupation as the first landscaper, and he was instructed not to eat from the tree of the knowledge of good and evil. It was then that God gave him a wife to help with all God had called Adam to accomplish. It was God's design from *the very beginning, before the fall and before the curse,* that a wife would be a helper to her husband. It is vital to realize that after God created Eve and assigned her role, *then* He said, "It is good."

Woman's role was not part of the curse of sin, but was part of the perfect design of God.

As God created the world, each step of creation built upon the last. He first created light and darkness, separated the waters and dry land, and then filled the land with grass and trees and plants. The sun and moon and stars were given to govern the days. After that, the waters were filled with swimming animals, the skies swarmed with flying things, and the land was inhabited with beasts and crawling creatures. Finally, God made man.

God didn't do all this creating—the crescendo getting more glorious with each new addition—and then decide, "Ah, well, I guess I'll throw in a lowly woman for the man." No! One of the definitions of the word "crown" is "the top or highest part of something." God made the woman to be the crown of His creation, not an afterthought. She was the highest point—the final touch on His masterpiece. God was *intentional* in how He created woman, and placing her in the role of a helper to her husband was the *very best* position God could have given her.

Rebellion Is Foolishness

In the original Hebrew, the word for "helper" is *ezer kenegdo.* It means "a helper like him, or worthy of him, suitable or adaptable to him." Eve was uniquely and perfectly designed to be a helper to her husband.

In nature, we see the males of a species perform different actions. A male lion protects and the lioness hunts and raises the cubs. The rooster protects the hens and chicks, and the hen lays eggs and broods over her babies. The female penguin lays the egg, then leaves it in the care of the husband while she hunts. There are clear male and female roles in the animal kingdom.

What if we started to question the order in the animal kingdom and demanded they have "equal" roles? What if we picketed the chicken coop and required the rooster to lay eggs and care for the chicks? Or what if we demanded equal hunting and childcare responsibilities for lions? The idea is ridiculous. Natural "laws" are followed because that's the way they were designed by the Creator.

Yet Satan has caused us to believe that God's structure of the human family is somehow demeaning and wrong, a trap designed to enslave and subdue us. On the contrary, embracing our God-given role is the only means to true freedom.

What Happens If We Are Out of Order?

The Genesis account demonstrates what happens if a wife decides to take the lead in her home. Adam was given the assigned role as the leader of his family, and Eve was to be his helper. Eve stepped out of the order God had given her, reached out for the forbidden fruit, and Adam followed her lead. Adam stood by and did nothing while his wife led them to destruction. The results were catastrophic, not only for Adam and Eve but for all subsequent generations.

In addition to Eve, the Bible gives several examples of a wife undermining or leading her husband instead of following him:

• **Sarah** decided God needed help in keeping His promises. She convinced Abraham to take Hagar as a second wife and have a child through her. The subsequent birth of Ishmael resulted in heartache for Abraham, Sarah, and Hagar and produced enemies for the descendants of Isaac that still exist today. (Gen. 16)

• **Rebekah** wanted to make sure her favorite son, Jacob, got more of an inheritance than his brother. She convinced Jacob to manipulate and deceive his father. The consequence was that her son had to flee from his vengeful brother, causing her family to be scattered. Jacob met years of heartache and struggle, and Rebekah died without ever seeing her beloved Jacob again. (Gen. 27)

• **Jezebel** not only incited her husband to abandon worship of the true God and go after idols, but she also encouraged her husband to commit murder in order to get the property he wanted. She eventually fell out of a window and was eaten by dogs. Her name is symbolic with carnality and everything Satanic in the book of Revelation. (1 Kings 18–19, 21; 2 Kings 9)

• **Delilah** manipulated and nagged Samson in order to find out the secret of his strength. This resulted in him being captured, tortured, and blinded, and eventually led not only to his death, but also to the deaths of the leaders of Delilah's people. (Judg. 16)

• **Michal** saw her husband, David, dancing before the Lord in what would have basically been his underwear. She despised him in her heart and mocked him to his face. The result was that Michal never had any children. (2 Sam. 6)

We will not find one biblical instance where a woman manipulated, nagged, undermined, usurped, or led her husband and the outcome was one of a blessing or peace. How silly to think the outcome would be any different for us.

We can be assured that if we choose rebellion against the order God has established for the family, catastrophe will also result in our own homes. A wife who "wears the pants" in her home, one who leads her husband (or who tries to have an equal leadership role with him), will ultimately find herself frustrated, angry, discontented, and lonely.

The Same Job Description as the Holy Spirit

Perhaps the most overlooked aspect of our role as a helper is the fact God bears the title Himself. In Jesus's last conversation with His disciples before His crucifixion, He comforts them by promising to send them the Helper, the Holy Spirit:

> Nevertheless, I tell you the truth: it is to your advantage that I go away, for if I do not go away, the Helper will not come to you. But if I go, I will send Him to you. (John 16:7)

In no way is the Holy Spirit inferior to God—He *is* God, our Helper. This third person of the Trinity bears the same job title as a wife! This should encourage us to embrace the title with absolute delight.

The Source of the Conflict

Where have we gotten this idea that being in charge is somehow superior to being behind the scenes? It is an idea older than earth itself.

Before the earth was created, Satan was actually an incredibly beautiful and gifted angel. Guided by pride, he wanted the credit, praise, and glory due to God. Other angels even agreed to follow him instead of God, and this is what led to Satan being cast out of heaven along with the demonic angels (Isa. 14:12–15 and Ezek. 28:11–19).

Satan whispers to women that God is unfair in calling them to be helpers and suggests we should be the ones in charge. Wanting to be the best, to be noticed, praised, and glorified—is a trait of Satan. When we seek these things, we are behaving like him.

Know Your Role and Shut Your Hole

My parents were very moral people, but the idea of biblical roles within marriage was totally foreign to them. My mom grew up in the '60s and was an adamant feminist. My passive father usually let her have her way because it was the path of least resistance. There was never any question about who "wore the pants" in our family. Screaming, slamming doors, not speaking to my dad for days, and threats of divorce were all standard ways of getting what she wanted. Their marriage ended in divorce when I was a teenager.**

My husband was a package deal. An adorable five-year-old blue-eyed blond boy named Joshua came with him, and I became an utterly unqualified wife and mother at twenty-three years old. Though I had been a Christian for a few years before I got married, I had little understanding of how to help, submit to, or honor my husband. For the first three years of marriage, whenever I didn't get my way, I would cry, scream, stomp my feet, slam doors, or threaten divorce. It had "worked" for my mom, and I assumed I could employ the same tactics and get my way.

I am so incredibly grateful my husband wasn't manipulated by me—not even once. He was an impenetrable force, and no matter how much I would storm, he would not be moved by his contentious wife.

One day I got angry because he had not taken out the trash. I was working full time, so I expected him to do his "fair share" of the housework. After exploding in screams and slamming a pan on the stove for effect, Brent got in his truck and left for work without saying a word to me. And he left the trash can overflowing in the kitchen.

I went into my room and tried to pray. Sobbing in self-pity, I asked God to fix it all (which meant, *Make Brent take out the trash like he's supposed to!*). I remembered a marriage book we had received as a wedding present, pulled it off the shelf, and opened to a section on what the Bible said about roles in marriage. I read about the helpful, submissive, respectful wife God expected me to be. It was like a spotlight on my unruly heart. Through the Scriptures, He exposed my self-centeredness, pride, and outright rebellion against His commands. I repented. I asked for His help. I yielded up my own will and committed to do things His way.

While I was reading, I'd let Joshua park in front of the TV, watching *WWF Superstars of Wrestling*. For those not in the know, there was an unfortunate era of choreographed wrestling where superhero-like "pro" wrestlers violently pummeled each other in a ring. Little boys loved it. Well, the wrestler in the particular episode being shown was nicknamed The Rock. The Rock had a catchphrase that he used to scream at his opponents: "Know your role and shut your hole!"

I found myself being ministered to by a WWF pro wrestler! Know your role—I am called to come alongside my husband and support and help him. Shut your hole—I am a contentious, rebellious, clamorous woman! I need to shut my mouth!

Decades have passed since that day, but the whole lesson is so firmly pressed into my heart. It began a transformation in our family that will bear fruit for decades. "Know your role and shut your hole" is still something I say to myself on a regular basis!

**I chose to include this truth about my family, not to dishonor my mother, but because I believe many women grow up with similar examples. In my mom's defense, she was not a Christian when I was growing up, and she was simply living by the feminist mantra of her generation. She got saved before she remarried, and her second marriage was very different. In one of my last conversations with her, she told me she regretted wasting so many good days of her life battling to be the boss, and she wished she had learned God was right sooner. My sweet mom is in heaven now, and I believe she would encourage me to share her struggle if it might lead to someone else's repentance and obedience.

LESSON 6 WIFE-CHANGING QUESTIONS

1. Why do you think the concept of being a helper is so offensive in our culture?

   pride

2. What is your biggest obstacle to surrendering to this calling on your life?

   My thought - I am older &
   entitled to ... He is younger
   and spoiled - always given
   what he wants. Where or is there

3. Were you able to identify any unbiblical perspectives in your own thinking as you read through this lesson? Is there anything you need to confess as sin?

   balance or is submission
   balance I seek?
   Selfish thinking that I need
   the help not that I am the
   help. If God Himself is the
   Helper - this is not too much
   for me to undertake here.

4. Do you think your husband would say that you are his help? Why or why not?

I think he would and at times he does. But his recognition should not be what I seek to fill me up.

5. Can you think of any examples of women in your own life who have played their part of helper well? What have they done to fulfill their role?

I don't have one "good example in my life. Mindi & Karen as pastor's wives have shown me.

6. Can you think of any bad examples of women who have rejected this calling on their life? What can you observe from their poor example?

Many girl friends, relatives my cry is how will my daughters answer this question?

7. Are you currently being the best possible helper to your husband in this season of your marriage?

Seeing th need & stepping toward it only through God's assistance + guidance.

LESSON 7

Fight the Right Enemy with the Right Weapons

As a follower of Christ, you are enlisted as a soldier in a very real battle. There is a fierce war going on around you. Your enemy wants your marriage destroyed and your witness for Christ eliminated. But God has not left you defenseless in this war. He has given you a full suit of armor and powerful weapons.

This lesson is under the "Help" section of this book because the most important way you can be a helper to your husband (and help yourself) is to engage in the battle with the spiritual weapons God has supplied. Ephesians 6:10–12 shows us four specific things we are to do in the battle:

> Finally, be strong in the Lord and in the strength of his might. Put on the whole armor of God, that you may be able to stand against the schemes of the devil. For we do not wrestle against flesh and blood, but against the rulers, against the authorities, against the cosmic powers over this present darkness, against the spiritual forces of evil in the heavenly places.

Battle Strategy #1—Identify Your True Enemy

Your husband may often seem to be the source of conflict in your life, but Ephesians chapter 6 says things are not what they appear to be. The truth is, your husband is *not* your real enemy. Your enemy is the same one that confronted Eve in the garden, and your conflict is actually with the cosmic powers and rulers of darkness. And they don't want you to know it. If you can be convinced your husband is the real problem, and if you continue to do battle with him, your marriage is exactly where Satan wants it to be—in the crossfire. You must fight the real enemy with the right weapons.

Battle Strategy #2—Use the Right Weapons

Just because you can't see something doesn't mean it's not there. You can't see the fierce spiritual battle going on around you because you are limited to your own senses. But the Word of God warns us that even though we are in fleshly bodies, we don't fight our battles with fleshly weapons.

Second Corinthians 10:3 tells us, "For though we walk in the flesh, we do not war according to the flesh."

What are fleshly weapons? Everything most women use to fight against their husbands! We manipulate, cry, rage, tell their friends, withhold sex, demand immediate change, and threaten divorce—all weapons that gain no victory in the battle, but instead lay a path for our own destruction.

As Christian women, however, we have been given powerfully effective weapons. 2 Corinthians 10:4 goes on to say, "For the weapons of our warfare are not carnal but mighty in God for pulling down strongholds."

What are these mighty weapons? Ephesians 6:13–17 describes them in detail. Let's unpack each of these and examine what they are and how they work.

> Therefore take up the whole armor of God, that you may be able to withstand in the evil day, and having done all, to stand firm. (vs. 13)

God has given you armor—isn't that marvelous? The Creator of the universe has equipped you with all you need to engage in the spiritual battle around you. You can't buy this in any store or make it yourself. The armor of God comes only as a gift from Him.

Paul begins this section on the armor of God by first saying what the full set of armor will do for us: If we take up the full set, we will be able to withstand the evil attacks of our enemy. That's quite a promise! If you take up this armor, you will be able to do all that is required of you as a soldier and to stand against your enemy. You are *assured* ultimate victory (in Christ) if you battle the right enemy with the right weapons!

We not only have weapons, but we also have spiritual armor. Paul wrote this while in a Roman prison, surrounded by armored guards. We can picture him studying the equipment of the soldiers around him and recognizing the way God has similarly equipped believers. In the next three verses of Ephesians 6, Paul describes each piece of the armor and weapons a believer has access to.

Belt of Truth

> Stand therefore, having fastened on the belt of truth. (Eph. 6:14)

The belt of a soldier was the first piece of equipment he put on, and all his other armor was attached to it in some way. Likewise, the belt of truth is what we must start with. Everything we do hangs on the truth of who we say God is and on His Word being absolute truth.

In spiritual battles, we may get confused by unbiblical opinions, and our feelings will lie to us. Therefore, we must be grounded in the truth of God's character and Word alone.

Are you grounded in the truth? Are you certain of God's character, His Word, and your identity in Him? This is where everything else attaches and stays in place.

Being equipped with truth is essential in combating the lies that are thrown at you in regard to your role in your marriage.

Breastplate of Righteousness

> . . . having put on the breastplate of righteousness. (Eph. 6:14)

A soldier's breastplate protected his vital organs. Without it, he would be essentially defenseless and could be easily killed in battle.

Righteousness is the breastplate of the Christian. We know that righteousness is only granted through faith in Jesus Christ—it cannot be earned. The righteousness we are given through faith in Christ gives us our identity. It is our basis for security.

When we are in battle, our enemy will often remind us of our past sin and current failures, and will predict our future ruin. To *put on* the breastplate of righteousness is to remind ourselves of where we stand before God—not based on our own performance, but on the finished work of Jesus on the cross. Jesus has given us *His own* righteousness. Like a Roman soldier wearing his breastplate, when we put on the breastplate of righteousness and wear it courageously, our spiritual "vital organs" are protected.

Shoes of the Gospel

> . . . and having shod your feet with the preparation of the gospel of peace.
> (Eph. 6:15)

Footwear was essential to a Roman soldier. If he didn't have shoes, he would be slow, slip, or step on something and injure himself in battle. No matter how well-equipped he was, if his feet were injured, he became an easy target for the enemy.

Have you ever tried to hike over a rugged landscape in plastic flip-flops? It's pretty much impossible to go very fast or very far. But a well-fitting pair of hiking shoes can quickly propel you over rough terrain.

The gospel is the symbolic pair of shoes for the believer. How secure is your footing? Are you able to define the gospel clearly? David Guzik says, "The gospel is the footing for everything else we do."[1]

In the introduction, I shared an acronym with you for the gospel to help you remember the essential points of the gospel. Can you remember them? Be sure you can articulate the gospel—it is your spiritual footwear and it needs to be in good condition for the rough terrain of this world.

The Shield of Faith

> In all circumstances take up the shield of faith, with which you can extinguish all the flaming darts of the evil one. (Eph. 6:16)

The shield a Roman soldier used was not like Captain America's, but rather, it was roughly the size of a soldier's full body. It was a mighty defense against arrows that were set on fire and launched at the soldier. The soldier could completely hide himself behind this defensive piece of armor, and often the flaming arrow would be extinguished as it hit the shield.

I love this symbolism so much. Our enemy fires flaming arrows, doesn't he? I am often hit with intense accusations, fears, doubts, emotions, or troubles. If I am not standing behind my shield of faith, then I can be set ablaze by the lies convincing me that the accusations are true, the fears are merited, the doubts are reality, and the emotions are justified—and I am convinced my troubles will overtake me.

However, if I am shielded by faith, I can stand firm against the fiery darts and claim that God knows the truth of the accusations and that He will reveal the right information in His time. I can fight my fear because I am confident God is with me and will never leave me. My doubts and wild feelings can be put to rest because I know the truth about God. Faith allows me to claim what I do not actually see, but still know to be true.

Candace's husband was frequently away on business trips. She shared how she would get hit with darts of insecurity and fear that would rapidly turn into unreasonable accusations and behaviors:

> I would be totally fine at home with the kids, and then I would have a thought like, *What if Richard is not really working, and he's just going off to a hotel with a mistress?* I would let my thoughts spiral totally out of control till I was a crying mess, frantically texting, demanding to see photographic proof of his whereabouts. I once drove six hours to spy on him and to see if he was really on a business trip.
>
> The constant accusing and questioning made Richard angry, and we started fighting all the time. This just convinced me that he was probably seeing other women when he was away. I heard a message at church about how the enemy will shoot fiery darts at us and how the shield of faith must be used to quench them. I realized I was letting the lies of the enemy set my thoughts on fire.
>
> I had to decide to apply faith to those thoughts, to remind myself of God's love and protection and of Richard's integrity. I started using my fears to prompt me to pray for my husband and my marriage instead of

freaking out. After a few months of that, I realized I wasn't having those types of insecurities as often. My faith had grown stronger, and the fiery darts were extinguished more quickly.

Helmet of Salvation

Ephesians 6:17 says, "And take the helmet of salvation." First Thessalonians 5:8 further describes this spiritual piece of armor as the helmet of "the hope of salvation."

The Roman helmet, similar to our modern-day motorcycle helmets, protected a soldier's entire head. Spiritually, it is symbolic of the hope we have of heaven. When we are growing weary in a long battle, remembering that our future is secure in a battle-free heaven will give us strength to continue in the fight.

We have a very sure and certain hope. "Blessed be the God and Father of our Lord Jesus Christ," Peter exults in his first epistle, "who according to His great mercy has caused us to be born again to a living hope through the resurrection of Jesus Christ from the dead, to obtain an inheritance which is imperishable and undefiled and will not fade away, reserved in heaven for you, who are protected by the power of God through faith for a salvation ready to be revealed in the last time" (1 Peter 1:3–5).

When the helmet of that hope is in place, we can

> Greatly rejoice, even though now for a little while, if necessary, we have been distressed by various trials, that the proof of our faith, being more precious than gold which is perishable, even though tested by fire, may be found to result in praise and glory and honor at the revelation of Jesus Christ; and though [we] have not seen Him, [we] love Him, and though we do not see Him now, but believe in Him, we greatly rejoice with joy inexpressible and full of glory, obtaining as the outcome of our faith the salvation of our souls" (1 Peter 1: 6-9).

Our helmet is the certain prospect of heaven, our ultimate salvation, which we have as an anchor of the soul. (Heb. 6:19)

> Often when a runner is on the home stretch of a race he suddenly "hits the wall," as the expression goes. His legs wobble and refuse to go any farther. The only hope for the runner is to keep his mind on the goal, on the victory to be won for himself and his team. It is that hope that keeps him going when every other part of his being wants to give up.[2]
> —John MacArthur

The Sword of the Spirit

> . . . and the sword of the Spirit, which is the word of God. (Eph. 6:17)

Your Bible is a weapon. Not the book itself, but the words contained in the pages.

Once you know the Word, you then have it as a ready weapon. Apply its truth to every battle in your life. There is nothing in your life that the Word of God does not address. It is living and active and can cut right to the heart of any matter. Use it in your marriage. Not just the verses about marriage—the whole of Scripture pertains to your life! (This does not mean you should quote Scripture at your husband every time he offends you! Rather, remind yourself and the real enemy—Satan—of what God has promised in His Word, pray Scripture over your marriage, and preach it to yourself.)

There is really no excuse for you to not know the Word of God. You have ready access to it, you are literate, you have twenty-four hours in a day to find time to read or listen to it, and you have the Holy Spirit to explain it to you—not to mention great Bible teachers, commentators, books, blogs, and websites at your fingertips. To remain ignorant of the Bible is a choice. It is a choice that many do not ever get to make because they have no access to the Word. Take advantage of the privilege you have to access the sword of the Spirit. Know the Word of God.

In Luke 4, Jesus demonstrated exactly how to combat our mutual enemy when we are hit with the lust of the flesh, the lust of the eyes, and the pride of life. Each time He was tempted, he responded to Satan by saying, "It is written. . . ." Jesus battled Satan using only the written Word of God. Oh, what an example to follow!

Prayer

> . . . praying always with all prayer and supplication in the Spirit, being watchful to this end with all perseverance and supplication for all the saints. (Eph. 6:18)

Prayer is our most effective tool in helping our husbands and bringing about real changes in our families, yet is often our last resort. After we have nagged, cried, and talked to our friends, we decide, *Well, all I can do now is pray.* Oh, how foolish! Prayer is a supernatural defensive weapon we can continually use to help mold and shape our families.

Sadly, prayer is often explained like a quaint little two-way chat with God. That's so trite and ridiculous. Prayer is war. Prayer is labor-intensive effort. Prayer takes concentration and perseverance. It is a battle to get into prayer, a battle to stay in prayer, and a battle to believe prayer is even accomplishing anything. That's why there is often so little of it in our lives! If it was easy, we would do it all the time. And yet we *must* pray if we want to see things change in our homes.

Prayer requires faith. It demands we believe what the Scriptures say is true, that we participate in spiritual things we can't see, and that we believe something we can't see is happening as a result.

I once heard prayer described as a Christian's "long-range artillery." Prayer is a way for us to do battle from great distances. It is limitless. There is no place too far for prayer to reach. Whether your husband is out of the country, out of town, or out of his mind—discharge prayer to wherever he is, and you are helping him there.

Be Ready for Battle

A soldier would be foolish to wait until the middle of a battle to put his armor on. Knowing the battle is sure to come, a wise soldier wears his armor at all times so he is ready to fight whenever his enemy strikes. If we aren't taking up the armor of God, then it will be impossible to stand against the spiritual forces coming against us when they arrive.

So how does a Christian wife put her spiritual armor on?

Belt of Truth. Remind yourself what is true, based on the Scriptures. God is ultimately good and right in everything He does. He loves you, and He will never forsake you. His Spirit is there to guide you, and His plans are always right and best.

Breastplate of Righteousness. Remember that you are in right standing with God, based on what Jesus did on the cross. You are forgiven and able to walk in holiness and obedience because His Spirit lives within you.

Shoes of the Gospel. Refresh yourself with the gospel. Preach it to yourself.

Shield of Faith. Apply what you know to those fiery darts and attacks that come your way. Believe God above every thought, feeling, circumstance, and opinion.

Helmet of Salvation. Take comfort in the truth that your eternity is secure in heaven.

Sword of the Spirit. Use the Word of God as a defensive and offensive weapon. Protect yourself with truth, and attack your enemy with it.

Prayer. Engage in the war with the weapon of prayer, remembering it's a struggle worth fighting.

LESSON 7 WIFE-CHANGING QUESTIONS

1. Have you been guilty of using fleshly weapons in your marriage? What has been the result?

_____

_____

_____

_____

2. In reviewing the armor and weapons you have been given, are there any weaknesses in your recent use of them?

_____

_____

_____

_____

3. Are you persistently, passionately engaging in battle through prayer, expecting God to answer? How can you improve in this area?

_____

_____

_____

_____

4. How can you specifically use each piece of spiritual armor in your marriage right now?

Belt of Truth:

_____

_____

Breastplate of Righteousness:

_____

_____

Shoes of the Gospel:

_____

_____

Shield of Faith:

_____

_____

Helmet of Salvation:

_____

_____

Sword of the Spirit:

_____

_____

Prayer:

_____

_____

5. What wife-changing adjustments need to be made to ensure you are continually fighting the right enemy with the right weapons?

_____

_____

_____

_____

LESSON 8

Lisa accomplished more in a day than most women do in a week. She was an expert planner, always punctual, and kept her home in perfect order. When she married Kyle, she was attracted to his spontaneous whims and found his disorganized habits adorable. She figured once they were married, Kyle would see the wisdom in being orderly and on time. She could fix him!

But instead of adapting to her schedule, Kyle called her a nag and a control freak. After countless battles about schedules and chore lists, Lisa decided Kyle was just ridiculously immature. That he could live his life without routine and leave tasks unfinished for weeks was just proof of his juvenile view of adulthood. Though she wouldn't say so out loud, Lisa believed she was superior to Kyle in intellect and spiritual maturity because she was more structured. She looked at his undone tasks with disgust and sighed at the thought of a future with someone not as sensible as she was.

What Lisa failed to understand was that her husband was uniquely created by God and was not supposed to be like her. His unstructured ways are not necessarily marks of immaturity, but rather are a reflection of the creativity of God and a way for Lisa to grow. While Kyle could likely benefit from his wife's perfect planning, Lisa could equally grow in letting go of control and being led more by the Spirit of God rather than her own schedule. God has brought the two of them together with their unique strengths and weaknesses and desires to make each other *better* because of the other.

Many times a wife will wrongly perceive a difference between herself and her husband as a fault that needs to be corrected. Often, these "faults" are actually God-given qualities that a wife can greatly benefit from if she can choose to let go of her own preferences and adapt to the man God has made for her.

> The more you look at your spouse and see the imprint of God's fingers and are amazed, the more you will be able to resist the temptation to try to remake him or her into your own image. The more you esteem what God has created, the less you will want to remake it. The more you see divine beauty and divine glory in the differences between you, the less you will be irritated by them.[3] —Paul David Tripp

There *should* be huge differences between you and your husband. You are individually designed to fit together into one complete unit. You are not independent clones of the same person. Each of you brings necessary strengths that the other needs. You also each bring weaknesses that can be protected by the other.

Expectations and Reality

Many women marry an *expectation* rather than an actual man. A young bride often has all kinds of ideas about how her marriage is going to be. But soon after the honeymoon, she starts to see that the guy she said "I do" to is not fitting into her plan, which must mean she has to work on him. She then spends the next several years trying to conform him to her expectations and lives in a perpetual state of frustration and disappointment. Many of us enter into marriage expecting our husbands to be like our fathers or brothers. If you grew up with a quiet, steady, passive father, you might be at a loss as to how to respond to your loud, impulsive, and aggressive husband. You may be tempted to tell him he is supposed to be quiet, steady, and passive. If you spend your marriage trying to make your husband act like your daddy, you'll be frustrated for the rest of your married life.

Some wives spend years trying to change their husbands into someone else. They believe if their husband would just be more outgoing, or less social, or harder working, or not work so much. If he would lose weight, or stop being obsessed with the gym, if he were wiser with money, or wasn't such a tightwad. If he were smarter, or not so smart, if he were more adventurous, or more spiritual, or more in touch with his feelings—*then* she would be a happy wife.

Some wives come into marriage with the perspective that their husband is like a fixer-upper house they get to go into and completely renovate. But that's not God's idea of how to be a helper to your husband. Your husband is not your "project." It is God's work to change him if he needs improvements.

For many women, their biggest obstacle in embracing their roles as helpers is letting go of their own expectations of who they want their husbands to be and choosing to serve them as they are. Ladies, your husband is who he is. Does he need improvement? Absolutely. But he is who he is today. And God expects you to help him *as he is*.

Know Your Own Husband

There are artistic men and athletic men, relational men and intellectual men, assertive men and adventurous men, methodical men and spontaneous men. There are countless qualities and temperaments and combinations of all of them. No man is alike! Your husband is unique to this world, and he is intentionally designed by God as he is.

How you help your husband is going to be different from how your friend helps hers. The way your talents fit with your husband's personality and temperament will be unique to your own relationship.

Are you an expert on your own husband? Who are you actually married to? What is your husband's personality like? What is his temperament? What are his strengths and weaknesses? What are his favorite things to do? What things annoy him?

It is absolutely necessary for you to know your own husband's unique personality and temperament, to understand his strengths and weaknesses. If you know who you're actually married to, then you can be busy helping him be all God has called him to be instead of trying to make him into someone else.

As his helper, it is your *job* to know him as well as you possibly can and to serve him according to the unique person he is.

Who Is Your Husband's Wife?

Your husband married a unique person also. Your temperament, quirks, talents, skills, preferences—he married all of them. Who is your husband actually married to? Knowing your own strengths and weaknesses can help you identify how you are uniquely designed to help your own husband.

My neighbor, Lori, is the most incredible homemaker I've ever known. She bakes her own bread after she grinds the grain herself. She grows vegetables in her organic backyard garden, keeps chickens, and sews most of the dresses worn by her three young daughters. Their church often meets in her sparkling-clean home. Her minivan is usually in her driveway because she is home. She embodies a "stereotypical homeschool mom"—right down to her ankle-length denim skirt. Lori is an altogether lovely woman.

I live down the street from Lori. I buy my bread and my clothes from the store, and I have killed every vegetable I have ever tried to grow myself. Most days, I'm in my minivan more than I'm in my home. Though I homeschooled, I've never owned an ankle-length denim skirt.

Years ago I tried to be more like a "real" homeschool mom—constructing elaborate lesson plans, baking (burning) my own bread, and planting a vegetable garden (which became infested with bugs and was entirely inedible). My husband hadn't asked me to do any of those things. I just compared myself to women like Lori and assumed doing those things would make me a better wife. I exhausted myself in trying to become someone my husband hadn't married and God hadn't called me to be. Brent finally had to remind me that he needed my help in ministry much more than he needed homegrown vegetables and freshly baked bread. What a relief! I'm not designed to be a domestic genius like Lori! I'm designed to be Pastor Brent's wife!

My role as a helper is identical to Lori's, but I go about fulfilling it in a different way. Lori's husband married Lori, and she is a fantastic helper to him. Brent married me, and he thinks I'm altogether lovely. Lori and I are both honoring God in how we each are living out our own calling to be helpers to our own husbands, according to the gifts He has given each of us.

You Are a Package Deal

When I got married, it didn't erase my love of reading, museums, board games, thrift stores, and long hikes. Brent married my grammar skills, organizational mania, love for hosting parties and houseguests, and my sharp memory. Unfortunately, he also married my extreme clumsiness, multitasking incompetence, math ineptitude, athletic inability, and technological uselessness. My unique capabilities and gifts, as well as my limitations and inabilities, came with the whole Nancy package. All of these things define my own identity and determine what kind of helper I am to Brent. I can truly help him in ministry and business, but if I tried to play on his basketball team or manage our finances, I would embarrass us both!

You are intentionally designed by God to help your own husband. Having an honest view of your husband and yourself is necessary for you to be the best helper you can be. You are as unique as he is. Together you form a unique, beautiful bond that has never been exactly duplicated on this earth. To try and change what God has created and intentionally designed is foolishness. But working together to maximize your joined strengths and cover one another's weaknesses results in a beautiful reflection of God's wisdom.

A Helper Suitable for Him

The truth of your identity as a wife is found in Genesis 2:18, when God said, "I will make him a helper suitable for him."

God created the woman with the primary purpose of being a helper, suited to her husband's needs. Eve was made *for* Adam and *from* Adam, and she was given *to* Adam. Her main purpose was for Adam's benefit. This wasn't an insult to Eve, but rather was a gift to her.

What does that mean for *you*? Of course, it's not your *only* function, but a central role of your life is to be a suitable, tailor-made, productive helper to your own husband.

I asked friends to comment on how they help their husbands, and I was bombarded with great answers. There were the standard domestic answers like housekeeping and shopping, but I was blessed by some of the more specific things that some of the ladies shared.

Susan was keenly aware of Tim's fear of financial failure. He'd been struggling to start his own business and was continually making comments that he wasn't sure they were going to make it. Susan wasn't so sure either, but she knew that more than anything, Tim needed her to believe in his future success. She earnestly guarded herself against voicing her own fears and chose to speak words of affirmation. She said to me, "It's so important that Tim knows that even if we lose everything, I'll be by his side and will support him no matter what."

Debbie's husband is severely dyslexic. She reads nearly everything for him, without treating him like he's a toddler. We have gone to dinner with them, and I watched in admiration as she casually read over the menu and then said, "Ooh! I bet you'd like the lasagna, but the salmon comes with sweet potatoes, and you love those." When they go to new places, she reads street names and storefront signs, all in a way most people looking on would have no idea she is actually reading to her husband.

Early in their marriage, Marianne's husband realized she was way better at managing their finances than he was. Without being controlling or condescending, she has handled their budget and investments for nearly thirty years.

Diane said her husband has huge fingers, and she realized he always had trouble getting the little pieces of communion bread when it came around at church. She started just grabbing two pieces so he didn't have to fumble anymore.

Amber's husband is super articulate but a terrible speller, and his grammar and punctuation skills are sometimes lacking. However, his job requires him to write newsletters and important emails. Several times a week, and sometimes several times a day, her husband asks her to review an email or newsletter, and she makes sure what he has written is correct. No one knows she does this, and she lets him take the credit for writing so well.

I was visiting my friend Maureen while she was undergoing radiation treatments for cancer. Her husband, John, was going to a wedding without her and started to leave. Maureen noticed he was wearing jeans and a striped polo shirt, and she gently told him jeans were not appropriate for a wedding—that he needed to wear slacks. John went into the closet and came out with a pair of striped slacks and asked if they would go with the striped shirt he was wearing, saying, "They are kind of the same color, right?" He was totally serious.

Maureen gently coached him through several wardrobe choices. Seeing my amusement, she whispered, "I usually have his clothes all picked out for him, but I was too sick this week to think about what he would wear today."

Here are some other ways you can be a helper to your husband:

- Praise him in front of others, especially to your children (double points if he hears you).
- Honor his wishes when he's not around.
- Dress in clothes he likes to see you in, not what you prefer.
- Participate in/learn about his hobbies.
- Give him time to himself when he needs it.
- Let him sleep in.
- Meet his sexual needs without him having to ask.
- Match his socks.
- Call his mother.
- Drop off his dry cleaning, or iron for him.
- Share his burdens.
- Know his fears and insecurities and guard them.
- Keep track of birthdays and special events and remind him to acknowledge them.
- Send him a list of upcoming events to put on his calendar.
- Remind him to put on sunscreen (and don't be a nag if he forgets).
- Ask him every day how you can pray for him (and then actually pray!).
- Kiss him when you part and when you meet.
- Pack his lunch (add a love note!).
- Update his wardrobe—keep him in style.
- Let him dream big (don't kill his dreams with practicality!).
- Encourage healthy habits without nagging.
- Sit with him while he does a "man chore."
- Learn how to do a "man chore" and do it for him.
- Listen to him without interrupting.
- Be able to engage him in rousing conversation (don't be a bore!).
- Choose to not be easily offended.
- Don't spend more than you agree upon together—stay within your financial means without complaint.

- Tell the truth.
- Keep his secrets.
- Make him more important than your housework.
- Bring him a cool drink without being asked.
- Ask his advice (and take it!).
- Prepare nutritious meals (ones he will actually eat).
- Go to parties or business obligations with him and look fantastic.
- Be his cheerleader.
- Make doctor/dentist appointments for him.
- Praise his strengths and overlook his weaknesses.
- Replace things he runs out of.
- Repair or replace things he breaks or damages (without grumbling).

These are just a few samples of how different women have come alongside their own husbands and occupied their God-given position of *helper*. There is not a one-size-fits-all job description for a Christian wife.

The way you help your husband is one area of marriage that continually needs wife-changing adjustments. Occupations, family dynamics, health, location, and other factors determine how each of us will occupy our role as helper in our own marriages from season to season. At all times, each of us is called to be a helper to our own husbands, and we are wise to examine our own lives and assess where we may need to refresh our commitment to this role.

His Helper, Not His Mother

With all this helping, I want to give you a word of caution. There is a delicate balance between helping and nagging. A wife will often cross this line and begin treating her husband like another one of her children. Don't turn into his second mom!

Joe has been a surfer his whole life. Being a blue-eyed blond, he has very fair skin and often gets horrible sunburns. His wife, Cathy, is concerned he is going to get skin cancer. "Don't forget to put on sunscreen!" she cheerfully warns as he is loading his board into his truck. But more often than not, he comes home bright red. Here is where Cathy has to be careful. She could easily turn into a nag, scolding him for his carelessness and reminding him he has four children to raise, and if he dies of skin cancer, he will leave her to do it alone. She would be trying to help him, but he will surely roll his eyes at her condescending lecture.

So what can she do to get him to wear sunscreen? First, she can ask him how she can help him to remember. He may ask her to not let him out of the house until she has put it on him herself. She can also leave a healthy supply of sunscreen in his truck, in his surf bag, and in his bathroom cabinet, and never say a word. The bottom line is—he's a man. He may tell her to leave it alone because he can choose to wear sunscreen or not. She can dishonor him by treating him like a child, or she can treat him like a man, offer her help, and then let him do what he's going to do.

Claire rarely consumes sugar, processed foods, or meat. She makes healthy meals for her family and ensures they are taking their supplements every day. However, her husband, Bruce, isn't as into clean eating as she would like. Sometimes, after picking at the kale and quinoa salad his wife serves for dinner, Bruce will run to the corner mini-mart, come home with a box of cupcakes, and eat them all in one sitting—in front of the kids. Claire often finds Bruce's supplements untouched on the bathroom counter after he leaves for work, and she discovers fast-food bags in his truck. He has gained twenty-five pounds since they got married, and she is terribly concerned about his health. She is often guilty of huffing disgustedly at what he chooses to put in his body. When she shows her disapproval, it just makes Bruce want to eat more junk because he wants to prove he can make his own choices whether she likes it or not.

How can Claire help him stay healthy and not act like his disapproving mother? The best thing she can do is to stop showing disapproval. Disrespect, even if motivated by genuine concern, will never motivate a husband to change. Bruce is quite aware of what his wife wants him to do. He knows he's gained weight, and he knows he should lay off the cupcakes. He knows. She can earnestly pray for God to convict him and determine to never nag him again about what he is eating or not eating. She can discover what healthy foods he will actually enjoy (it's probably not her kale and quinoa salad) and provide those for him. Not being a nag is the best thing Claire can do for her marriage and for Bruce's health.

More often than not, we learn to be responsible by suffering the consequences of irresponsibility. We get sunburned or we gain weight and feel terrible—and then we make changes to avoid those same uncomfortable circumstances. It is important to let our husbands learn their own lessons, free from our nagging.

You Are Your Husband's Helper—He Is Not Yours!

Julia began our meeting by saying, "I'm just exhausted. I work all day cleaning my house and taking care of the kids. I'm also working three mornings a week to help pay our bills. Simon is working overtime, but he's not helping me with the house or the kids. He expects me to still make dinner every night and get the kids to bed. And he slept in on Saturday! It's not fair! I think he should at least offer to do more around the house. If I'm working too, shouldn't he have to help me?"

I have heard versions of this scenario countless times. I've lived this scenario myself. Wives everywhere are crying out, "It's not fair!" And you know what? They're right! If we are looking to keep score, I would wager women are doing more than their "fair share" of house cleaning, child-rearing, shopping, laundry, and cooking. Many wives are doing all of the work at home and working full- or part-time jobs. They are working hard and are often taken advantage of. If we are keeping score, we are certainly being cheated.

But friends, why are we keeping score? Why are we trying to make things "fair?" Hasn't Jesus called us to be servants—to give, expecting nothing in return? Should we not let *Him* be the one keeping score? We are called to lay down our lives to serve our King! We are not called to lives of equality or fairness, but lives of giving, sacrifice, and service.

There is an enormous lie in our society that tells us that we should have some sort of fifty-fifty arrangement when it comes to our marriages. I have known women who developed detailed chore charts and cooking schedules to ensure their husbands did their "fair share." I've even heard of women keeping track of who has to change the next diaper or alternating who has to drive the kids to school to make sure they don't end up doing more work than their husbands.

Sisters, this is not a business partnership; it's a marriage!

Can your husband help you? Absolutely! (If my husband were speaking to your husband, he'd be the first to tell him to grab a broom!) I have friends who have shopping-loving husbands or husbands who are the cooks in their families. Brent does all our laundry. These are all blessings, and we can be grateful that our husbands choose to serve this way.

It is absolutely great if your husband offers to be the trashman or the chef or the chief duster—you're a blessed woman and should take him up on that—but to demand a balance of the workload in the name of "fairness" is setting yourself up for constant discontent and strife in your home.

By divine design, you are your husband's helper. He is not yours. For you to demand fairness is essentially disagreeing with God. Instead, choose to be a willing helper, and leave the score keeping up to God.

LESSON 8 WIFE-CHANGING QUESTIONS

1. Have you battled with feeling disappointed because your husband hasn't met your expectations? Do you need to surrender your expectations to the Lord and decide to help your husband as he is today? Write a prayer of surrender here.

_____

_____

_____

_____

2. What wife-changes can you make to be a more capable helper? Think of two things you can learn to do or get better at in order to be a more capable helper to your husband.

_____

_____

_____

_____

3. What are your strengths? What are five things you are really good at and enjoy doing?

_____

_____

_____

_____

4. How can you use these strengths to better help your husband?

_____

_____

_____

_____

5. What are your three biggest weaknesses?

_____

_____

_____

_____

6. How do these weaknesses limit you as a helper?

_____

_____

_____

_____

7. What weaknesses does your husband have that you can help him with? (Write these on your list.)

_____

_____

_____

_____

8. Write down at least ten ways you can help your own husband.

_____

_____

_____

_____

9. In the next twenty-four hours, go to your husband and tell him that your assignment for this lesson was to make a list of the ways you can be a helper to him. Read him your list. Then ask him what else should be on it.

_____

_____

_____

_____

10. Are there things your husband would like your help with, but you have been reluctant because it's "not your thing"? Can you work on being more capable or willing in this area? Write a commitment to serve the Lord by helping your husband.

_____

_____

_____

_____

11. Are you ever guilty of being a nagging wife? Are your good intentions possibly pushing him away from you? Write a commitment to change your approach to helping him.

_____

_____

_____

_____

12. Have you been guilty of expecting your husband to be your helper? Confess your sin to God. Confess your sin to your husband. Write a prayer of repentance here.

_____

_____

_____

_____

LESSON 9

One of my favorite pictures of my sister is when she was three years old and had buttoned her own sweater. The photo shows her with a cheesy grin, pushing out her belly, proudly showing off her ability to get the buttons in the holes, totally unconcerned that two of the buttons were dangling below the last buttonhole.

The way you understand submission is like buttoning a sweater. If you line up the first button with the right hole, then it's easy to get the other buttons straight, but if you don't start out right, then the rest of the buttons won't match up. Aligning your own perspective with how God sees submission is essential to how everything else lines up in your marriage; therefore, every Christian wife needs to understand submission and confidently live by this principle in her own marriage.

Slavery or Pseudo-spiritual?

We live in a culture that greatly values autonomy and independence, so when we talk about things like being a helper or submitting, it's no wonder we encounter opposition. Our culture wants us to believe we must fight for our rights and demand to be treated fairly.

Marital advice from worldly talk shows or blogs will tell you what your flesh wants to hear: You deserve to be treated like a princess every day. You are entitled to time to yourself. You should only have to do 50 percent of the housework. Your husband is selfish if he doesn't live to cater to your needs.

Spend fifteen minutes reading secular marriage blogs, and you will be convinced that if you're following the Bible, you're doing it all wrong!

The world's ideas of how a marriage is "supposed" to work and what a good wife is changes from generation to generation. Articles my grandmother read differed greatly from the ones written for my mother's generation. The current culture questions whether marriage even needs to be between people of the opposite sex. In contrast, God's instructions about how a wife should operate have not changed since the Garden of Eden. How foolish we are to take any counsel from the unsteady, unbelieving world around us!

It's not just the secular world that misunderstands the biblical command of submission. There is an equally disturbing trend among Christian circles. Some Christian women adopt a sort of mindless "I-traded-my-brains-for-a-wedding-ring" attitude and call it "biblical submission." In an attempt to be spiritual, these ladies behave as if their sole purpose for existence is to do whatever their husband orders. They won't leave the house, make a sandwich, or choose a dress to wear without first checking that their husbands approve. While this might appear to be super-Christian, this is not the biblical standard of submission either.

Submission: What's the Point?

Wives, submit to your own husbands, as to the Lord. (Eph. 5:22)

In order for a society to function properly, there must be people in authority, as well as people in submission to that authority. Students are to follow their teachers' instructions; employees submit to the demands of their employers; soldiers obey orders from their superiors; all of us yield to the police officer who stands in the middle of the busy intersection and holds his hand in the "stop" position.

Submission is all about order.

In any business, organization, school, or institution, there must be a chain of command. There has to be a president, a CEO, a principal, a boss, or a director. Someone has to have authority to be the final decision maker.

Though democracy is great and we all should have an opportunity to voice our opinion at times, there are certain times when we just won't be able to agree on a decision. To avoid gridlock, it is necessary to have one final authority who can make the decision.

Our society is accustomed to submitting to authority outside the home , but often reacts with disgust at the suggestion that such authority should exist within a marriage. Yet a family is an organization with a need to be governed just like other institutions.

God has declared that the husband is the final authority within a family.

Submission Defined

"Submission" literally means "to order under." It is a military word referring to the way a military is organized according to rank. The level of authority a person has depends on his rank, and those who are of lesser rank are required to submit to those above them. A private in the army may be smarter, more talented, a more capable leader, or more spiritually stable than his general; however, because of the rank of the general, the private must submit to the general's authority.

Within a marriage, submission doesn't have anything to do with the man being smarter, more talented, more capable, or more spiritual than his wife. Nor is it a mark of inferiority, an admission of stupidity, or a punishment for femininity. Submission has everything to do with God's designated order.

When Paul instructed wives to submit to their husbands, he was teaching that submission is based on the God-given rank of the husband and not on his personal qualifications. It is our God-breathed command to respect our husband's God-appointed position.

The opposite of the word "submit" is "rebel." If I'm not submitting, I'm rebelling—both against God and my husband.

Jesus—Always the Best Example

Do you realize Jesus submitted? Jesus, the eternal creator of the universe, willingly laid down His own rights and submitted to the authorities in His human life.

- Jesus obeyed His parents. In Luke 2, we read that Jesus was submissive to His parents when He was a child. Jesus honored the roles within the family that He Himself set in place when He formed the first family. He was certainly superior to His parents, yet He was "subject to them" because of the position they were in.
- Jesus paid taxes. In Matthew 17, we find that the ruler of the universe submitted to the authority of the tax collectors.
- Jesus submitted to governing authorities(John 18). Before Jesus was crucified, He allowed those in authority to arrest Him. He went through the trial process (though it was illegal and unjust), and ultimately let the government murder Him. Jesus was the supreme King, yet He submitted Himself to human government.

In all of these ways, we see Jesus willingly lay aside His own rights and submit to those in positions of human authority. He did this *because He was ultimately submitting to the Father.* That's the key. Submission is possible if we are ultimately submitting to God. Pastor and Bible commentator David Guzik says:

> Submission does not mean inferiority. As well, submission does not mean silence. Submission means "sub-mission." There is a mission for the Christian marriage, and that mission is obeying and glorifying God. The wife says, "I'm going to put myself under that mission. That mission is more important than my individual desires. I'm not putting myself below my husband, I'm putting myself below the mission God has for our marriage, for my life."⁴

Submission or Silence?

Submission does not mean a wife must always agree with her husband, never share her opinions, or never communicate her ideas with him. A wife is not forbidden to give her perspective or appeal to her husband with her concerns about a decision. Her husband is wise to take her counsel into consideration; she is, after all, his own God-given helper!

When a decision must be made and the husband and wife cannot agree, then it is up to the husband to lead his family in the way he believes God is leading him. The husband then answers to God for whatever ultimate decision is made.

Some women's minds are filled with fear that their husband will dictate their entire lives. Images of him sitting in his easy chair while he tells her what she is allowed to eat, what she has to wear, who she can associate with, where she can go, and what she is allowed to think are often what is conjured up in the minds of fearful women. This is not the picture of a godly marriage!

Submission itself isn't actually what we struggle with. Being in submission to our husbands is easy when we are in agreement, but when we have a conflict and must surrender our own wills, that's when the curse comes into play. Submission is only difficult when we disagree!

The need to lay down your will may arise often in certain seasons, and in other seasons you may be in agreement with your husband in every area. Each marriage is unique in what circumstances surrender is required. In most cases, much of what a wife chooses to do or not do will not need to be brought to her husband for approval. However, if there are decisions your husband makes and you disagree with him, then it is God's command for you to lay down your own will and submit to the authority He has given to your husband.

The flooring contractor said they would start the project on Monday. As soon as he left, I decided the best thing for me to do would be to paint the bedrooms before they ripped out the carpet. I figured it would take me a whole day, but it would be totally worth it to have fresh walls to go with the new floors. Before lunch, I had picked out the colors, purchased four gallons of paint, and loaded up on masking tape and paintbrushes.

When Brent called that afternoon, I enthusiastically shared my plans with him. He quenched my painting fire hard: "Babe, I don't want you taking on a big painting project right now. You haven't rested all summer. School starts soon, the kids are off right now, you have that retreat to prepare for, and you're going to get worn out. I'd rather hire someone to paint."

I countered by telling him I was already prepared and had my schedule all laid out. It was going to be easy. He wasn't impressed and was really firm that he didn't want me painting. Oh, I was so frustrated!

Friday morning, I woke up and so badly wanted to roll that lovely yellow on the walls. I could have just done it. Brent was already at work, and I would have been nearly done when he got home. He would have been upset, but I'd have my yellow walls! I chose to die to my own will, honor him, and take his counsel.

The flooring guys came and went and my walls were still gray. A few weeks later, Brent hired an out-of-work painter to do not only the bedrooms, but also the bathroom and all the doors, windows, and baseboards. He painted for six full days. I received way more blessings than I would have if I had insisted on my own way.

"To Your Own Husbands"

It is important to note that wives are instructed to submit to their *own* husbands in Ephesians 5:22. Women are not mandated to submit to every man, but only to their own husbands. Male headship is a principle for the family and the church, but not for society as a whole. It is absolutely acceptable for a woman to be the president of a company or a country, the director of an organization, or the leader of a club or team. In those cases, the men she oversees will submit to her authority. It is only mandated that a wife submits to her own husband.

"As to the Lord"

There are many absurd interpretations of this phrase. Some commentators teach that a wife is to submit to her husband as if he is God Himself. Ha! Your husband is a fallen, sinful man, and both of you are in desperate need of a Savior. You aren't married to God!

Another interpretation is that a wife is to submit to her husband as long as he is doing what God wants. (This, of course, is up to the wife's determination!) According to this theology, if a husband isn't doing things the way a wife decides is "the Lord's way," then she is not under obligation to submit to him.

Neither one of these interpretations is accurate.

The phrase "as to the Lord" identifies what a wife's *motive* is in submitting to her husband. Dr. Martin Lloyd-Jones explains:

> It means, Wives, submit yourselves unto your own husbands because it is a part of your duty to the Lord, because it is an expression of your submission to the Lord. Or, Wives, submit yourselves to your own husbands; do it in this way, do it as a part of your submission to the Lord. In other words, you are not doing it only for the husband, you are doing it primarily for the Lord Himself. You are doing it for Christ's sake, you are doing it because you know that He exhorts you to do it, because it is well-pleasing in His sight that you should be doing it. It is part of your Christian behavior, it is a part of your discipleship.[5]

When a wife chooses to obey God's order for her family and submits herself under her husband's authority, she is actually demonstrating that her trust is in God—in His ability to direct her husband and in His promises to provide for her and protect her.

A wife must remember that when she submits herself to her husband, regardless of his spiritual condition, she is ultimately submitting herself to God. As Christians, our highest goal in life is to honor and glorify God. God says that being willing to submit to the authority He has given to our husbands is a way we can honor and glorify Him in our marriages. That should be all the motivation we need.

Elisabeth Elliot says, "The woman who accepts the limitations of womanhood finds in those very limitations her gifts, her special calling—wings, in fact, which bear her up into perfect freedom, into the will of God."[6]

LESSON 9 WIFE-CHANGING QUESTIONS

1. Has your understanding of the concept of submission been biblically accurate?

_____

_____

_____

_____

2. What are some of the negative ideas you have had personally or have heard others say about submission?

_____

_____

_____

_____

3. Is there something in your perspective about submission that has been "off"? Do you need to realign your buttons and make some wife-changing adjustments?

_____

_____

_____

_____

4. How would you define biblical submission to a friend asking about it?

_____

_____

_____

_____

5. Can you think of a time when you refused to submit to your husband? What was the outcome?

_____

_____

_____

_____

6. Can you think of a time when you biblically submitted to your husband? Was it difficult? Why or why not? What was the outcome?

_____

_____

_____

_____

7. Is there currently an issue in your marriage where you need to submit to your husband? Write a prayer of surrender here.

_____

_____

_____

_____

LESSON 10

The Response That Fits

My mom used to say there should be two signs posted in every dressing room offering words of wisdom to women who are trying on clothes. The signs would read:

> Just because you can get it on your body does not mean it fits you.
> Just because it's in style doesn't mean you should wear it.

We would quote one of these sayings to one another whenever we saw a woman who had sausaged herself into a too-tight dress, or a seventy-five-year-old wearing a trendy top made for a teenager. Some things are just not appropriate for certain ladies, and some things are just not appropriate for anyone!

Colossians 3:18 says, *"Wives, be subject to your husbands, as is fitting in the Lord."* Consider the expression "as is fitting in the Lord." As a Christian wife, what attitude "fits" you? You might be able to convince your husband to let you lead, but that doesn't mean the role fits you. It might be in style for you to be in charge of your house, but it doesn't mean you should be.

Why Submission Bugs You

My son got stung by a wasp when he was six years old. With red, tear-stained cheeks, he asked, "Why did God even make wasps? Just so they can sting us?" I didn't know how to answer him, so I did some research and discovered that wasps are incredibly complex creatures that are indispensable to the ecosystem of our planet. If we didn't have wasps, farmlands would be overrun with pests, and the crops we depend upon for food would be eaten up by the bugs the wasps eat. The way wasps form colonies and reproduce is blatant proof of a wise Creator. (Look into wasps for yourselves. I promise you will be amazed!) Even though they can sting, wasps are a vital part of God's master plan of creation.

Many women respond to the command to submit to their husbands in the same way my son did to wasps. When they hear their God-given assignment is to be a submissive helper, it stings! Their hearts cry out, "Why did God tell me to submit? Just so He can hurt me?"

The answer goes back to Eve. Our rebellion against our role is part of the curse.

We learned in the previous lessons that God declared Eve to be a helper comparable to Adam. This was done while the world was still perfect and the curse of sin had not yet been introduced. From the very beginning, Eve was to follow her husband's leading and help him accomplish the tasks that God had assigned to Adam. This was all working perfectly until that blasted forbidden fruit.

Remember when God was handing down the curse for Eve's sin? One of the things He said to her was, "Your desire shall be for your husband, and he shall rule over you" (Gen. 3:16).

When Eve chose to disobey God, she did so in direct contradiction to the commands of God and the instruction of her husband. Eve was led by the serpent, and Adam was led by his wife. The whole God-ordained leadership structure was reversed. The consequence from then on was a wife's heart would desire to be out from under her husband's authority.

The ESV translation of Genesis 3:16 puts a little footnote at the bottom of the verse, indicating that the word "for" can also be translated "against." That translation makes things a lot clearer. *"Your desire shall be against your husband, and he shall rule over you"* (emphasis added). How clarifying! The woman's desire is now *against* his God-given position of leadership and authority.

Eve's role as a helper was not changed after the fall, but her *feelings* about her role were affected. The curse brought a desire for a woman to dominate her husband. Submitting to Adam wasn't part of the curse. The curse was that now Eve wouldn't *want* to submit. She would rebel and want power and authority for herself.

It is a terrifying thing to be sinful women in a fallen world. We are now equipped with a fallen, sinful nature and a propensity toward wanting to dominate in our marriages, and we are married to fallen, sinful men. Yet we are still called to submit to our own husbands. And because of the curse, that stings!

Being in Hot Water

A few years into our marriage, Brent came home and announced he had decided to buy a hot tub. He was working hard as a landscaper at the time, and he loved the thought of coming home and relaxing in hot bubbling water in our backyard. After careful research, he decided which one to buy. He tried to sell me on the deal by saying it would be something we could enjoy together.

Now I have never liked hot tubs because I don't like being hot on purpose. I was pregnant at the time, and pregnant women can't even get into hot tubs. The whole idea seemed silly to me. When he told me how much he was going to spend on it, I nearly fainted.

After praying and deciding God agreed with me, I lovingly, respectfully told Brent that I thought a hot tub was a really bad idea. I reasoned with him that we couldn't afford it, I wouldn't enjoy it, and since he'd be alone in hot water, why didn't he just take a bath every night? Oh, and did I mention we really couldn't afford it? I listed all the expenses that were ahead of us that summer and explained why we should at least wait until after the baby was born to spend so much money on a large luxury item. I was very sweet and respectful through the whole conversation.

The hot tub was installed two days later.

Brent was grinning ear to ear as the workers installed it. I was very clear about how I felt, and he chose to make a decision that was entirely against my wishes. Oh, I was so mad! I could have easily pitched a fit. I could have made sure that the workmen knew I was not happy to have them there as I pouted or slammed pots on the stove. I could have yelled at my husband in front of them to embarrass him. I could have called my momma and cried about it or burned his dinner intentionally. Doing all of those things had crossed my mind, but instead I submitted. I had been overruled, and my only godly choice was to trust God and let Him work it out.

That summer was financially difficult. We struggled for months to catch up. There were plenty of opportunities for me to tell him I told him so, but what purpose would that have served?

One night, after a very sparse meal and after explaining that I had no more laundry soap or bread and no money to buy more, Brent scooped me up in a big hug in the kitchen and said, "It's okay! I'm just going to relax in my financial mistake, and we will figure it out!"

The hot-tub incident ended up being a huge marker in our marriage. After that, Brent decided, *without my prodding,* that he would never again make a huge financial decision unless we both agreed. Through making that mistake, he learned that he would be wise to listen to my advice on financial matters.

I can't say the hot tub was the last financial mistake we made or the last time I had to submit, but the hot tub grew us as a married couple. I believe God honored my choice to submit *as unto the Lord,* and our family was ultimately better in the long run *because* of the mistake he made and my response to it.

But what if . . . ?

Every time I teach on the subject of submission, I get a list of "but what if" questions.

Of course, I cannot address every possible scenario or specifically address every circumstance, but I will attempt to answer a few general questions.

What if my husband won't lead?

Leslie's husband goes to church with the family on Sundays and coaches their boys' soccer team. He's home for dinner most nights and is typically kind and easygoing. Whenever Leslie asks him for his input on an issue, his typical response is, "Whatever you think, Hon!" But Leslie is desperate for him to be more of a leader. She longs for him to lead the family in devotions, to pray with her, to be more involved with the kids, and to just be more driven in his life overall. She believes his constantly passive and agreeable attitude is actually due to laziness and a lack of genuine care for his family.

I will readily admit there is a shortage of strong, godly men in Christian homes today. It is quite common for a woman to say she would follow her husband, but he won't take any initiative to lead. To those women:

- Pray, pray, pray. There is genuine power in bringing your requests to God. Ask God to build your husband into the godly leader He wants him to be. Ask God to show you specific ways to follow your husband's lead. Pray for patience to wait on God to work.
- Often a wife will jump in and lead when her husband won't. If your husband won't lead, do not decide to lead your family yourself. Leave the leader position in your family vacant in every area possible until your husband occupies it.
- Your obedience to your role is not dependent on your husband fulfilling his. If your husband has failed to provide, protect, and lead, you are not excused from helping him or following him. Choose to follow the leader God has given you in obedience to God's command to you.
- Continue to ask your husband's opinion and to check for his approval, even if you know he's going to say, "Whatever you think, Hon!" Be sure to follow his wishes, especially when you don't agree with him. The more he knows he will be respected and followed, the more likely he will be to lead.
- If he is being indecisive, don't pressure him. He doesn't have to operate on your timeline.
- If your husband tells you to do whatever you want, that can still be his leading. If you ask your husband which dress to wear and he tells you both look good on you, don't take that as a lack of leadership. If he tells you he doesn't care if you go to that luncheon or if your sister comes to visit, he's still leading. However, make sure he's not being indifferent because he knows if you don't like what he says, you'll pitch a fit.

- Encourage your husband in small ways by showing confidence in his decisions. Something as simple as saying, "That was a great restaurant. I'm glad you chose it" will go a long way in demonstrating your willingness to follow.
- Admit when you don't follow his leading, and tell him you should have.
- Remember that you can't say, "You're the leader, now lead!" because if he does, then that means he's actually obeying you.
- Many men give up trying to lead their families because their wives throw a tantrum if they don't agree with a decision. Men will often take the path of least resistance. Make sure your sour attitude toward his decisions isn't what is keeping him from leading well.
- Don't compare your husband to the men you perceive as "leading the right way." Remember, your family is unique. You honestly don't know the details of what is actually happening in the homes of the people you perceive are doing it all right.

What if my husband isn't being the spiritual leader in our home?

The "spiritual leader" model that women often revere prays fervently with his wife every morning, reads Scripture with her every night, does nightly devotions with the children, and makes sure the family is in church together twice a week. When their own husbands fail to perform to this ideal, they decode they are not married to a "spiritual leader."

The expectation of intimate prayer, family devotions, and regular Bible reading is what we would all love, but the Scriptures never say a husband is required to do any of these things. Your husband is not in sin if he fails to "wash you in the Word." (By the way, that verse Ephesians 5:26, is talking about *you* becoming holy—and your husband making sure *you* are doing what *you* need to do according to the Scriptures. We are often far more concerned with our husband's lack of spirituality than our own.)

Of course, men should be encouraged to do all these things in their families. Christian homes are greatly strengthened this way, and it falls on the men to lead these practices. But I'm not writing to the men. I'm writing to the women, encouraging them to seek God themselves, submit to their husbands, and cheerfully follow whatever spiritual leadership their husbands provide.

A spiritual leader is not measured by how often he prays with his wife or how faithful he is in family devotions. Leadership goes beyond external exercises.

If your husband is not willing to lead the family in devotions, then you can read the Scriptures and pray with your children. I suggest you do this when your husband is not home so as not to be tempted to make a production of it. "Come, children [sigh deeply and roll eyes]. We are going to seek the Lord together while your father watches that ungodly TV show."

Many Christian women actually repel their husbands from praying with them or reading the Word with them because they know their wives' expectations are so high. I have heard of women correcting their husband's grammar or theology in the middle of a prayer (which is a great way to ensure you will always pray alone). If a wife has a superhero expectation that her mere mortal husband can never live up to, then he's a fool for even trying. Don't expect a superhero. Ultimately, God is your spiritual leader. Joyfully follow whatever leadership your mortal man supplies, and seek Christ yourself for all the rest.

How can I submit to my husband when he _____?

This is probably the most common opposition I hear from wives. How they are supposed to submit to a man who is lazy, a workaholic, a drunk, a mama's boy, using pornography, is a liar, obsessed with sports, or is a nonbeliever, a hypocrite, or . . . ? Hoping that somehow their husband's behavior voids God's command to submit as a wife, they want some sort of escape clause.

Here's the deal: God knew the circumstances that you would be in when He wrote His Word. You are not the exception to His plan. To "stand up for your rights" might make you shine in our culture, but it will not make you stand out in God's kingdom.

Let me soften that a bit. If your husband is immature, lazy, or weak, or even if he's not a Christian, that doesn't mean that you are excused from being submissive. You can't justify your own disobedience by someone else's. Your husband's qualifications for the role are unimportant. God has called him to be the leader, and you are assigned the role as his helper. Do it for the Lord's sake. It is God who has asked this response from you, and He knows best.

Our husbands *will* mess up. They will make bad financial decisions, be poor spiritual leaders, fail as fathers, mistreat our mothers, and overall, act like sinners.

Friends, you married a sinner. Your husband is married to a sinner too. That's all there is to marry! Waiting for your husband to obey God before you will obey Him is just downright foolish. Somebody has to go first, and it might as well be you.

How can I submit when my husband has hurt me so deeply?

I have wept with dear sisters who have been victims of their husband's sin. Wives are often left to pick up the pieces of their husband's sinful choices and bad decisions. And it's not fair. It's really not.

There is no "out" clause. Oh, but there is hope!

Isaiah 61:1–3 gives us a picture of what Jesus came to do for His people:

> The Spirit of the Lord God is upon me, because the Lord has anointed me to bring good news to the poor; He has sent me to bind up the brokenhearted, to proclaim liberty to the captives, and the opening of the prison to those who are bound; to proclaim the year of the Lord's favor, and the day of vengeance of our God; to comfort all who mourn; to grant to those who mourn in Zion—to give them a beautiful headdress instead of ashes, the oil of gladness instead of mourning, the garment of praise instead of a faint spirit; that they may be called oaks of righteousness, the planting of the Lord, that He may be glorified.

You may be experiencing deep pain because of something your husband has done. Your pain is part of the consequences of his sin. My heart breaks with yours. But my heart also clings to Jesus for you—the One who came to comfort those who mourn, heal the brokenhearted, console, and give beauty for ashes and praise for heaviness. No matter what your husband has done, Jesus will *not* fail you. He is unable to fail you. He can't be anything but faithful to you because Faithful is who He is. He is with you in your pain and wants to be your Comforter and Helper. He specializes in transforming tragedy into victory.

Your calling is to obey God because He is worthy of your obedience, not because your husband deserves it. Submit to and help your husband "as to the Lord." Your motivation is to please God. He will give you the ability to obey Him as you lean into Him.

Choose obedience. Your submissive, helpful attitude toward your husband may be the tool God uses to turn your husband's heart toward Christ. You can be the door that God comes through to heal your entire family.

What if my husband is making a decision that will surely ruin us?

Many women are terrified that if they let their husbands make the final decisions in their families, they will be homeless, penniless, friendless, or possibly dead. The thought of not being in control paralyzes them with fear. They are sure, if given the opportunity, their husband will lead their family to destruction.

I wonder what Sarah thought when Abraham came to her with the big idea of leaving their home and going out to the land God would eventually show him? Can you imagine the conversation for a moment? "Pack the camel, Sweetie! We're going in that direction, and I don't know what's out there, but God spoke to me!"

What fear gripped Sarah's heart when Abraham told her to say she was his sister to the kings of the land, and ended up with her being taken into the royal harem—twice!

Being married to the patriarch of God's chosen people was not easy! Yet we see God's hand of protection on Sarah again and again, in spite of Abraham's shortcomings. The only long-term tragedy that plagued Sarah's life was when she led her husband to sleep with her handmaid and produce a son instead of waiting on God! When Sarah decided she was going to make things happen her own way, she ended up bringing lasting pain to her family.

But that's not what Sarah is remembered for. The Scriptures point to her as an example of a submissive wife:

> For this is how the holy women who hoped in God used to adorn themselves, by submitting to their own husbands, as Sarah obeyed Abraham, calling him lord. And you are her children, if you do good and do not fear anything that is frightening. (1 Peter 3:5–6)

How can we willingly choose to follow men who may lead us into financial ruin, spiritual dryness, or worse—and not be gripped by fear? The same way Sarah did. Look at the first part of that verse. It says the holy women *who hoped in God* submitted to their husbands and were not frightened.

Well-placed hope is the key to fearlessness. If your hope is placed in your husband, then you have every reason to be terrified! But as a Christian, your hope is not in your husband, your bank account, your government, your church, or yourself. Your hope is in God Himself.

Did you know the command to "fear not," or "do not be afraid" appears 365 times in the Bible? There is not a day all year that we need to be afraid.

The counter command to "fear not" is always to "place your hope in God." Placing your hope in God can only happen if you truly know Him. You can't trust someone you don't know. Get to know your trustworthy God and see your fears decrease. Increase your Bible reading and your prayer life, and you will be able to confidently place your hope in your God the way Sarah did.

Exceptions to Submission

If your husband is demanding you to sin, in direct contradiction to His Word, then you are released from the command to submit. If your husband is asking you to steal, to murder, to bring anyone else into your sexual relationship, or to blatantly lie, then you need to obey God and not your husband.

If you see your husband is about to sin against God, then your unwillingness to submit may be what causes him to recognize his sin. A wife is a poor helper if she stands by silently and watches her husband disobey God. We are called to be helpers, not blind, silent submitters!

But let me caution you to make sure it is outright sin your husband is asking of you before you choose not to submit. Women often search for some hint of sin in their husband's request as an excuse to rebel against him.

In all my years of ministry, I can only remember two women I counseled to not submit to their husbands. One woman's husband was demanding she get a job as a stripper to help provide for the family, and the other was a woman whose husband wanted her to get an abortion. That means that all the rest of the women were able to find a way to honor God and submit to their husbands.

Embrace Your Calling with Joy!

I hope that in going through the last five lessons, the following things were accomplished in you:

1. You understand you are called by God to be a helper to your husband

2. You will seek to practically fulfill the role of being a helper in ways suited to your own strengths and your husband's unique fashioning.

3. You understand God has wisely and kindly commanded you to submit to your husband.

4. You joyfully embrace God's wisdom in the design of roles within marriage and trust Him to ultimately lead your family through your husband.

5. If you are able to embrace these concepts and apply them to your own life, then you will be building your marriage in a way that will honor God and reflect Him to the lost world around you.

LESSON 10 WIFE-CHANGING QUESTIONS

1. Have you been guilty of looking for an exception to God's command for you to submit to your husband?

_____

_____

_____

_____

2. Is there something specific you are afraid of happening if you submit to your husband?

_____

_____

_____

_____

3. Look up some of the "fear not" commands in the Bible, including the counter command to put your hope in God. Write out at least three of them that minister to you specifically.

_____

_____

_____

_____

4. Are there any other "What if" questions you have in regard to submission? Can you answer them yourself now, based on this content?

_____

_____

_____

_____

5. Do you understand the four objectives mentioned above, and are you willing to apply what you have learned?

_____

_____

_____

_____

SMILE

LESSON 11

When Brandon met Katie, he knew he wanted to spend the rest of his life with her. She was so full of life and laughter, and their conversations were invigorating. Katie would light up when he walked into a room, and her genuine, sweet smile made him want to do anything for her. Katie loved Jesus, and to Brandon, she fit the profile of everything a godly woman should be. At times, Brandon would be overcome with the fact that someone so incredible would choose to be with him. He couldn't wait to marry her so he could come home to her loveliness every day.

Shortly after the wedding, Katie stopped smiling so much. Everything seemed to irritate her. Brandon didn't hang his clothes up right, he didn't help her enough around the house, he spent money foolishly, he worked too much, he spent too much time with his parents, and he chewed too loudly.

Brandon began to dread going home from work because he knew Katie would lay into him about whatever had offended her that day. After the baby came, it got worse. Their once-stimulating conversations were now centered on her giving him his chore list. When he tried sharing a new business idea or a dream for the future, or when he wanted to discuss something about the baby with Katie, she made him feel stupid or incompetent. When they were in public, she made her annoyance toward him known with heavy sighs and eye rolls. Their sex life had started out passionate and intense, but now, if he approached her, she shot him a look that said, "Are you kidding me?"

Brandon wondered what happened to the lovely girl he had fallen in love with. Where was the radiant smile that used to make him feel like the most blessed man alive? Now he only saw that smile when she gave it to other people. He had wanted to spend his life with the vibrant, laughing, brilliant girl who thought he was amazing, but in a few short years she had transformed into an annoyed shrew who made him wish he wasn't married.

None of us leave our wedding receptions expecting to have fights about money, wet towels, or where to spend Mother's Day. Everyone hopes for a marriage filled with joy and laughter and romance, but many end up with a home full of the stench of mutual discontent, frustration, anger, nagging, bitterness, and loneliness.

The issue of attitude is largely overlooked in Christian messages on being a wife. We can often focus so much on what we do that we neglect the attitude with which we do it. However, our actions go hand in hand with our attitudes.

Let's get building on the next wall of our houses—and get to work on our smiles!

> smile—*noun:* An expression of joy or pleasure on the face in which the ends of the mouth curve up slightly, often with the lips moving apart so the teeth can be seen.
> *She flashed him a radiant smile.*
> smile—*verb:* The external expressing of internal positive emotions, esp. happiness, pleasure, amusement, or a friendly feeling through facial expression.
> *He smiles sweetly when he sees his grandbaby.*

In this chapter, we will focus on our own responses and choices in our attitudes and how those may be perceived by our husbands. We will explore what the Bible says about a wife's attitude, discover how we can walk in obedience and joy, and cause God to be the One who smiles.

Oh, It's Just You

I learned a valuable lesson in the years I worked in the corporate world. For eight hours a day, I would hear Kelly in the cubicle next to me answering her phone in a singsong voice: "Good morning! This is Kelly! How may I help you?" Most of the time, she would cheerfully talk with whoever was on the line: "Oh! Hi, there! Yes, I'll have that project done for you this afternoon: Have a great day!"

But at least once a day I would hear, "Good morning! This is Kelly! . . . [then flatly] What? . . . Yeah . . . Mhmm . . . Okay . . . Can't you take care of that yourself? . . . [Sigh] . . . Okay, yeah . . . Whatever . . ." Click. That's when I knew Kelly was talking to her husband.

Every time her husband called, she lost all the singsong sweetness, and she spoke to him with irritation in her voice. She didn't know I was listening, but Kelly made it clear that she didn't much like the guy on the other end of the phone.

I witnessed something similar at a party years ago. Julia had arrived early with her kids, and her husband was going to meet them there later. We sat chatting by the front door and greeted everyone who arrived with smiles and hugs.

Julia's husband eventually came in, and I got up to say hello. But Julia didn't even acknowledge he'd arrived—she didn't get up, and didn't even say hi. She parked in her folding chair, waiting for me to come back from greeting her husband.

After her husband had left the entryway, I said, "You greeted everyone who came through the door, but when Steve got here, you ignored him. What's up with that?"

She laughed. "What? It's just Steve!" Her answer spoke loud and clear about the state of her heart toward her husband.

With their words and actions, these women are telling their husbands, "You are *just* my husband, and you don't really matter. You aren't as important as my customers, my coworkers, or anyone else who might walk through the door." These women are tearing down their homes with their own hands, and they don't even know it.

Do you remember when you were first being pursued by your husband? You couldn't wait to hear from him. You were anxious to see him. You smiled at him all the time just because you were so happy to be in his presence. Guess what? He still wants to be married to the girl who makes him feel like he is the most attractive, important, brilliant man alive.

What Did You Expect?

We can easily forget that the curse that brought pain, sickness, and hard work, with little to show for it, this was all the consequence of Eve's choice to disobey. When you made your vows, you said something like, "I take this man to be my husband, to love, honor, and cherish, for better or worse, in sickness and in health, in poverty and prosperity, till death do us part." However, many women sign up for marriage and actually only plan to be married for better, for health, and for prosperity. Any bit of for worse, sickness, or poverty is not in their plan, and they behave as if the curse was supposed to skip them.

Hardship and suffering are part of every marriage, and we all vowed to love, honor, and cherish through the good *and* the bad. So why are we surprised when things are hard? Only in Disney princess movies do women get to follow their hearts and live happily ever after (and have talking animals do their housework!). In the real world, two sinful people join their lives together and have to work very hard to learn to live together in harmony.

God has promised you an abundant life, not a work-free, battle-free life. There will be trials and hardships and suffering and sickness and pain in your future. Being a follower of Jesus does not make us immune to these basic tenets of human existence. Being a follower of Jesus makes us more than conquerors *in* all of these things (Rom. 8:37). You vowed to *love* your husband no matter what adversity came into your life. Friend, your smile communicates how committed you are to that vow.

Don't Follow Your Heart!

Every Disney movie has the same message: follow your heart. Every beautiful princess ends up getting whatever prize she is after as soon as she listens to her own heart and follows whatever it tells her—what a ridiculous notion!

> The heart is deceitful above all things, and desperately sick; who can understand it? (Jer. 17:9)

The Bible tells me my heart is exceedingly deceitful and desperately sick! If I follow my heart, I will surely bring destruction on my life. Eve followed her heart, and look where it got her. It appears Eve's disobedience in the garden was quite impulsive. She didn't stop to think about what the consequences of her choice would be or get counsel from her husband. If Eve could have foreseen the horrible aftermath of her impulsiveness—not just in her own life but in the lives of countless generations to follow, she surely would have chosen differently. Ladies, it is still our enemy's tactic to get us to impulsively follow our hearts, to act on how we feel to be true rather than what we *know* to be true.

But there is good news! Being a Christian means we don't have to be a slave to our emotions or be ruled by our wicked hearts. We have a way of escape.

Be a Control Freak

Some of you may describe yourselves as "control freaks." While that normally refers to a woman who has to have things done her way or she goes crazy (which is *not* a good thing), I want to encourage you to be a *self-control freak.*

The first step in self-control is to *acknowledge that you are responsible for your own responses.* It is never anyone else's fault that you give in to the temptation to rage, nag, manipulate, or complain. You alone are accountable for your actions, moods, and words.

1 Thessalonians 4:4 says, "Each of you should know how to possess his own vessel in sanctification and honor." Your "vessel" is not only your body, but your emotions as well.

The second step is to *transfer the governing of your spirit to the Holy Spirit.* You do this by putting off the old self, renewing your mind to agree with God, and then putting on the new self. All of these things are choices that involve self-control by the power of the Holy Spirit.

> . . . to put off your old self, which belongs to your former manner of life and is corrupt through deceitful desires, and to be renewed in the spirit of your

minds, and to put on the new self, created after the likeness of God in true righteousness and holiness. (Eph. 4:22–24)

When it comes to being cheerful, choose to walk in obedience to God and not in obedience to your feelings. Now you might say, Is the pastor's wife telling me to lie? Am I supposed to be untruthful about how I feel?

Yes! Your feelings are not the controlling force of your life; obedience to God is! It may feel like a lie to act contrary to how you feel, but it is actually obeying the command to take every thought captive to obey Christ, to deny yourself and pick up your cross (2 Cor. 10:5; Matt. 16:24).

Dress Up like Jesus

When my daughter was little, she had a giant box full of dress-up clothes. She could be a princess, a cowgirl, and a marine in the span of twenty minutes. With each costume she put on, she would then act like whatever character she looked like.

As Christians, we are encouraged to "dress up" like Jesus, to put on His very nature and to not obey our flesh.

But put on the Lord Jesus Christ, and make no provision for the flesh, to fulfill its lust. (Rom. 13:14)

We are told to "put on" the Lord Jesus Christ—to wear His character and act like Him. This is an intentional act that is not governed by how we feel. It's not lying—it's obedience.

1 Peter 5:5 commands us to "clothe yourselves, all of you, with humility toward one another, for 'God opposes the proud but gives grace to the humble.'"

Your feelings may tell you to oppose your husband, scream at your kids, demand your rights, or withdraw your love from anyone who hurts you. However, if you instead choose to act like Jesus, to deny yourself, and to treat those around you like He would, you are "dressing up" like Jesus. When you choose to behave in a way contrary to what you feel like doing, it's not lying—it's the fruit of the Spirit.

Manipulation Disguised as "Communication"

There is definitely room for sharing concerns and letting your husband know that your feelings have been hurt over something. Communication is important, but some women feel a need to communicate every tiny inconvenience or hurt. This can come in many forms besides conversation: eye rolls, deep sighs, withholding affection, or saying nothing at all with the hope that the silence will let him know he's failed to please you. These are all ways of manipulation and nagging, and they are not effective or God-honoring.

Some women think their attitude doesn't matter if it comes in the form of a text:

- Wet towel on the floor . . . again. Really?
- Hope you enjoyed your fancy business lunch. I ate Timmy's leftover chicken nuggets.
- The dishwasher's broken. Wish you'd gotten that promotion.
- You're not the only one who needs a day off, you know.
- Need to work late. Can you pick up the kids for once?

I saw one woman's social media post with a photo of her disaster of a house with the caption, "I leave him home with the kids for two hours, and I come home to this."

One wife honestly said to me, "If he does what he's supposed to do, then I'm nice to him. How else can I train him to be a good boy?"

Oh, foolish women! We tear down our homes with our own hands.

Drip, Drip, Drip

Your husband is the head of your home, but you are the *heart*. Your husband has the authority to decide what direction your family will take, but you have the power to influence how everyone in your home will *feel*. As a woman who says she believes and lives by the Scriptures, you are wise to heed the biblical warnings about the mood you set in your home.

Proverbs has many warnings about a wife's power over the heart of her family:

> The contentions of a wife are a continual dripping. (Prov. 19:13)

> It is better to live in a corner of the house-top than in a house shared with a quarrelsome wife. (Prov. 21:9)

> It is better to live in a desert land than with a quarrelsome and fretful woman. (Prov. 21:19)

> A continual dripping on a rainy day and a quarrelsome wife are alike; to restrain her is to restrain the wind or to grasp oil in one's right hand. (Prov. 27:15-16)

Do you see the theme here? Like a constant, irritating dripping, the contentious, quarrelsome, fretful, unrestrained wife is a woman everyone wants to escape from. A woman who demands her own way, pouts when she isn't given what she wants, and manipulates her husband with her moods is what Proverbs warns against.

Is this how your family would describe you? I encourage you to genuinely consider how your family would define your "normal" mood. Can they even predict how you will be from day to day or hour to hour? What scent is your attitude filling up your home with?

I read about a man who called his wife Peg, even though that wasn't her name. When asked why he called her that, he said, "Well, Peg is short for Pegasus, and Pegasus was an immortal horse, and an immortal horse is an everlasting nag, so that's why I call my wife Peg!"

Women are often stereotyped as nags, and with good reason. Nagging is a form of manipulation. A wife employs endless suggesting, complaining, or whining to get what she wants. We somehow think if we keep saying the same thing, with increased intensity, we will get the response we want. However, it rarely, if ever, produces results we want, and it chips away at our relationships.

So what is a dripping, nagging, contentious wife to do?

Feelings Follow Action

Your husband doesn't always deserve your help or to be treated with sweetness. You might be married to the biggest toad ever, and he's the last guy who has earned your favor this week, yet just as in the case with being a submissive helper, God does not give us a "follow your heart" pass when our husbands are being less than loveable.

We don't always feel cheerful, and our husbands often don't "deserve" our smiles, but there is so much we lose when we try to manipulate things with our moods. Often when we make a conscious decision to smile when we feel like crying, to answer sweetly when we feel like rolling our eyes, to serve joyfully when we are feeling unappreciated, or to praise when we feel like complaining, it is then that God will put the emotion behind the act of obedience. Feelings often change when we sacrifice our fleshly desires to be negative, angry, sarcastic, or distant, and instead put on Jesus and love the people around us. Improving our marriages can begin with denying ourselves and choosing to smile. It is not natural, but it is absolutely possible by the power of the Holy Spirit. Joanne says,

> Sometimes I make it my project to influence his rotten mood just by being sweet, smiling, and affectionate. I sometimes just "get into his boat" for a while and identify where he is, what has happened, and what he's feeling—until he feels "heard." After almost thirty-eight years of marriage, I've learned I have a dramatic influence for his good.

Fresh Fruit

We can only fake being joyful and thankful for so long. There must be a deeper dimension to our attitudes than just saying we will try harder to be nice.

But the fruit of the Spirit is love, joy, peace, patience, kindness, goodness, faithfulness, gentleness, self-control; against such things there is no law. (Gal. 5:22–23)

We don't have it in ourselves to be loving, joyful, kind, good, faithful, gentle, self-controlled women. We need the power of the Holy Spirit. If we seek Him, God will provide all we need to be the genuinely smiling women we are called to be.

Get an Accent!

My big sister moved to Tennessee after she got married. We both grew up in California, but after living in the south for so many years, she now has a Southern drawl as thick as Scarlett O'Hara's. I love my sister and I want to be adorable and charming like she is, so I automatically imitate her. When she comes to visit, within a few hours I'm saying "y'all" and "fixin'," and everything else.

It's the same way when we spend time with Jesus. We start acting like Him. We pick up His accents of joy and kindness and thanksgiving. The fruit of the Spirit is transferred to us as we spend time with Him. When we see those things that make Him so lovely and wonderful and we imitate Him without even realizing it, we become conformed to His image and are able to treat people the way He does.

Light Up

I want to give you an assignment. Every time you see your husband, make it a point to *light up*. If you don't feel like it, do it anyway. Decide your first reaction to seeing your husband or hearing his voice will be to smile. In doing this, you are conditioning yourself to be intentionally happy around him.

- If he calls you during the day, sound like you are delighted to hear from him. Make sure there is no hint of "it's just you" when you speak to him. Answer your phone as if you are getting a call from the most important person in your life—because you are.
- Change your husband's contact name to something that will make you automatically smile. (When I was newly married, my husband playfully changed his contact name in my phone to A Hot Stud. I left it that way because it reminded me of how he wanted me to think of him when he called. When I see A Hot Stud is calling, I'm more likely to answer excitedly.)
- If you're in another room when he comes home, make it a point to stop what you are doing and intentionally connect with the person you vowed to love and cherish for the rest of your life. If he gets home

before you, intentionally greet him with a kiss and a smile before you do anything else. Choose to treat him like he's the most important person in the world to you because he is.

- When you are at an event together and you catch his eye, smile, wink, or give him some indication you think he's special and you're glad he's yours.

PMS and Chemical Imbalances Don't Justify Sin

I remember hearing a pastor say he believed PMS and depression were something women had made up in order to justify their sinful behaviors. Yes, I wanted to slap him, as I'm sure the rest of the females in the room did. Sisters, PMS and hormonal imbalances are real. They can make the most docile woman feel like ripping the cute little heads off her children. They can make us cry uncontrollably, sleep endlessly, and eat recklessly.

Women frequently justify erratic, violent, or outrageous behavior by blaming it on "that time of the month" or a "chemical imbalance." But consider this: women throughout history have had to deal with the same hormones you and I have today. PMS, menopause, and other imbalances are nothing new. God could have given us a chemical imbalance loophole or a PMS pass, but He didn't. Therefore, we are not excused from the command to love people and be self-controlled because our chemicals are off.

Taking care of your body by eating well and exercising can contribute to being emotionally balanced, but ultimately, your emotions are subject to your will. Your hormones do not run your life; *you* are in control of your own behavior. You may not be able to help how you *feel* at a certain time of the month, but you can absolutely control how you respond to your feelings. But *only through the power of the Holy Spirit.*

I have an acronym for PMS: **P**leading for the **M**ercy of the **S**avior.

When you're feeling out of sorts because of your hormones, you are even more desperate for the power of the Holy Spirit than you are on other days. Let your PMS be a trigger to bring you to your knees, a force that drives you to seek the Lord all the more.

It is impossible in your own strength to act nicely when you don't particularly like the people in your house that day. But you *can* do all things through Christ. It is essential that you be consistently near to Jesus so you can rely on His strength when you are weak.

The hard thing about PMS and menopause is our emotions feel so real. However, our feelings often have very little to do with reality. Those little habits that mildly bug you one day can feel like grounds for divorce the next day. Romans 13:14 instructs us to "put on the Lord Jesus Christ, and make no provision for the flesh, to gratify its desires." When you're "chemically offended," remind yourself the problem is not them—it's you! Admit that to the Lord. Track your cycle on your calendar and recognize those days you will likely be more emotional or irritable. Don't schedule too much activity on those days if you can avoid it. Do schedule extra time for prayer and reading the Scriptures. Apologize to your family as many times as you need to. Tell your little ones Mommy needs a time out, put yourself in one, and seek the Lord while you're there.

As we get older, the predictable patterns of PMS give way to the sometimes unpredictable season of menopause. Some women struggle with sleeplessness, weepiness, anger, and sexual issues. Take good care of your body and seek medical help if necessary, but don't let up in your spiritual battling. We must not allow ourselves to be governed by our hormones and emotions. You are in desperate need of your Savior in every season of life.

Salty Speech

> More of a man is seen in his words than in anything else belonging to him; you may look into his face and be mistaken, you may visit his house and not discover him, you may scan his business and misunderstand him; but if you hear his daily conversation you shall soon know him. The heart babbles out its secret when the tongue is in motion.[1] —Charles Spurgeon

I grew up with a bar of soap in my mouth. Sassiness, disrespect, lying, and complaining were all met with a wide slab of Palmolive and no mercy. Mom actually dragged the bar across my teeth as she released me from my tongue cleansing, just to make sure there was a lingering consequence to my offense.

I wish I could say this punishment cured me from future verbal sin, but I have been a reluctant learner. As a wife, I have certainly been guilty of sassiness, disrespect, lying, and complaining.

At the root of all this ungodliness is my pride. My pride demands I be treated with all I feel I deserve and that my husband do what I expect. When I don't get my own way, the pride in my heart flows out of my mouth in various forms of verbal unloveliness.

But the Scriptures tell me it is possible to never raise my voice, never use a curse word, and never call my husband an unkind name. It is not only possible, but expected, that gracious speech should *always* flow from the mouths of Christian women.

Let your speech always be gracious, seasoned with salt, so that you may know how you ought to answer each person. (Col. 4:6)

Let no unwholesome word proceed from your mouth, but only such a word as is good for edification according to the need of the moment, that it may give grace to those who hear. (Eph. 4:29)

If we are born again, there is no excuse for our mouths to remain unredeemed. No matter the circumstance, we have the ability to speak with grace. Notice both of these challenging verses begin with the word "let." This word means we have a choice. We can either *let* our words be gracious, wholesome, edifying, and grace-infusing, or we can *let* our words tear down our loved ones. What speech are we letting out of our mouths?

The speech of a redeemed wife must also be "seasoned with salt." Salt is an effective seasoning because it is purifying, cleansing, and flavorful and brings enjoyment of what could be otherwise bland. Are we *letting* our words be effective to purify and cleanse those who hear us, bringing flavor and enjoyment to a conversation?

May God use the sanctifying "soap" of His Holy Spirit to cleanse our mouths and cause gracious words to flow from our lips. Oh, may we be women who choose to fill our homes with life-giving, home-building, God-glorifying, graciously salty speech.

Let us choose:

- Compliment instead of complaining
- Praising instead of pouting
- Respecting instead of retorting
- Delighting instead of discouraging
- Singing instead of sassing

LESSON 11 WIFE-CHANGING QUESTIONS

1. Is your current attitude a sweet aroma, or does it downright stink? What is the source of your attitude?

   _____

   _____

   _____

   _____

2. Are you guilty of behaving as if you deserve to not have any hardships? Can you think of a time when you behaved this way?

   _____

   _____

   _____

   _____

3. What would your family say is your "normal" mood? (If you're really brave, ask them!)

   _____

   _____

   _____

   _____

4. What are your common bad-attitude practices (eye rolling, silent treatment, screaming, manipulating, etc. ?)

   _____

_____

_____

_____

5. Explain what it means to "put on the Lord Jesus Christ."

_____

_____

_____

_____

6. What is your biggest challenge to "dressing up like Jesus?"

_____

_____

_____

_____

7. What would being "clothed with humility" in your marriage actually look like? What wife-changes do you need to incorporate to make this a normal attitude for you?

_____

_____

_____

_____

8. How do your emotions or hormones affect your perception of reality? How do you typically respond to this?

_____

_____

_____

_____

9. In what ways do you need to deliberately guard yourself against acting on your feelings?

_____

_____

_____

_____

10. Are you in need of a Holy Spirit mouth-washing? How are you doing with filling your home with gracious speech? What wife-changes do you need to make in regard to your words?

_____

_____

_____

_____

LESSON 12

Holy Happiness

After our oldest son got married, I was reading some well-wishes addressed to the bride and groom: *Wishing you a lifetime of happiness!* . . . *May the years ahead be filled with lasting happiness . . . Be blessed with a long and happy marriage . . . May the happiness you have today continue through your life together.* They were all lovely sentiments. But it got me thinking about the fact that hoping for perpetual happiness isn't very realistic when two sinners commit to live together for the rest of their lives.

Yet many women expect their husbands to live entirely for their happiness. Unfortunately, when these wives aren't happy, they insist it's the fault of an insensitive, happiness-robbing husband.

In the linen department at the department store, my daughter and I awkwardly looked at towels alongside the arguing couple.

Flipping her long hair and dramatically rolling her eyes, the woman spat, "We are getting bath *sheets*. They're so much better than towels. And that's final!"

The muscular young man stammered, "I—I don't really want a sheet. How about you get a sheet thingy, and I'll get a regular towel?"

Raising her voice so everyone within a four-aisle radius could hear her declaration, she announced, "If you expect this relationship to work, then you are going to have to make some adjustments! We are getting *bath sheets*!"

This woman was hinging the success of her entire relationship on what kind of towel the guy wanted. How ridiculous. Yet how many wives hang the success of each day on whether or not their husbands give in to their demands.

Bob was kind and hardworking and provided a comfortable life for Annie and her two boys. He coached the boys' baseball team, served in the church, and prayed with his wife regularly. But in women's ministry meetings, Annie was continually asking for prayer for her marriage, implying to her church friends that things were not healthy at home.

When Annie came to me for counseling, she acknowledged that Bob was great in many areas. "But," she said, "I'm just not happy. He doesn't always listen to me or meet all my needs. He never gives me enough money. Playing golf on the weekends is more important to him than I am. He doesn't read the Bible to us as much as he should. When he prays with me, he just says the same things over and over. Whenever I tell him I'm upset, he just gets mad and doesn't want to change. He has canceled our last two date nights. I don't think he's loving me like Christ loves the church, and that's why I'm so unhappy. I keep praying, but I won't be happy till he obeys God."

As much as happiness is a lovely thought and the pursuit of it is even an American right, it is not the ultimate life goal for a Christian. Rather, the ultimate pursuit for a follower of Jesus is holiness, and when this goal is sought after above personal happiness in marriage, the result is a happiness that can't be described in a wedding card.

As Christ Loves the Church

> Husbands, love your wives, just as Christ also loved the church and gave Himself for her. (Eph. 5:25)

Women love this passage of Scripture. I have been quoted this verse by discontent wives more times than I can count. This is the only marriage verse some women have memorized! Citing their own unhappiness as evidence of their husband's disobedience, churches are full of women who are quite sure they are not being loved like Christ loves the church. They believe their husbands are to be the source of their unbroken happiness, and when these wives are unhappy, they pout. They compare. They demand. They give the silent treatment. They post about it on social media. They are unhappy, and it's all his fault.

We are wise to pay attention to punctuation in Scripture. Notice that the end of verse 25 has a comma, which tells us, "Wait, there's more!" Here's what the rest of the next two verses say:

> That He might sanctify and cleanse her with the washing of water by the word, that He might present her to Himself a glorious church, not having spot or wrinkle or any such thing, but that she should be holy and without blemish. (Eph. 5:26–27)

The first way a husband demonstrates love for his wife is what Jesus does in His church—He gives Himself to the pursuit of cleansing her (which [ahem] implies she's dirty) and making sure she is as spot-free spiritually as she can be. It is his wife's *holiness,* rather than her happiness, that a godly husband is to keep as his priority. Ephesians 5 continues:

> In the same way husbands should love their wives as their own bodies. He who loves his wife loves himself. For no one ever hated his own flesh, but nourishes and cherishes it, just as Christ does the church. (Eph. 5:28–29)

Second to his wife's holiness, a husband is called to treat his wife with love by nourishing and cherishing her as Christ does the church. A husband *should* be devoted to his wife's holiness, and he *should* treat her with tenderness and affection.

Now, I can hear wives wailing, "But that's just it! He doesn't care for my holiness or my happiness! He doesn't pray with me or read the Bible with me, and most of the time, he's not even nice! He doesn't do a thing to help me be holy or happy, and *that's* why I'm so miserable!"

To be treated as a valuable, cherished bride and to have holiness be at the forefront of her husband's priorities are biblical desires that a wife should have because God has instructed this to be the standard for godly husbands. Yet many women are married to men who don't devote themselves to spiritual things and are primarily self-serving in their marriages. This is a shameful thing, and it grieves our heavenly Father. If you are married to a negligent, unkind, or selfish man, God sees your loneliness and hurt, and your husband will answer to Him for his disobedience.

However, dear sister, as difficult as it is for you, your husband's disobedience does not justify your own. A spiritually weak husband is not an excuse for an unholy wife.

Although there is a certain void and real pain if your husband is disobedient to God, a deep degree of happiness is still possible for you. Both sanctification and happiness can still be found in your personal pursuit of holiness. Regardless of a husband's behavior, each of us must be committed to personal intimacy with Jesus, knowing He sees any unmet needs and will meet us in them.

Pour out your heart to the Lord in prayer about these things, and knowing that God hears you and is working in ways you don't see. When occasional opportunities arise with your husband, respectfully communicate your need to be spiritually, emotionally, and physically nourished and cherished. Resisting the temptation to manipulate your husband by guilt or pity is challenging, but your ultimate desire should be that he is moved by the Holy Spirit, rather than by your nagging, to change. Any lasting change will be because God did a work. The objective is not for your husband to become the man you think he should be, but rather to participate in the sanctification process God has lined up for him to become the man He wants him to be.

Even if your husband is wonderfully attentive to your heart and soul, to expect perpetual happiness in your marriage is quite unreasonable. This unrealistic expectation can actually border on idolatry and can cause a wife to require her husband to provide for her what he was never intended to.

A Husband Is a Poor Substitute for a Savior

More often than not, when things seem "off" in my marriage, it's really not my marriage causing the imbalance. Things are usually "off" in my relationship with God, and I am looking to my husband to make up the difference. While my husband is a loving, godly, considerate man who wants me holy and happy, he's a poor replacement for Jesus in my life.

I absolutely love what Paul Tripp has to say about this idea:

> There are many, many Christian relationships that are painful and marked by conflict and disappointment because one person, or both people, in those relationships are placing a burden on the other person that no human can bear:
>
> > No person can be the foundation of your identity.
> > No person can provide the source for your joy.
> > No person can give you a reason to get up in the morning.
> > No person can give you a reason to continue in the midst of difficulty.
> > No person can be the carrier of your hope.
> > No person can give your heart peace and rest.
> > No person can change you from the inside out.
> > No person can alter your past.
> > No person can atone for your wrongs.
>
> And yet . . . we have all asked someone, at some point and in some way, to be the fourth member of the Trinity for us! It's simply a relationship doomed for failure. When we ask a person to do for us what only Christ can do, we place a crushing and impossible burden on them, and then judge them when they fall short. It's vital to remember that human love is a wonderful thing—you should pursue people who love you, and you should be pursued by people because you're loving. But you will only ever find life—real, heart-changing, soul-satisfying life—in a vertical relationship with one Person.
>
> Only Christ can be your source of spiritual vitality and strength. Only Christ can save you, change you, and deliver you from you. Only Christ can give your soul what it's desperately seeking. Could it be that the disappointment you experience in your relationships is the product of unrealistic and unattainable expectations? Could it be that you have unwittingly put people in God's place? Could it be that you ask the people to do what only Christ can do for you? There is but one Savior, and He is yours forever. You don't need to put that burden on the person next to you.[2]

The Way to Happiness Is through Holiness

In Jesus's most famous sermon, He began by giving us the secret of happiness. Be mindful as you read this that His description does not fit a standard worldly pursuit of happiness.

In Matthew 5:3–12, the word "blessed" is the same word for "happy".

> Blessed [happy] are the poor in spirit, for theirs is the kingdom of heaven. Blessed are those who mourn, for they shall be comforted. Blessed are the meek, for they shall inherit the earth. Blessed are those who hunger and thirst for righteousness, for they shall be filled. Blessed are the merciful, for they shall obtain mercy. Blessed are the pure in heart, for they shall see God. Blessed are the peacemakers, for they shall be called sons of God. Blessed are those who are persecuted for righteousness' sake, for theirs is the kingdom of heaven. Blessed are you when they revile and persecute you and say all kinds of evil against you falsely for My sake. Rejoice and be exceedingly glad, for great is your reward in heaven, for so they persecuted the prophets who were before you.

Notice Jesus did not say "Blessed are those who always get their way," "Blessed are those who never have to suffer," or even "Blessed are you when your husband does whatever you want him to." Instead, He said those who mourn and those who are persecuted, reviled, and slandered are blessed. Why? Because suffering draws us close to God and makes us holy—and holiness brings happiness.

Marriage is a sanctifying relationship. The trials of marriage are often the means by which we are made to be poor in spirit, mournful, meek, hungry and thirsty for righteousness, merciful, pure in heart, peacemakers, persecuted, and reviled. Marriage often displays how much personal holiness we are lacking, and it can also show us how sufficient Jesus is to meet our needs. Sher Pai says,

> My husband is a dedicated financial provider for our family and he diligently loves our children, but he is not an emotional investor. As a young wife and new Christian, I would look at the married couples in my church and watch the way husbands seemed to spiritually and emotionally nurture their wives. It made me feel as though I was missing something.
>
> Feeling sorry for myself, I would go to God and ask Him to change my husband. When years went by and nothing changed, I grew discouraged and even hopeless. It wasn't until I cried out to God and asked Him to fill me that my heart was changed and the way I thought about my husband changed too. Now I appreciate the special way God made him. My husband's strengths are powerful, but his weaknesses have allowed me access to intimacy with God that I would not have experienced otherwise.

I am grateful for the unique traits of the man God has given me—the things that at first made me feel as though something was missing later became the opportunity for God to prove He is more than enough for me.

Your husband may be the main tool God uses to make you holy. He knows what He's doing. Happiness is a blessed by-product of fixing your eyes on Jesus rather on than your husband.

Holiness How-Tos

The book of Psalms begins by telling us what the happy, or blessed, man does *not* do.

Blessed is the man who walks not in the counsel of the ungodly, nor stands in the path of sinners, nor sits in the seat of the scornful. (Ps. 1:1)

The happy believer does not walk, stand, or sit with those who do not want to obey God. The blessed woman is blessed because she chooses to reject the counsel of the ungodly, to stay off the same path as sinners who are rejecting God, and to not hang around scornful people. Of course, this is a challenge when the scornful person is your husband! Even though you may not be able to avoid the company of a sinful, scornful person, you can choose to not participate in their practices. Choosing what *not* to do allows a believer to remain unhindered by ungodly thoughts and behaviors, and therefore, the path of blessing stays open.

Psalm 1 goes on to tell us what the happy believer *does* do:

But his delight is in the law of the Lord, and in His law he meditates day and night. (Ps. 1:2)

The holy, happy woman chooses what she thinks about day and night—the Word of God. So much of our unhappiness stems from what we choose to think about. The biblical recipe for happiness is:

Holy Living + Holy Thinking = Blessedness (Happiness)

If you want to be happy, then seek to be holy. Be as set apart from this sin-sick world as possible. Draw nearer and nearer to Jesus through His Word, and act like He does toward the people around you. This may be difficult when you seem to be the only one walking in holiness, but the eventual by-product of obedience is contentment. The holier you are, the happier you will be.

Holiness is primarily a personal pursuit—one that every believer chooses when they follow Christ as Savior—whether they are married or single. Each of us is ultimately responsible for our own holiness, and therefore, our own happiness.

LESSON 12 WIFE-CHANGING QUESTIONS

1. How has being married caused you to become more holy?

_____

_____

_____

_____

2. In your own words, explain how happiness and holiness are connected?

_____

_____

_____

_____

3. In what ways are you currently pursuing personal holiness?

_____

_____

_____

_____

4. Write a prayer asking the Lord to work in your husband's heart in the area of loving you well (be specific in asking God what you want to see Him do), and also for your own pursuit of holiness to be your focus as God works in your husband.

_____

_____

_____

_____

LESSON 13

Get Out of Debt

Madison sat across from me, recounting how many times that month Jacob had raised his voice, canceled their plans, forgotten something she had asked him to do, not returned her texts, and had not eaten the meals she prepared. She had a running mental scoreboard of all the things he had done wrong. (I honestly wondered if she had an actual spreadsheet somewhere.) And that was just the account from the previous month. She also shared details about the wedding he made them all late to last year and how long he left the Christmas lights up. She ended her list of offenses with, "See? All Jacob cares about is himself!"

This miserable woman had spent months (perhaps years) reviewing her husband's wrongs. She had devoted herself to proving her case, building her argument, is all she could declare was, "See? He's selfish!" Perhaps he was, and all of the things she said he did, he probably did. Madison had spent so much time and energy rehearsing the wrongs Jacob had committed against her. The "offenses" she had listed weren't horrible. Many of them were likely unintentional. How much freer would Madison be if she chose to forgive her husband for his petty wrongs and just smiled and enjoyed him instead?

Contrary to the declaration in 1 Corinthians 13:5 that "love keeps no record of wrongs," many women keep detailed accounts of the offenses committed by their husbands. Rather than letting things go and choosing real forgiveness, a wife will keep score, determined to make him "pay off" what he has done.

Why are we often so slow to forgive when it truly makes things so much better? Perhaps it's because holding on to our anger makes us feel powerful. We feel like we are in control and can protect ourselves from being hurt. We convince ourselves we have to remember the offense so it doesn't happen again. We keep score, adding up offenses and building a "case" to prove he's a monster. Somehow this makes us feel better. However, it doesn't make us smiling, lovely women, does it? It actually puts us in deep bondage.

Wanting to be in control over our marriages was actually predicted for us. Remember, God said to Eve, "Your desire shall be for your husband." That means Eve's heart (and yours and mine) wants to be the boss. When we hang on to his offenses, demanding that he "pay" for whatever he did, we're playing right along with our cursed nature.

Petty Pet Peeves

It can be downright maddening to live with a man. Perhaps he will leave the toilet seat up, will not rinse his shaving remains down the sink, won't text back (and when he does three hours later, it's with "k"), will blow his nose in restaurants, will fall asleep on top of the top sheet, won't close drawers or cabinets, and will think a dirty shirt next to the hamper is "close enough."

Petty offenses—the minor things that are super annoying but not sinful, can quickly be transformed into major marital issues. Our prideful hearts want to take them as personal assaults and indications of deep character issues. We are wise to develop some practical strategies to deal with petty pet peeves.

The Three-Day Rule

Let's say that on a Tuesday morning you go into the bathroom to find that your husband left his wet towel on the floor on top of his once-worn pajamas, didn't wipe off the shower door, and left the remnants of his morning shave in the sink. Your immediate reaction is anger. You shouldn't have to pick up after a grown man like he's a toddler. How hard is it to hang up a towel and put away pajamas? And really, hair in the sink? That's just gross! So you clean it up, all the while brooding over all that his behavior implies. *He thinks my whole purpose in life is to be his personal maid. He has no clue what I even do all day. I'm sick of being unappreciated. How nice that he gets to go off to his fancy office and have lunch in swanky restaurants every day with interesting people, while his little servant is home cleaning up his disgusting messes and eating dinosaur chicken nuggets with his sick kids!*

When he texts later in the day to ask how your day is going, you answer with, "Still cleaning your beard hair out of the sink." You stew about it all day, noticing every microscopic indication of his inconsiderate abuse. By dinnertime, you're contemplating separating from him for a while so he can see what it's like to live without you. When he calls to say he's going to be late for dinner, you blurt out, "I'm not your dinner slave or your maid! You can just eat in your office! I'm done!" And your dear husband replies, "Are you about to start your period?"

The spiral is real, isn't it?

So here's a little strategy I've used to help myself navigate which issues to address and which ones to let go: When I'm irritated or offended by something my husband has done, I determine to not say anything to him about it for three days.

Yes. For seventy-two hours, I don't say a thing. (This does *not* mean I give him the silent treatment or let it fester and grow for three days.) I hang up the towel, put away his pajamas, and rinse out the sink. It only takes two minutes, and I have the rest of the day to be a smiling wife.

I carry on as if he had not done anything to offend me, and I commit the matter to prayer, asking God to convict him. Giving things a little time allows me to determine if I'm overreacting, responding with hormones, or if my husband has just had an off day. Usually it's just not worth disrupting the peace in my home.

On Thursday, if I'm still upset about Monday's mess, I look for a good time to address the situation. Most of the things that had bugged me on Monday have been replaced with other things (and by then, I'm waiting to see if those things are bothering me on Sunday). This one rule has preserved much peace in my house.

A fool gives full vent to his spirit, but a wise man quietly holds it back. (Prov. 29:11)

What Do I Want Him to Do?

Sometimes I can end up blowing up a little thing into a much bigger issue if I don't stop and consider what I actually want from my husband. Another highly effective way of dealing with petty offenses is to simply ask yourself this question: What do I want him to do?

Brent has the annoying habit of not pulling his car up into the driveway far enough. He parks his car right in the middle like it's all his, and I end up having to parallel park in front of our house—and I'm awful at parallel parking. The temptation is to start stewing on all that his parking job implies. *He acts like he's the only one who lives here. He doesn't even care that I have kids and groceries to unload or that I hate parallel parking. He's probably inside right now watching me try to park my van and laughing at me . . .*

See what I'm doing? How much simpler would it be to just go inside and cheerfully say, "Hey, babe! Man, I hate parallel parking. I stink at it. Could you please try to remember to park further up the driveway so I can park behind you?" That's really all I want him to do. It's so much easier to just ask for what I want than to turn it into an issue where I question his character and the stability of our relationship.

Don't imply he's a horrible selfish monster or bring it up every time he has let you down in the last two years because of a small infraction. Perhaps you can say, "I want to ask if you would spend some time teaching Billy how to catch better. You're so great at sports, and he said he's been teased at school about not being good with a ball," rather than, "You aren't spending enough time with our son, and haven't done anything with him since last summer. Now he's being picked on and will probably end up a drug addict because you never spent time with him when he was nine."

What do you want him to do? Ask for it directly. Don't just sigh deeply and hope he asks why. Expecting him to decipher your hints and innuendos is setting you both up for disappointment. Simply and sweetly ask for what you want. Lay it out for him. You may need to ask several times (with respect and not nagging), but it's so much easier than manipulation and quarreling!

Rein In Those Thoughts

Vanessa stood in her closet shuffling through the rack, trying to find something to wear to church. *I have fifteen minutes to get ready. It's too hot for that. I don't have shoes that go with those pants. Everything is so old and out of style. Except for that dress, but I look like a flowered sausage in it 'cause I'm so fat. Ugh. I really have no clothes, and I wish Tim made more money so I could either buy new clothes, or at least join the gym. It's not fair he gets to go to the gym and I don't. He spends way more money on himself than me. If I get that promotion, I'm not even going to tell him. I'm just going to spend it all on myself like he would if it were him!*

Those mental spirals can escalate quickly, can't they?

If we are honest, the real problem is not usually our husbands. It's our own self-pity and pride. We feel bad, and we want to blame someone else—and our husbands are the easiest target.

Many of us go into each day *expecting* to be offended. We assume a defensive stance and keep our fists up, ready to punch back at the first hint of opposition. How much easier would it be to rather *expect* our husbands to not want to hurt us on purpose, and to seek to be his teammate rather than his opponent?

The trick is to stop the spiral before it makes its first loop:

I have fifteen minutes to get ready. It's too hot for that. I don't have shoes that go with those pants—Oh, Lord, help me! I don't want to be discouraged about this. I'm looking at a closet full of clothes. Show me what to wear to church today, and by the way, I'd really like something new. Could You please provide for me? I'm also discouraged by this extra weight. Lord, show me what I need to do to get it off so I can wear all the clothes in my closet.

When I feel myself getting ready to spiral, when I'm starting to slip down the hole of self-pity and blame, I need to rein in my thoughts. I need to *choose* to not be easily offended, and to instead cry out to the Lord and invite Him to intervene, knowing that He is wanting to help me in every single area of my life. If I do this continually, I'm not only avoiding that ugly coil of selfishness and pride, but I'm drawing closer to the Lord, which only fuels my smile.

Is It Worth I t?

Getting into an insult-slinging match with your husband because he forgot to take the trashcans to the curb is absurd, but it happens, doesn't it? We decide we would rather prove our point and be right than have peace in our homes. Friend, it is better to be kind than to be right. It is better to have peace than to get your own way. It's not worth it to win a fight and repel your husband.

When it comes to those annoying little things and you're tempted to mention how frustrated you are, ask yourself, "Is it worth it?" Is addressing this offense worth disrupting the peace in our house? Is this an issue that really needs to be communicated through, or is it something I can choose to die to myself on?

Most of the time (almost *all* of the time), it's just not worth it. Sometimes I am just being nit-picky. Sometimes I am being selfish. Sometimes it's just never going to change, so I should just let it go and choose to smile instead! Rose says,

> My husband has always had a beard of some sort. I like his beard. Hygiene is a huge priority for him (I'm so grateful!), and he keeps his beard neatly trimmed at all times. Unfortunately, he has the super annoying habit of leaving the bathroom drawers open when he trims his beard. Yeah. Yuck. I have gotten mad and pointed out how gross it is. I have sweetly asked him to try and remember to close the drawers. I have even texted photos of the hairy drawer to him with the word "Really?" But you know what? It's probably not going to change. In twenty years, I'll probably still be sweeping out the drawers after he shaves. So what? It's really not that big of a deal! I've decided that every time I do it, I'm going to just thank God for my husband!

I love Proverbs 14:4: *"Where there are no oxen, the manger is clean, but abundant crops come by the strength of the ox."* What the writer of that Proverb is saying is that the stables are clean when you don't have animals, but without the animals, you don't get much work done! You can't harvest your crops without the ox that dirties up the stable. You can't have a clean stable and an ox at the same time, and the benefit of the ox outweighs the benefits of a clean stable.

Oh, wives, keep this in mind. How many widows wish they had their husband's messes to pick up or annoying habits to tolerate? Their houses might be spotless and annoyance-free, but these widows are lonely. Be grateful for your big ox of a husband. Choose to let the petty things go, and rejoice that you get to live out your life with him as a crowning, smiling wife.

Major Offenses

What if the issues you are contending with are not petty pet peeves? What if he did something huge that is life-altering or devastating? How can you forgive when your pain is so real or your fear of a repeat offense is so intense? Sometimes a husband makes a choice that causes tremendous pain to his wife, as well as causing long-term consequences to his whole family.

When a wife has been deeply offended by her husband, her command from God is to forgive. But forgiveness is not easy, and the deeper the pain, the more difficult it is to forgive. However, forgiveness is *always* possible. *Always.* God would never command us to do something we are unable to obey.

> Put on then, as God's chosen ones, holy and beloved, compassionate hearts, kindness, humility, meekness, and patience, bearing with one another and, if one has a complaint against another, forgiving each other; as the Lord has forgiven you, so you also must forgive. (Col. 3:12–13)

Decisions, Decisions

There are five things to remember when it comes to forgiveness:

1. Forgiveness is entirely possible by the power of the Holy Spirit.

Forgiveness—a true and complete dismissal of an offense, with no demand for compensation—does not come naturally. To be able to forgive a horrific offense that has caused you incredible suffering is totally against your nature. Naturally, you are defensive, bitter, and angry and will stay that way until you die. However, *because of the Holy Spirit who dwells in you*, you have the power to do what you can't do on your own.

> And when he had said this, he breathed on them and said to them, "Receive the Holy Spirit. If you forgive the sins of any, they are forgiven them; if you withhold forgiveness from any, it is withheld." (John 20:22–23)

Jesus breathed on His disciples, and they received the Holy Spirit. In the very next sentence, He tells them they have the power to forgive. There is a very firm connection between the power of the Holy Spirit and the ability to forgive. If left to yourself, you will remain bitter, angry, and defensive about whatever happened.

But glory and hallelujah! You haven't been left to yourself! Apart from Him, you can't forgive, but through Him and by Him, you most certainly can.

2. You have been forgiven by God.

Don't forget that you have committed sin that warrants you to spend eternity in hell, separated from God. Whatever your husband (or anyone else) has done to you, keep in mind you have committed cosmic treason against a holy God and have been forgiven for it. Not just forgiven, but you've been given grace—unmerited favor from your Creator. Therefore, you have all the example you need to extend the same kind of grace to those who have offended you.

Forgiveness in your marriage begins with your relationship with God. When you have been offended, taking the offense to God before you take it to your husband is essential. When we go to Jesus with another's offense, we are reminded that we are sinners in need of grace ourselves, and we are then able to extend the grace we have received to another.

> Be kind to one another, tenderhearted, forgiving one another, *as God in Christ forgave you.* (Eph. 4:32, emphasis added)

> Bearing with one another and, if one has a complaint against another, forgiving each other; *as the Lord has forgiven you, so you also must forgive.* (Col. 3:13, emphasis added)

> And forgive us our debts, *as we also have forgiven our debtors.* (Matt. 6:12, emphasis added)

3. Forgiveness is costly.

To willingly choose to lay aside your right to be treated fairly, honestly, or lovingly is expensive. It comes at an enormous and heavy personal price. You pay for forgiving someone by swallowing your pride, giving up your rights, and surrendering your pain. That's why forgiving is so terribly hard.

Jesus is our ultimate example of forgiveness. Granting us forgiveness cost Him everything, and He will forever bear the marks that our forgiveness cost Him.

> We rightly celebrate what Jesus did, but let us remember that it resulted in Him bearing permanent scars on His body. Within God Himself, there is a constant memorial to the heavy cost of forgiving us.[3] —Vernon Pierre

4. Forgiveness is not a feeling—it is a choice.

Forgiveness is a decision, and it is often one you must make again and again. It will be combatted by memories and feelings on a regular basis, and it will need to be *chosen* repeatedly. When that bitterness rises up in you again, then you must actively choose to lay it down and forgive.

If you are experiencing the pain of someone else's sin, you aren't required to respond to that pain. I love the wisdom in this quote by Maureen Schaffer:

> Pain, emotional or physical, can be very loud. Loud enough to demand we believe its conclusions about God, ourselves, our situations, or others. Remember that just because something is loud doesn't mean it is truth. When we are in pain we had best ignore the assessments and conclusions that present themselves through the filter of pain. The still, small voice of God is still more authoritative than the loud, bullying voice of pain.

Scarlett got a call from a collections agent telling her that Luke, her husband, had opened a credit card in her name without her knowing, and he had pulled out dozens of cash advances on that card. Upon investigating, she soon learned Luke had been participating in online gambling, had two other secret credit cards, and they were over $65,000 in debt.

When Scarlett confronted Luke about the gambling and credit cards, he was deeply repentant, but the consequences of his offense were huge. Their credit was destroyed along with their marital trust. The rebuilding would be a long, painful climb.

In her pastor's office, Scarlett said, "I know I have to forgive him and work on restoring everything, but I sure don't *feel* forgiving right now. I'm so angry and hurt that every time I look at him, I just want to punch him in the face! I want to leave him and let him fend for himself! But I know I won't do that. I know I will forgive him. That's the choice I'm making in my head, but my feelings are going to need to catch up, and I'm not sure how long that will take."

Scarlett's reaction was so healthy. She would be downright crazy to just smile sweetly at Luke and say, "Well, God tells me to forgive you, so I do. Let's just forget it. What would you like for dinner, Sweetheart?" Her anger, hurt, and pain were the natural consequences to Luke's sin. They were the right way for her to feel; however, she couldn't let her feelings govern whether or not she obeyed God.

She had to *choose* forgiveness.

About eighteen months later, Scarlett shared, "We had to sell our house and start over. It was so humiliating to tell our neighbors and our family. There were days I was so angry that he did this to us that I considered leaving. But I chose to forgive him instead. I had to keep reminding myself of all God has forgiven me for, and to ask Him to help me to love Luke like He does. It was so hard at first, but I saw real change in Luke. He was so humble, and he started seeking God like I had always wanted him to. It's strange to say it, but I think that the whole financial crisis was an answer to my prayers for God to really get to my husband's heart. He's accountable to men in our church in a way he really needed. I'm actually grateful the whole mess happened. I still have waves of fear that he'll do this to us again, and I sometimes check our credit online just to make sure, but I am starting to trust him again."

Part of being a helper to your husband is not excusing sinful behavior. If he has done something sinful against you or someone else, don't pretend it is okay when it isn't. Nowhere in Scripture are we called to deny reality for the sake of preserving a relationship. Call sinful actions what they are—with an attitude of humility and gentleness. Your husband needs correction as much as you do.

Sometimes whatever your husband has done will never be able to be repaired. Maybe he brought financial ruin, destroyed your family's reputation, or lost friendships and family relationships. His offense may have essentially destroyed your life—perhaps cost you years of hardship and sleepless nights—and there's nothing that will ever bring it all back.

You may feel like your husband doesn't really understand what he did to you. You may want to make him see how much you're suffering. Maybe you think he should be more heartbroken than he is. You might think, *If I forgive him, then that means it's all okay. He'll start thinking what he did wasn't a big deal, and then maybe it will all happen again. I can't go through something like this ever again. I have to make sure he never forgets what he did!*

Dear Sister, you must first accept that he may not be able to restore to you what has been lost through his offense. There are some tragic things that happen in life that can't be remedied, no matter how much sorrow there is. Surrender to the truth that your life is permanently changed because of what has happened.

The good news is our suffering is never wasted. God is an expert at turning ashes into something beautiful. He can turn a painful situation around and make it into an experience that causes you to know Him more intimately and allows you to minister to others more compassionately.

5. Forgiveness is not the same as reconciliation.

There is a difference between forgiveness and reconciliation. Forgiveness is always required by God. Reconciliation is not.

Is it possible to forgive someone and remain unreconciled? Yes. Reconciliation means repairing and restoring a broken relationship. Forgiveness does not always lead to reconciliation.

Jesus didn't require people to be sorry before He forgave them. On the cross, Jesus asked God to forgive those who put Him there, saying, "Father, forgive them, for they know not what they do" (Luke 23:34). These people crucified their Savior, and He extended forgiveness to them without them being sorry.

However, Jesus didn't say those He had extended forgiveness to were in a right relationship with Him. They could only have restoration in their relationship with Him if they repented from their sin. Reconciliation requires repentance. If someone is unwilling to repent, we are still required to forgive them, but the relationship can't be restored unless there is reconciliation. While there may be forgiveness, the relationship remains broken until there is acknowledgment of the offense and repentance from the sin.

It should always be our desire to be reconciled to people. That's the heart Jesus has for every single person. However, we are only responsible for our own part in a conflict. The Scripture instructs us, "If possible, so far as it depends on you, live peaceably with all" (Rom. 12:18). Notice two things about this verse. Paul wrote, "If possible," which means sometimes it *won't* be possible. Secondly, he said, "As far as it depends on you," which means there is another side. There is an "as much as it depends on them." Before the Lord, we are only responsible for doing what we can on our end to have peaceable relationships with people. Sometimes, because of what depends on *them*, living at peace is not possible.

If your husband has sinned against you in a deep way, you are commanded to forgive and then to pursue restoring the relationship. This is a long process. Trust takes time to be restored, and it is only done through proven trustworthiness. It is okay to grieve what sin has destroyed, but don't remain in the grief. Process the reality of what has happened, with your heart set on eventual restoration. Jesus knows what it is like to be betrayed and sinned against by those He loves most. Go to Him with your burdens, seek out wise counsel, and pursue restoration, as much as it depends on you.

May God help us to be women who do all we can to seek peace with all men, and when that is not possible, to rest confidently in Him who sees all things and does not stop working miracles.

When You're the Offender

Sometimes it's not your husband who has sinned. It's you.

I have said and done some really damaging, hurtful things to my husband over the years. He has been on the receiving end of my cutting remarks, my foolish choices, my deliberate rebellion, and my careless mistakes. Brent Kaser married a wretched sinner.

Your husband is married to a wretched sinner too.

So what do we do when we have sinned against our husbands?

1. Confess immediately.

This can be the hardest part. Often, I will start justifying my actions, reasoning why it's not really my fault I did what I did. I blame someone else or make excuses for why it's not a big deal. I need to just stop and face reality. I blew it. I need to call my sin what it is.

When you see you have sinned, you should be sorry about it and say so. Take full responsibility for what happened. Be humble and sincere. You were wrong. Admit it without explaining your reasons or justifying why it was a natural reaction.

With your confession and apology, ask for forgiveness. Your husband needs an opportunity to choose to let it go and not hold it against you. Don't demand that he forgive you immediately. He may need time to cool off and reset.

Let's say I disrespected my husband in front of my kids. I recognize my behavior is sinful, so I say to him (while my kids listen), "I disrespected you when I argued with you about it. I'm sorry. Will you please forgive me?"

No excuses. No saying, "I'm sorry, but you were still wrong."

Confess. Apologize. Ask for forgiveness.

2. Repent.

Repentance should immediately follow confession. Repentance means to turn away. It means that I stop doing whatever I was doing and turn away from it. If I don't repent, then my confession is worthless. I can't say, "I disrespected you. I'm sorry. But you're such an idiot!" Repentance means turning from my sin and not continuing in it any longer.

3. Expect and embrace consequences.

Just because I admit my sin and repent from it doesn't mean I won't suffer consequences for my actions. Just like Eve in the garden, I don't get to choose the consequences for my sin.

If you have sinned, then be prepared to suffer the penalties. Sometimes God is incredibly gracious to us and we don't suffer consequences. However, you will likely have to pay that fine, lose that job, be removed from a leadership position, or be ostracized from that group. You may need to do the work of repairing the damages you caused—either relationally or practically. Resist the urge to run from the cost of your sin. Embrace the cost instead. Our God-ordained consequences are often the teachers we need to keep us from sinning in the same way again.

4. Pursue reconciliation.

Reconciliation is a process, and depending on the offense, it can be a long one. Sometimes the pain of a harsh word or sinful action lingers, and it is very difficult to go "back to normal" because the sting remains. Just like a scraped knee or a broken bone, healing from an emotional wound takes time.

I remember a conversation I once had with Lauren after she flipped out on her husband, cussed him out, and shattered a dish that she threw at him in anger.

She piously said, "Well, it's not my problem now. I told God I was sorry, and I told Trevor I was sorry. He has to forgive me. If he's still mad, then he's the one in sin!"

Lauren had just torn down her husband, behaved like a maniac, and then shrugged it off, saying, "Sorry. Now you have to forgive me." Her husband needed time to recover from her tantrum. He needed to see her sincerity and her genuine repentance before he could be reconciled to his wife.

We are being terribly immature if we demand everyone else turn on the forgiveness just because we are ready to start acting like godly women again. Relationships aren't automatically restored the second an apology is uttered. Trust is earned, and sometimes it takes time for it to be restored. That's a consequence of sin.

Sometimes we turn a fire hose of emotions on our husbands, blasting them with pent-up frustrations and hurts. When they are dripping wet and stunned by the unexpected drenching, we shouldn't be upset when it takes a while for them to recover. They are wisely hesitant to come close to us for fear of another dousing.

If you hurt your husband in some way and he takes a while to reset back to normal, don't accuse him of not forgiving you. Sometimes that distance is a consequence of your sin. Don't misuse use the whole "do not let the sun go down on your anger" verse. That verse means *you* need to get over *your* anger. It's not sinful to choose quietness for the night, or even a day or two, and allow the Lord to work in both of you. Don't demand reconciliation on your own time frame. Stop talking, and leave room and time for the Holy Spirit to speak to both of you.

Do all you can to assure your husband of your repentance, and give him the space he needs to heal.

In the course of your marriage, there will be plenty of opportunities to extend and receive forgiveness. There will be countless petty issues, a handful of major offenses, and plenty of sin of varying degrees in between. The glorious news is you don't need to walk through life bearing the burden of all of those offenses. Because of Jesus, you have the power to forgive and to walk through this life as a woman who smiles at her future.

LESSON 13 WIFE-CHANGING QUESTIONS

1. What are two petty offenses that really get under your skin?

_____

_____

_____

_____

2. How can you better react to these petty offenses and maintain your smile?

_____

_____

_____

_____

3. Can you recall the five things that are key to understanding forgiveness?

_____

_____

_____

_____

4. Examine your heart. Are you holding on to unforgiveness toward your husband? Toward anyone else? If so, how are you going to pursue forgiveness?

_____

_____

_____

_____

5. Is there something you have done against your husband (or anyone else) for which you need to seek forgiveness? What are the three steps to proceed with that?

_____

_____

_____

_____

6. Did you learn anything new regarding forgiveness, and/or are there any wife-changing adjustments you need to make in this area?

_____

_____

_____

_____

LESSON 14

Carissa and Jack had been married for six years when they came for counseling. It seemed as if it had been just one big trial with only a few good days in between.

As we were discussing the need for a wife to respect her husband, Jack blurted, "It's pretty obvious that she doesn't respect me at all. There's no pleasing her because she thinks I'm a total failure."

Carissa retorted, "I do respect him! He is just such a jerk all the time that I don't have any opportunity to show it! Maybe if he were nice for a day, I could show some respect!"

Carissa communicated disrespect in nearly every word of that counseling appointment but swore that she respected her husband. Her actions and words completely denied her claim, and little by little, day by day, she was destroying her marriage.

Respect is something we all know we are required to show our husbands, but many of us don't know what that looks like in practice. We are wise to examine ourselves in our current season of marriage and determine what wife-changes we need to make to ensure we are showing our husbands the respect they need.

Respect—See to It!

Pay attention to the last sentence in Ephesians 5:32–33, particularly the part after the second comma:

> This mystery is great; but I am speaking with reference to Christ and the church. Nevertheless, each individual among you also is to love his own wife even as himself, *and let the wife see to it that she respect her husband.* (emphasis added)

A wife's respect is mentioned as the parallel to the husband's call to love his wife. A wife is to "see to it," meaning she is to pay careful attention to this matter, that she should *make sure* respecting her husband is happening.

Many women would much rather "see to" a lot of other things than respecting their husbands. They see to it that their house is decorated properly, that their hair is styled and their makeup is on, that their children are in the right schools or activities, that their careers are moving forward, that the women's ministry luncheon is lovely, and that they are at that prayer meeting or that Bible study or that community event. They are busy "seeing to it" in many areas, but are neglecting the one area to which Scripture commands they see.

Your Half of the Sandwich

This verse in Ephesians is kind of like a sandwich. One slice of bread is the husband loving his wife, the other slice of bread is the wife's respect, and the whole thing being a picture of Christ and the church, is the "mystery meat" in the middle that we will discuss in chapter six.

When women point out their husband's "disobedience" to loving them "like Christ loves the church," they usually fail to mention their disobedience to the command to see that they respect their husbands. They only want to discuss one side of the sandwich—*his*!

In order for the whole picture of marriage as a symbol of Christ and the church to work, both sides must be working together to make the picture clear. There must be the sacrificial, nurturing love of the husband doing all he can to ensure his wife's holiness, and there must be the respectful, submissive actions and attitude of the wife toward her husband. The husband represents God's care for the church, and the wife represents the response of the church toward God. If either of us doesn't do our part, we mess up the symbolism.

You can only control your own part. You only get one side of the sandwich! Leave the "loving you" part between God and your husband. *You see to it* that you respect your husband.

Respect is *not* earned in a marriage. God commands a wife to respect her husband without any conditions. She is to respect him simply because she is married to him. This is a man's greatest need from his wife. Respect is too vital for it to come and go based on his performance.

Many wives make the mistake of withholding respect from their husbands in an effort to make them change. They say things like, "Everyone thinks you're a nice guy, but I know the truth!," or "Why can't you be more like the pastor? He prays with his wife every morning." Their reasoning is that he will be motivated to be a nicer guy and to pray more with his wife if she says these things to him. But it doesn't work that way. Manipulation is always counterproductive. He feels disrespected, instantly gets angry and defensive, and may respond with emotional distance and a desire to increase the very behavior she is trying to make him change.

When you disrespect your husband by being unappreciative, corrective, demeaning, ridiculing, ignoring, or dismissing, it will hurt him and your marriage. Disrespecting your husband will only rob you of his desire to love you.

It is often easier to identify the absence of respect than to identify its practice. How can you tell if you're treating your husband disrespectfully?

The Disrespect Test

The goal of the Disrespect Test is to see if there are disrespectful behaviors you can correct in order to display more respect to your husband. Answer these questions honestly. (If you really want to know, ask your husband to answer.)

- Do you ask him questions you really don't want answers to? (Do you not see the hamper in the closet? Are you going to stay on the couch all day? Do you think the trash is going to take itself out?)
- Do you roll your eyes at him?
- Do you interfere when he's disciplining the kids?
- Do you interrupt him when he's talking?
- Do you say "I told you so" in any form?
- Do you tell your mother, sister, or girlfriends about his mistakes?
- Do you ever suggest he shouldn't eat something because of his weight?
- Do you withhold praising him or smiling at him because you don't want him to think everything is okay?
- Do you make him feel as if sex is a reward for him being a "good boy"?
- Do you expect him to be sensitive to your moods but expect him to never have an off day?
- Do you compare him (either verbally or silently) to your pastor, your friend's husband, or to fictional characters you admire?
- Do you manipulate him by crying, threatening, or verbally attacking?
- Do you get disgruntled if he spends time enjoying activities that don't include you?
- Do you complain that you don't have enough money?
- Do you forget to say "thank you" for the things he does?
- Do you disregard his requests if he's not around?
- Do you think he should "earn" your respect before you give it to him?
- Do you talk to your husband with a condescending tone?
- Do you choose not to get dressed or not to do your hair and makeup if your husband is the only one you'll see all day?
- Do you get up and greet him when you see him after a few hours, or do you barely look up from whatever you're doing with an "Oh, it's just you" expression?
- Do you share "funny" stories with other people that make your husband look like a fool?
- Do you do anything else that you know makes your husband feel disrespected?

We sat across from Deb at a church potluck when her husband came back to the table with a heaping plateful of food.

"Seriously?" Deb said to him with a huff of disgust.

No one at the table knew the details that were contained in that one word, but it was clear she disapproved of his plate, and she made sure we all knew about it. Deb's husband sat in silence through the rest of the evening and left during the closing prayer.

At a home fellowship, I was in the kitchen helping to clean up after dinner. Mia's husband came in and asked what he could do to help.

With a severe eye roll, she snarled, "Really? You want to help me now that you have someone here to impress? No thanks. I got it!"

Women also ruthlessly disrespect their husbands on social media:

"I just wish I had someone I could trust."

"Someone is going to enjoy sleeping on the sofa tonight."

"At least one of us got what they wanted for Christmas."

"*Someone* always seems to find time to golf, but the time to fix the dishwasher hasn't been there for two months."

"Must be nice to sleep till seven, only have to work eight hours, come home to dinner, and then lay on the sofa all night."

If these wives are so brazenly disrespecting their husbands in public, I shudder to think how they behave in their own homes.

Damaging Stereotype

The current American stereotype of a husband is that of an overweight, witless, couch potato who is constantly getting in trouble with his smart, sophisticated wife who puts him in time-out when she makes him sleep on the sofa. Think about how many times you have seen this scene in memes, sitcoms, commercials, or comedy performances. It's been the caricature of the American family for the last three decades and has contributed to the vast respect deficiency given to husbands, even in Christian homes.

Look at what blogger Matt Walsh said about this depiction of marriage:

> These cultural messages aren't harmful because they hurt my manly feelings; they're harmful because of what they do to young girls. Society tells our daughters that men are boorish dolts who need to be herded like goats and lectured like schoolboys. Then they grow up and enter into

marriage wholly unprepared and unwilling to accept the biblical notion that "wives should submit to their husbands" because "the husband is the head of the wife" (Eph. 5).

It is a fatal problem, because the one thing that is consistently withheld from men and husbands—respect—is the one thing we need the most.

Respect is our language. If it isn't said with respect, we can't hear it. This is why nagging is ineffective and self-defeating. This is why statements made in sarcastic tones, or with rolling eyes, will never be received well. We have a filter in our brains, and a statement made in disrespect will be filtered out like the poison it is.[4]

A wife must be vigilant to guard any hint of disrespect toward her husband in her words, her actions, and her expressions. This is a commandment for every Christian wife. To disobey this command is sin. If you are guilty of any form of disrespect toward your husband, like any other sin, there is only one thing to do: repent.

Honor

Honor and respect are related, but honor goes beyond outward respect. While respect is commanded toward outward behavior, honor refers to internally revering and applying worth and value to someone. Honor recognizes the qualities in another person and esteems them with genuine admiration. It means you admire and appreciate someone so much that it comes out in your words and actions naturally. It's not lip service, and it's not obedience out of a command or submission to authority.

It's one thing to respect the police officer holding up his hand telling you to stop. You respect his authority because of his badge and what it means. However, if that same police officer happens to be your friend and you know how hard he works and that last year he almost lost his life in the line of duty, you have an admiration for him that goes beyond external respect. You honor him.

Within a marriage, honor goes beyond the expected "duties" of a wife because honor reveals her real heart toward her husband. Your husband doesn't just want your outward respect, does he? To merely respect him for no reason other than God commands it isn't what your husband is after. He wants you to admire him, value him, and esteem him. Your husband wants to be not only outwardly respected, but he also wants to be truly honored.

Honoring your husband by esteeming his opinions, character, and personality is of great worth. Doing this means looking beyond his momentary lapses in character and seeing him for who God is calling him to be. Honor is promoting and magnifying the best about him while minimizing the negative. It's treating him as the man you know he really wants to be.

An honored husband is convinced that his wife thinks highly of him. Do you *honor* your husband? Do you have genuine admiration for him? Often when you start to really think about the man you are married to, you can recognize honorable things about him. Philippians 4:8 encourages us to train our minds to think about the things that are honorable:

> Finally, brothers, whatever is true, whatever is **honorable**, whatever is just, whatever is pure, whatever is lovely, whatever is commendable, if there is any excellence, if there is anything worthy of praise, think about these things. (Phil. 4:8, emphasis added)

What is honorable, just, pure, lovely, commendable, excellent, and praiseworthy about your husband? When you choose to think about these things, the admiration for the man you married will grow, and your inward honoring of him will be externally evident to him.

I asked a group of ladies to share some of the things they find honorable about their husbands. Here is just a sampling of their list:

- He keeps working a job he doesn't like in order to provide for us.
- He gets two weeks off a year and chooses to spend them doing something that will be fun for the kids.
- He is generous.
- He knows how to fix stuff.
- He stays calm in a crisis.
- He puts others before himself.
- He leaves notes for me when I am feeling down.
- He really listens and remembers what people say.
- He keeps His word.
- He will help anyone, even at great cost to himself.
- He works long hours and comes home and plays with the kids.
- He doesn't say unkind things about people.
- He rarely complains.
- He knows how to cook and clean.
- He doesn't make a commitment he's not confident he can meet.
- He guards his eyes and mind from impurity.

- He is intelligent, yet values my thoughts and opinions.
- He honors my parents like they are his own.
- He's emotionally steady.
- He's patient.
- He points me to Jesus.

Consider those things that are honorable about your own husband, and dwell on them. Some women may read over the above list and say, "Well, my husband does none of those things, so that's why I don't honor him." To those women, I would encourage you to ask the Lord to show you what you *can* honor him for. You may be surprised what you suddenly end up noticing. Work toward not just externally respecting your husband, but work toward inwardly honoring him.

Honor him verbally. Verbal honor is like a magnet because it draws your husband toward you. Acknowledge when he does something admirable by telling him he did a great job. Let him know that you noticed and admire him. If you want more honorable behavior from your husband, be sure to point out when he does something you love. Compliments are addictive—they make us want to repeat whatever it is that gets us admired. Here are some examples:

"That was a great idea to take the boys to a hockey game so you could have some manly bonding time with them."

"You're so kind to elderly people. I love that about you."

"I'm so blessed to be married to a handy-man. You've saved us so much money over the years, and our house looks amazing because of you."

"I hope our daughter marries a man as generous as you."

Honor him intellectually. Appreciate his point of view. You don't always have to agree with him, but his opinions aren't foolish because they are different from yours. Validate his ideas rather than mock them. He's a unique individual, and he has his own way of seeing the world. Enjoy that about him.

In addition, remember that men like to fix stuff. It's part of how they're wired. Honor your husband by asking for his opinion and following his advice on how to solve problems or make things better. Your husband knows you. He knows other stuff too. Listen to his suggestions and validate his intellect by following them. You show him great honor when you value and implement his advice. For example:

"I have to drive to an appointment downtown. Can you please tell me the best route to get there so I don't get lost? You're way better at directions than I am."

"Mary asked me for advice on her finances. I told her she and Jackson should really talk to you since you're the one who handles our money so well."

"Can you explain what is going on politically in a way I can understand it? I just don't get it, and I need your help."

"I have a situation at work I'd like your counsel on."

Honor him physically. Deliberately choose to light up when you see him, as this communicates honor to your husband. Get up to greet him, reach for his hand for no reason, sit next to him on the sofa, put your hand on his knee in church. Kiss him hello and goodbye, and for no reason at all. Sincere and genuine affection shows honor to your husband.

Do not reject your husband's touch—sexual or otherwise. His need to be honored in this way is immense. We will discuss this in detail in chapter five, but remember *only you* can meet his need for physical intimacy. Don't dishonor him by withholding it. You will only damage your marriage by doing so.

Keep smiling. Your smile communicates respect and honor to your husband. Don't make your husband earn your smile. Give it to him freely—not because he always deserves it or because he is always brilliant or loving or attractive, but give your smile because it communicates respect and honor, which is his greatest need.

Respect. Honor. Smile. All three of these are nouns—they are *things* your husband needs. They are also verbs—*actions* that are demonstrated by your behavior that fulfill those very needs.

Respect. Honor. Smile. Repeat. That's your recipe for pleasing God in your marriage! It's simple, but not always easy, because it requires concentrated effort, dying to yourself, and seeking supernatural empowerment. But the fruit in your marriage that results will make you, your husband, and God smile.

LESSON 14 WIFE-CHANGING QUESTIONS

1. Are you guilty of any type of disrespect toward your husband? If so, write a prayer of repentance here.

_____

_____

_____

_____

2. What ways do you think your husband needs you to respect him most? Are you doing those things?

_____

_____

_____

_____

3. Ask your husband in what ways he feels respected by you and how you can grow in showing him respect. Write what he says here.

_____

_____

_____

_____

4. In your own words, explain the difference between respect and honor.

_____

_____

_____

_____

5. Do you think your husband feels honored by you?

_____

_____

_____

_____

6. Make your own list of at least honorable qualities about your husband.

_____

_____

_____

_____

7. When you have finished your list, and when the time is right, share it with him!

_____

_____

_____

_____

LESSON 15

Be His Friend

In the craziness of life—in raising kids, working, school schedules, housework, caring for elderly parents—and dozens of other things that make up our lives, we can often take friendship with our husbands for granted. We can be guilty of assuming our marriage relationship is fine because we are still together and we aren't fighting. However, maintaining a deep friendship with your husband isn't automatic. Are you a good friend to your husband?

Friends Do Stuff Together

My cousin Jennifer is part of a group of ladies who call themselves The Fun Wives Club. It all stemmed from some conversations about being unwilling to do things with their husbands that were out of their comfort zones. They started challenging one another to show respect to their husbands and be willing to do things they wouldn't choose to do ordinarily. Jennifer is married to Scott, a hardworking man who owns and operates a big construction company and races cars for fun. I asked her for some examples of what being in The Fun Wives Club has pushed her to do. Here is Jennifer's answer:

> I just completed a pistol training class and loved it. I drove his off-road race car in two races and ended up winning one of them! We just got back from taking the kids to San Felipe to be there with him for a race—I was a little afraid of taking the kids to Mexico, but it was beautiful and no big deal.
>
> I've learned to operate a skip loader and excavator, and I can hitch, back up, and drive all kinds of trailers. Oh, and he's hired me to design and implement the landscape for one of his projects! This has all been a huge blessing in our marriage, and I actually enjoy all the things I'm learning. It turns out it's way more fun being a fun wife than being left behind!

This has been a real challenge in my marriage. Brent and I honestly don't have a lot in common. I'm a complete nerd, and Brent is a total jock. We connected through ministry, and that is still our main common interest. Ministry is also our work, and there have been seasons where it seemed like we were more ministry partners than friends. It takes intentional effort to find things to enjoy together outside of work.

Even when I try to do something to promote our friendship, it doesn't always turn out like I envisioned it. About eight years into our marriage, Brent started playing golf. I decided that even though I am an athletic disgrace, I could possibly learn to use a stick to hit a little ball into a hole. I secretly took golf lessons for two months, and then I surprised Brent with a weekend getaway at a golf resort.

He was amazed! Feeling like a superstar wife, I put on my extremely cute new golf outfit and headed out to the golf course expecting to totally impress my man. At the first hole, I got out my club and assumed the position I had learned in my lessons. My dear husband actually fell on the ground laughing. He thought the sight of me with a club in my hand was the most hysterical thing he'd ever seen. He giggled through the first nine holes.

I was completely awful. Most of the par 3s took me at least eight or nine shots. It was hot. My arms hurt.

Brent finally said, "Nance, I love that you did this for me, but you're just *not* an athletic girl. I appreciate the surprise, really I do, but maybe we should do something else the rest of the weekend." My attempt at being his golfing buddy was a total bust, but I showed my husband that I wanted to be his friend, and he loved me for it.

Be a fun wife! Be adventurous, interesting, playful, and someone he wants to hang out with. Look for ways to connect with your husband that don't involve your work, your bedroom, your house, or your kids.

Friends Aren't Dream Killers

If you had a friend call and share some wild business idea, ministry opportunity, or a crazy adventurous camping-trip plan, chances are you wouldn't shoot her down with practical reasons why her ideas won't work. You would be excited for her, encourage her, and perhaps contribute a few practical suggestions, all with the intention of promoting her dreams. However, how would you react if your husband called you with those same ideas? Would you be a safe place for him to bounce ideas and dream, or would he be met with an automatic "Don't be ridiculous!"?

Is your husband a dreamer? Mine is. "Know what I want to do? I want to buy an RV and ride my bike across America for a year promoting missions!" Or, "I think we should adopt a child from Uganda." These are the kinds of regular sentences that have come out of Brent Kaser's mouth.

In the early years, I would immediately point out how completely absurd the ideas were. "Are you nuts? We would go crazy with our tribe of kids in an RV after a week, let alone a year, and what am I supposed to do while you are riding your bike? Hang out in the campground? No thanks." Or, "Do you know how much foreign adoptions cost? The friends we have who have done it say it's super hard."

After dousing his dreams with practicality so often, he stopped wanting to share them with me. I've learned he sometimes just wants to live through the experience in his head and share it with me. So now I let him dream, and I participate. "I'd love to adopt! Would we want a baby or an older child, or would we just let God decide for us?"

I gently bring up the practical things if his dreams start to turn into actions. Coming to him and saying, "I've been thinking about that RV idea, and I'm a little concerned about how we would all get along in such a small space. I'm not sure what I'd do all day while you were riding. What did you have in mind?" Asking questions like "Have you thought about . . ." or "I love the idea, but what would we do about . . .?" rather than directly pointing out the faults in his plan communicates respect and allows him to receive the practical aspects without feeling like he's being called a fool. Joanne says,

> While Mark was finishing his teaching credential, he would often come home proposing we move to various places he believed had better opportunities for new teachers. I would begin researching the pros and cons of the new "Promised Land," only to have a new nirvana proposed. I finally recognized he was dreaming and needed to bounce the idea off me, so I could relax until the moving truck actually backed up to my door!

Let your husband dream, and dream with him. If he knows you are willing to dream with him, he will plan all his dreams to include you!

Be His Cheerleader

Your husband should expect his wife to be his biggest supporter. Whether it's going to his softball games and cheering for him or giving him a pep talk before his sales meeting at work, being your husband's biggest fan should be a priority.

I remember hearing a woman saying she didn't give her husband a lot of praise because "He's already an egomaniac. I don't need him to have an even bigger head. If I compliment him, he'll only believe me and be more full of himself!" How silly! Your husband wants to know you think he's amazing. Be his fan! Cheer him on! He needs that from you!

Show up to his games, ask him how his presentation went at work, and be genuinely interested. Go listen to him teach the Sunday school class and tell him what you loved about it. Aubree says,

> Matt is super athletic. I hate sports. He wanted me to play softball with him so bad. I tried, but he soon realized I would not be able to have a ball thrown at me without screaming and running the opposite way.

Instead, I go to every single one of his games. I know every member of the team and cheer for them all. I bring snacks for the whole team. They call me their #1 cheerleader. I scream extra loud for Matt and always compliment him after the game on what he did well. He has accepted my lack of athletic ability and loves me as his cheerleader.

Just Be Nice!

Are you just plain nice to your husband? Do you treat him with the same niceness you treat the checker at the grocery store, the delivery guy, or the coffeeshop barista? Sometimes we end up being nicer to strangers than we do to the men we vowed to spend our lives with.

Are your husband's coworkers nicer to him than his wife? Do you jump up to refill a guest's coffee cup but expect your husband to get his own?

While we are on the subject, are you polite to your husband? Do you say "please" and "thank you"? Many women decide manners and politeness are wasted on their husbands. Stop it! Be nice! Be as courteous, kind, and friendly as you would be to anyone else. Or be even nicer.

Resist the Urge to Correct

Brent and I once went out to dinner with a couple I never want to be around again. The entire night, the wife interrupted her husband to correct him on meaningless details of every story:

"It wasn't on a Monday—it was a Wednesday."

"It wasn't orange—it was coral."

"She's not his niece—she's his cousin."

It was absolutely infuriating! I don't remember any of the stories he told that night, but I totally remember how rude and disrespectful her constant correction was.

Resist the urge to correct your husband in things that don't really matter. Let the trivial things go. Smile and enjoy him, and let him tell the story his way.

Correct Graciously

Sometimes though, there's a big error in something a husband says or does, and we are a terrible friend if we don't correct him.

My husband was invited to speak to a large crowd about our nonprofit organization. The room was full of potential ministry partners, and the presentation could benefit the lives of thousands of hurting people around the world. In the middle of the presentation, Brent got his words mixed up and accidentally misspoke about an important theological issue. He didn't realize his mistake and kept talking. In this crowd of biblically conservative people, this was a huge deal breaker.

I watched in horror as couples looked at each other with raised eyebrows that said, "They're not a ministry we can get behind."

Brent was completely unaware that he had made this error. I had to do something. I tried to get him to look at me, but I was in the back and couldn't catch his eye. So I walked right up the center aisle in the middle of his presentation. My husband was totally stunned. I went right up on the stage and whispered in his ear what he had said.

"I did?" was his reply. He laughingly said, "There's only one reason my wife would interrupt me in the middle of a presentation. I guess I just said something totally unbiblical!" Then he corrected his mistake.

The relief that spread over the room was tangible. We ended up securing a lasting partnership with that group of people. That wouldn't have happened if I hadn't corrected him.

We all need correction in big things from time to time, and we all regularly need little corrections only a good friend can give. A good friend tells you when you have something stuck in your teeth, when you need a mint, when you're talking too loudly, when you said something offensive, or when you're tagged in a bad photo. We treasure friends who love us enough to give us needed correction.

We would never think to insult our girlfriends by pointing out their stupidity, accusing them of immaturity, or insulting their character. If we treat our husbands like our friends, we will correct them with humility, tenderness, and respect.

Cover Him

We see people's sins displayed on newsfeeds, and we comment about how horrible they are. Women disguise gossip as "prayer requests" in church circles. All around us are examples of messed-up people, and we know all about them because people have shared the story.

But how many things have people *not* shared? How many examples can you think of where a person's reputation was preserved because those who knew about their offense chose not to conceal it? You probably can't think of many outside of your own family. And that's the whole point. By definition, *covering* hides an offense from the view of others. We don't know what they did because it was covered by people who chose not to make another's mistake public knowledge.

Your husband is going to do some foolish things over the course of his life. He will make bad decisions, say ridiculous things, and act in ungodly ways. You will know about most of his mistakes, and many of them will be known *only* by you. So what is a wife to do when her husband blows it?

Love covers a multitude of sins. (1 Peter 4:8)

He who covers a transgression seeks love, but he who repeats a matter separates friends. (Prov. 17:9)

Love covers. Covering is seeking to love. Covering does not mean ignoring. You can't cover up something unless you acknowledge it's there. Covering goes beyond forgiveness. It keeps sin private and protects the offender's reputation.

Does your husband trust that you will cover him? Can he be vulnerable and real and raw with you? Does he know his heart is safe with you? Does he trust you to guard his weaknesses, his reputation, and his dreams?

Or does his heart *not* trust you? Is he insecure about what you will do or say? Is he worried you will manipulate him, tarnish his reputation, or ridicule his dreams with your friends?

To be trusted with your husband's heart is a great honor. It is not to be assumed you deserve it or you get to keep his trust unconditionally. Your husband's trust is something you need to earn, treasure, and maintain. Covering for him is part of honoring him.

Desiree's husband, Mario, is a respected man in their community. He owns the local auto repair shop and teaches Sunday school. Everybody considers Mario one of the most genuinely joyful Christians they know. And he truly is. Only Desiree knows of her husband's silent battle with depression—days and weeks when Mario is overcome with feelings of deep despair.

Through the years, he has had some very dark times. Desiree has walked through each valley with him, at times fearing they would stay there forever. God has been faithful to be the One to lift Mario's head and pull him out of that place, and then Desiree rejoices with her husband and enjoys the mountaintop.

She has kept her husband's struggles between them, not denying they happen, but choosing to keep them private out of love for him. To share with her church or the community that he is sometimes depressed could cost him his reputation or his ministry. Because of her support, Mario has learned to identify his spirals and to know he won't stay down. He knows his wife will be by his side and will cover him when he needs it.

One of the most charming places we have ever stayed was a little cottage in the Georgia woods. It had a giant stone fireplace that took up one whole wall, and there was a lovely claw-foot tub in the bathroom. Brent suggested I go enjoy the bathtub while he started a fire.

Being from California, I was skeptical about his ability to light a fire with just wood and matches. "Do you know how to light that kind of fire?" I asked.

"C'mon, babe. I'm like Daniel Boone!" was his answer. I was submerged in lavender-scented bubbles when Brent called out, "Um, babe? I think we have a problem!"

When I came out in my towel, the entire room was filled with thick black smoke, and the flames of the fire were licking the carpet. As I threw some clothes on, I called the front desk and told them what was happening.

When the maintenance man arrived, my husband disappeared into the bathroom, totally embarrassed at his fire-making failure. I stood there while the burly mountain man scolded me about how "I" had lit the fire too far out and the smoke wasn't escaping through the chimney. I endured a thirty-minute fire-safety lesson.

When he finally left, I called down the hall, "Mr. Boone! You can come out now!"

He sheepishly opened the door and thanked me for taking the blame for him.

We had to sleep with the windows and doors open, even though it was hailing and twenty degrees outside. We laughed hysterically under that smoke-scented down comforter. We had to throw away our luggage when we got home because we couldn't get the smoke smell out of it.

A week later, I found a coonskin cap in a costume shop and bought it for him.

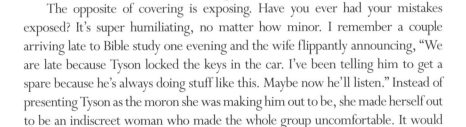

The opposite of covering is exposing. Have you ever had your mistakes exposed? It's super humiliating, no matter how minor. I remember a couple arriving late to Bible study one evening and the wife flippantly announcing, "We are late because Tyson locked the keys in the car. I've been telling him to get a spare because he's always doing stuff like this. Maybe now he'll listen." Instead of presenting Tyson as the moron she was making him out to be, she made herself out to be an indiscreet woman who made the whole group uncomfortable. It would have been better for her to simply apologize for being late with no reason and cover her husband.

Oh, may we be excellent wives who cover our husbands in grace!

Be Trustworthy

During a season when money was really tight, I started saving every spare dollar to buy myself something that cost $100. After six weeks, I had a fat pile of money stashed under my bedroom chair and was excited to make my purchase.

This particular morning, I sat in my chair reading my Bible. Brent came into our room and said, "We have $18 in our account till Friday. I have a lunch meeting today. Do you have any cash?"

I was sitting on $100, but I knew if I pulled out the stash, he would ask for all of it to pay for things we needed that week. I sat on my chair, Bible in my lap, and sweetly said, "Sorry, honey. I don't have anything. Maybe you can just go for coffee?"

I had lied, but it was *my* money! I had denied myself coffee with friends, cut coupons, and walked to the store to save gas money in order to save for what I wanted. I had worked hard to save it! I was fully justified in what I did, right?

Wrong.

All morning I kept trying to justify my lie. Then I realized I would have to hide my purchase from him for a while because if he came home and saw it, he would ask me how I paid for it. That meant I'd have to go shopping without the kids so they wouldn't tell him we had gone shopping. I would need to keep the package in my car for at least a week, which meant I had to make sure he didn't use my car.

By lunchtime, I had a detailed strategy about how I could keep my lie covered and still get what I wanted. I even thought of what I would say if he accidentally found my purchase or if he happened to call and ask what I was doing while I was out buying it.

As the time came closer for me to leave to spend my money, I had to surrender to the fact that I was being downright deceitful. I had lied to my husband and was orchestrating a web of deceit to cover myself. I was in sin. If I went out and spent that money on myself, I would have my prize, but it would cost me more than the one hundred dollars.

So I called him. After some small talk, I blurted out, "I lied to you this morning when you asked me if I had any money. I have saved a hundred dollars, and I was planning on spending it on myself today. I didn't want to share it with you. But it's all your money, too, so if you need it, you can have it all! I'm sorry I lied to you."

After a moment of silence, he laughed. "You're such a sinner! Thanks for confessing, babe. Go buy whatever you want with that money!"

It was humbling to admit my sin, but I went shopping that day with so much joy. I had invested in my marriage by being willing to part with something far less important. I enjoyed my purchase far more because I bought it with a clear conscience before God and my husband.

> *The heart of her husband safely trusts her, and he will have no lack of gain.*
> (Prov. 31:11)

Does your husband trust you? Is his heart safe with you? How about his bank account? His reputation? Is he assured he is gaining in all of these areas because you are his wife?

Our culture touts the whole "What he doesn't know won't hurt him" philosophy, but that's a lie. There should be nothing in your life your husband can't know about (birthday-gift secrets and fun surprises excluded). As a rule, if there is a need to keep something from your husband, then it is probably not something you should participate in.

Be Loyal

Loyalty is the idea that you come alongside someone and say, "I'm on your side. I'm for you. Count on me." There will likely be a time in your life when your husband is accused wrongly or is criticized unfairly. He needs to know his wife will back him. Does your husband know you will defend him and side with him—that you will believe his side of the story, even if nobody else does? Can he count on your loyalty?

Sometimes the criticism and accusations will be justified. Your husband may fail in a huge way. You don't need to be happy about it or pretend the failure didn't happen. You do need to comfort him and assure him you will help him work through the consequences, you still believe in him, and you'll be by his side to help him try again. Elisabeth Elliot says,

> When he fails, you cannot be proud of his failure. But you can be loyal. You can maintain that faith in the idea that God had when He made him, and you can comfort and support him, giving him the strength of your love, and the incentive which your pride in him will always instill.[5]

Keep Smiling

> Strength and dignity are her clothing, *And she smiles at the future.* (Prov. 31:25, emphasis added)

We can smile at the future because our eternity is secure. No matter how dark the world becomes, no matter how corrupt our government or how bleak our personal circumstances might be, we have a very real and sure hope that cannot be taken from us.

Not only that, but we have the very real assurance that God is with us right now. That sense of peace no matter what the circumstances is called the *joy of the Lord*. The joy of the Lord is the internal and genuine gladness of heart that comes only from truly knowing God, actively abiding in Christ, and being filled with the Holy Spirit.

> As I think about the bleakness of the landscape in which we live today, we desperately need women who are filled with hope in our great God—women of strength and dignity; women whose hearts are grounded in the Word of God; women of holy boldness. Feminine warriors who hope in the Lord, who, when things are falling apart around them, they fall to their knees, they cry out to the Lord, and they get up off their knees to minister hope and grace and peace and strength and dignity to their husband, to their children, to others around them—women who speak faith and hope and courage into the lives of the men and others around us.[6] —Nancy Leigh DeMoss

The position you have as a daughter of the King of kings is an anchor for your soul. Sister, no matter how defeated your circumstances might tempt you to feel, there is true cause to rejoice, because no matter what, your soul is secure and you have the sure hope of heaven. If you are a saved woman, then you have reason to smile.

LESSON 15 WIFE-CHANGING QUESTIONS

1. Being a friend to your husband means:
   • Doing stuff together

   _____

   _____

   • Being his cheerleader

   _____

   _____

   • Being nice

   _____

   _____

   • Resisting the urge to correct

   _____

   _____

   • Correcting graciously

   _____

   _____

   • Covering for him

   _____

   _____

• Being trustworthy

_____

_____

• Being loyal

_____

_____

2. Review this list, and think of at least one way in which you can more fully demonstrate this quality to your husband. Write that idea next to the quality.

_____

_____

_____

_____

3. In which areas do you need to grow as his friend?

_____

_____

_____

_____

4. Do you genuinely have the joy of the Lord? How is this demonstrated in your life?

_____

_____

_____

_____

ORDER

LESSON 16

Victoria wakes up at 5:00 a.m., entirely rested. She spends two hours at the feet of Jesus, interceding for her family, friends, and the lost world. She is never distracted during this time and finishes her devotions by memorizing a new verse every day.

Victoria's kids wake up at 7:00 a.m. and are cheerful. At 7:30 they are on time for the balanced breakfast she has prepared from scratch. By eight they are completely dressed, have their hair and teeth brushed, and leave for school with smiles and kisses every morning. Her children never misplace their shoes, bicker with each other, or forget to make their beds.

After Victoria spends an hour at the gym maintaining her flawless figure, she has time to tend to her appearance every morning. She does not have gray hair, wrinkles, or wire-like hairs growing out of her chin. Her clothes are the current style, ironed perfectly, and they always fit, no matter what time of the month it is. Her purse and her shoes match her nail polish.

Victoria's house is perpetually clean because she has an impeccable system that everyone in her house participates in. It only takes her twenty minutes a day to keep everything spotless. There is never a ring in her toilet, a dirty dish in her sink, or overflowing baskets in her laundry room. And of course, she recycles.

Victoria is also an excellent cook. She makes all her nutritionally balanced meals from scratch. Her children love vegetables. In fact, they love everything she puts on the table, and nobody ever complains about what she serves. She can welcome people to her elegantly set dinner table every night because she always has extra for guests. Most of her produce comes from her own backyard gardening, and what she doesn't grow herself is organic, because she can afford to buy whatever she wants at the local farmer's market.

Maintaining relationships is easy for Victoria. She calls her mother-in-law twice a week, has weekly coffee dates with girlfriends, answers every email promptly, never forgets to send a thank-you card, and always RSVPs. She has lunch with friends, weekly date nights with her husband, and plans special days each month when she can spend individual time with each of her children.

Of course, Victoria is also active in her church. She never misses Bible study, and she has her homework done every week. She attends the midweek service the church offers and is never distracted when the pastor goes long. She serves at a homeless shelter, teaches Sunday school, and goes on at least two short-term mission trips a year, as long as she can get time off from her part-time job at the animal shelter.

Of course, at the end of the day, Victoria has plenty of energy left over to put on lingerie, light candles, and have incredible sex with her husband.

Victoria is the perfect Christian woman.

And she's a big, big problem for me.

Friends, Victoria is not a real person! Yet how many of us believe we are failing because we aren't living up to this idealized standard?

The Big Picture

A friend once posted a picture of some flowers her kids had picked for her. The crude little bouquet looked adorable in a mason jar on her kitchen windowsill. It had a cute little sentence about how sweet her boys were to pick the flowers for her. A few minutes later, she had another post that read:

> I spent the last ten minutes cropping out reality to display the little highlight of what has been a horrible day. I realized I'm not showing the truth of my life on social media. So here's what I cropped out:

In the next picture, there was the same little bouquet on her windowsill, but she had included the rest of her kitchen in the frame. Under the window was a sink full of dirty dishes, and something was dripping down the front of the cabinets. There was food left out on the counters. The trashcan in the kitchen was overflowing, and there was spilled cereal on the floor. It was a total mess.

This started a trend of friends posting photos of our chaotic realities—kids fighting and crying, overflowing laundry baskets, and burned dinners. It was quite refreshing! My friend Daphna once said, "Don't compare your "behind the scenes" with everyone else's "highlight reel.""

How many of us are comparing the reality of our daily lives to the cropped, edited, and filtered images of the lives we see around us, convincing ourselves everyone is doing life so much better than we are? How often do we look at our to-do list and feel defeated before we even get dressed because we know there is no way we will be able to get it all done? Most women I know are moving through their lives feeling defeated and in a mild state of panic.

So how do we break free from this trend? Each of us is called to govern our own life in a way that honors God and reflects Him to the world around us. We are called to walk in obedience and to have a certain order to our lives.

In the next five lessons, we will examine what the Bible says about the priorities of a married woman and discover practical ways to put those priorities into practice in God's prescribed order. Elisabeth Elliot says,

> The way you keep your house, the way you organize your time, the care you take in your personal appearance, the things you spend your money on all speak loudly about what you believe. "The beauty of thy peace" shines forth in an ordered life. A disordered life speaks loudly of disorder in the soul.[1]

Order

The word "order" is one of my favorites. As a verb, "order" has three meanings:

1. To put something in an organized pattern or structure.
She ordered the contents of the sock drawer.
2. To give a command.
The officer ordered the driver to stop.
3. To request that something be made, supplied, or served.
She ordered two coffees to go.

"Order" also has four meanings as a noun:

1. The arrangement of people or things in sequence to one another.
I filed the cards in alphabetical order.
2. An authoritative command, direction, or instruction.
The sergeant's order was to march back to the base.
3. The condition of something working the way it is expected to.
The mechanic said the car was in working order.
4. The state of being organized, balanced, or in harmonious arrangement.
Her calendar brought order to her life.

Our God is a God of order. He fits every single definition of order listed above. (Go back and look—He does or is every one of these descriptions!) Therefore, as women who are created in the image of God, it is fitting that we reflect this order in our own lives.

The goal of this section is to examine how God is *ordering* your life—to determine in what ways you are being uniquely *ordered* to bring *order* to your own life in this current season of your life.

Order Begins with God Being Central

You will need your Bible to get the most out of this section!

The book of Numbers is where God organized, commanded, and governed the newly freed Israelites. Remember that when the Israelites were in Egypt, they were slaves. After being told what to do by cruel masters for four hundred years, they likely imagined "freedom" as the absence of rules and orders. However, a life without restrictions and organization leads people to chaos, not freedom.

Almost immediately, God sets out bringing order to the people. The way God organized the camps in Numbers 2 and 3 is very insightful. Go read the second and third chapters of Numbers right now.

Ordered to Be Free

From the start, all the tribes were arranged around the tabernacle—the tangible presence of God. Is your life arranged this way—with God as the central reference point?

Structure within the camps of Israel promoted unity, clarity, and purpose. God organized His people so they could be truly free. The same is true in the lives of God's people as individuals, and for any family, organization, business, ministry, or church. Order is essential!

> For slaves, it is simple—slaves are always told what to do and don't need to be ordered and organized. But free men must be taught order and organization and must submit to it. There is a limit to what we can be and what we can do for the Lord without order and organization. It isn't that order and organization are requirements for progress in the Christian life; they *are* progress in the Christian life, becoming more like the Lord.[2]
> —David Guzik

In Numbers 3, God gives a list of duties and responsibilities for each of the families. To be a priest, a man had to be a descendant of Aaron. Not just anyone could sign up for that job. Aaron had three sons, and each had a specific role in the temple. The family of Gershon took care of the skins of the tabernacle, Kohath's family was responsible for the things inside the tabernacle, and the family of Merari was to maintain the structural aspects. God's order continued to be laid down for the specific jobs certain people were to do. This wasn't volunteer work offered to whoever felt like doing these tasks. The positions were assigned to these men according to whom God decided was best suited.

Likewise, God has assigned each of us specific roles and duties. If you are reading this book, then you are likely a wife. Not everyone gets that role. Just as

God gave specific orders for how each role was to be played in Numbers, He has given specific orders for how to prioritize our lives as wives.

Let Me Give You a Hand

Years ago, I was about to teach a Bible study on biblical priorities to a beautiful group of illiterate, ex-Hindu tribal women in Nepal. Since they could not take notes, I wanted to give them a visual reminder of what our biblical priorities are as wives. As I was going through my notes, a thought came to me that I could use my hand to make a point they could remember. I have returned to that same village several times, and they can still hold up their hands and tell me exactly what order their priorities need to be in.

Whether you are a village woman in Nepal, a housewife in North Dakota, or an executive in New York, your God-ordered priorities are the same, so I will give you the same lesson.

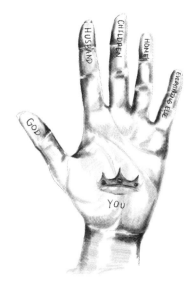

Thumbs Up

Have you ever considered that your thumbs are absolutely necessary for nearly everything you do with your hands? Try buttoning your blouse without using your thumbs! Try holding a coffee cup, chopping an onion, answering your phone, or starting your car—all of these simple tasks are dependent on your thumbs.

Your thumbs touch every one of your fingers and allow them to work efficiently. This is like your connection with God. Having a vibrant relationship with God allows all of your other relationships and responsibilities to work successfully. God meant it when He said,"Seek first the kingdom of God and His righteousness, and all these *things* will be added to you" (Matt. 6:33, emphasis added).

Daily communication with God is the key to your success as a Christian, as a wife, mother, employee, and friend, and as a representative of the gospel to the world. Jesus said, *"Apart from Me you can do nothing"* (John 15:5). Do you believe you can do nothing of eternal worth apart from Him?

I love this quote from Wendy Speake:

> Hurried, harried, and horrible: they go together. But hurried and holy rarely co-exist. Holy and hallowed and hushed, now those are true companions. They meet together in the morning hours before the sun steals past the beauty of dawn. We need to join them there. We need to fellowship with the Holy One—slowing down, sitting down, and coming down off our cram-packed agendas to seek Him on the floor.
>
> On the floor.
>
> Because that's where every person is going to end up, eventually. Either on purpose, prostrating oneself in worship, intentionally in the morning hours; or at night in a tearful puddle; or, and this is a frightening thought, they're going to find themselves on the ground like the discarded branch that's not bearing fruit—cut off and cast down.[3]

Friends, we are going to end up on our faces one way or another, aren't we? We can either intentionally spend time at the feet of Jesus, or our out-of-control lives will shove us there after we are spent and sin-sick. We get to choose which way we will arrive at His feet. Let's choose the better part!

In chapter 1, lesson 5, we spent some time detailing this first priority. If you have not begun the discipline of spending time with God every day, then go back and read that section again. Just like your thumb is essential to everything you touch, there is nothing more essential to your marriage or your family than you being in the presence of God on a regular basis.

Brake and Bow

For many of us, we begin each day with every intention of having God be central. We may start with time in the Word and in prayer, and we sincerely want God to be glorified in how we live. But as the day gets rolling, our intentions are replaced by frustrations and distractions. Suddenly, it's bedtime, and we haven't given much thought to God at all through the day. Again.

This describes every day of my life—*unless I am intentional about remembering that I am a disciple of Jesus.* I need to remember who I represent and that my ultimate goal in life is to glorify Him. I need to remember my commitment to walk in obedience.

As my day flies from one activity to the next, how do I remind myself of that early morning commitment to remain connected to my God? I intentionally Brake and Bow.

brake—*verb.* To slow down or stop something that is moving.

I must slow down, come to a complete stop, and remember I'm a disciple of Jesus. In the middle of my fast-moving day, it is essential for me to slam on the brakes of my heart and my mind and remind myself who I am living for.

bow—*verb.* To bend or incline in worship, submission, respect, and agreement.

That's precisely what I need—not only to brake, but also to bow—to stop and incline my heart and mind in worship, submission, respect, and agreement with the One whom I want to please.

On my phone, I set an alarm that goes off twice a day. On the screen it simply reads "Brake & Bow." This is my reminder to realign my thinking and my focus. I simply take a moment to acknowledge that no matter what is going on at that moment, God is there, I am His, and I live to please Him. It only takes a few seconds, but those few seconds of intentionally braking and bowing make all the difference to my frazzled heart and mind.

My first Brake and Bow happens at 12:15 p.m., typically when I'm in full swing at work or at home. At this time, I'm surrounded by people who need me to pour love and gentle instruction into their lives. It's also right around lunchtime, when I see other teachers or parents, or when I need to feed my own people at home. Those few seconds of braking and bowing remind me to represent Jesus to those I encounter.

The second alarm goes off at a similarly crazy time of day. At 4:45 p.m. is when the evening activities begin. It is yet another reminder for me to transition with my heart and mind set on pleasing the Lord and loving the people He has allowed me to serve.

I encourage you to evaluate your schedule and see if you might benefit from reminding yourself to Brake and Bow, to intentionally invite God to touch every aspect of your life throughout your day.

Few Things Are Necessary—Really Only One

To further emphasize the fact that seeking God is as essential as your thumbs, let's look at Luke 10:38–42. We read the story about a woman who was outwardly doing all the right things, but inwardly she was out of line in her relationship with Jesus:

> Now as they went on their way, Jesus entered a village. And a woman named Martha welcomed Him into her house. And she had a sister called Mary, who sat at the Lord's feet and listened to His teaching. But Martha was distracted with much serving. And she went up to Him and said, "Lord, do You not care that my sister has left me to serve alone? Tell her then to help me." But the Lord answered her, "Martha, Martha, you are anxious and troubled about many things, but one thing is necessary. Mary has chosen the good portion, which will not be taken away from her."

We see it was Martha who welcomed Jesus (and very likely the seventy-plus men He was traveling with) into her house. She likely had no prior notice that her guests were coming. Consider that level of hospitality! What would you do if you had Jesus over for dinner? What would you serve Him? You probably would do all you could to make the best meal possible. No boxed macaroni and cheese for the King of kings! No, you'd make your famous chicken enchiladas or your grandma's lasagna recipe. Likewise, Martha wanted to offer her very best for her most honored guest and His friends.

Martha began doing a good thing. The trouble was not with her desire to give her best to Jesus, but rather with her attitude in her serving. It says, "But Martha was distracted with much serving." Other translations say she was "cumbered about much serving" or "distracted with all her preparations."

Just think about how this scene likely unfolded:

Martha's slaving away in the hot kitchen. There are pots going all over the place. There is raw meat needing to be prepared on the counters and bread waiting to be kneaded, while everyone else is sitting around enjoying themselves, waiting for her to serve them. (Have you ever found yourself alone in the kitchen?)

Peeking around the corner, she sees Mary just listening to Jesus when there is a houseful of people to be fed. *Just listening!* The woman who should have been helping her is not working at all! If Martha was like me, she would have banged a few pots in the kitchen, hoping Mary would get the hint and get to work. When Mary didn't get up, Martha's inner dialogue would have started, perhaps like this:

Bang. Bang. Bang. I can't believe how lazy my sister is. Is she just going sit there all night and let me do all this work by myself? Jesus wouldn't want me to do this by myself! Oh, forget this!

Stomp! Stomp! Stomp!

Then with a deep sigh and a dramatic entrance, "Lord, do You not care that my sister has left me to serve alone? Tell her then to help me."

Martha likely expected Jesus to be on her side and to hear Him say, "Mary, Mary—get in the kitchen and help your hardworking sister!"

Instead, Jesus says to her, "Martha, Martha, you are anxious and troubled about many things, but one thing is necessary." (How many times have I gone to the Lord about somebody else, only to find the whole problem was me?)

Where Martha went wrong was when her desire to serve Jesus became a distraction and she became worried and troubled. Martha became more concerned with the work itself rather than who it was for. She had complicated her service *to* Jesus and missed being *with* Jesus.

"Mary has chosen the good portion, which will not be taken away from her." Jesus pointed out that Mary had made a conscious decision between two alternatives—she chose enjoying Jesus over an elaborate meal.

Remember, Martha said that Mary "*has left* me to do all the serving," meaning Mary had done some work and then left to sit with Jesus.

Mary served, and then chose the better part. It could have been that Mary was saying, "Hey, Martha, the stew is enough. Let's go sit with Jesus."

And Martha's attitude was, "No way! This is Jesus! We also need roast lamb, and raisin cakes, and fresh bread . . ."

Mary and Martha were each presented with a choice about how they would spend their evening. They could either knock themselves out serving and be identified as fine housekeepers and cooks, or they could sit at Jesus's feet and be identified as His disciples.

Which would you prefer to be identified by?

While much of this chapter will focus on the responsibilities we have in managing our homes in a way that honors the Lord, let us keep at the forefront of our minds that, above all else, we are disciples of Jesus. Everything else is secondary. When we choose the better part—making it our aim to listen to our Master, sit at His feet, and take in all He has to say to us—then the rest of our life will have far more order than if we attempt to order it ourselves.

LESSON 16 WIFE-CHANGING QUESTIONS

Seek first the kingdom of God and His righteousness, and all these things will be added to you. (Matt. 6:33)

1. Do you believe this verse is true? How are you demonstrating this?

_____

_____

_____

_____

2. Sincerely examine your life and determine if your life is ordered around God. If it isn't, what is it ordered around?

_____

_____

_____

_____

3. What wife-changes do you need to make to rearrange your life so that God is central?

_____

_____

_____

_____

4. Since you began reading this book, have you been more intentional about seeking the Lord personally? Have you been consistent? What are the common hindrances to your consistent time in God's presence?

_____

_____

_____

_____

5. Is there anything you can do to make your devotional time more beneficial?

_____

_____

_____

_____

6. Did you like the idea of incorporating a Brake and Bow into your life? If so, what time/times will you do this? Take a minute right now to go and set that alarm on your phone.

7. In what ways can you identify with Martha?

_____

_____

_____

_____

8. In what ways can you identify with Mary?

_____

_____

_____

_____

9. Can you think of some area of your life where you need to have less of a "Martha mentality" and have an attitude like Mary's?

_____

_____

_____

_____

LESSON 17

Pointers

Continuing with the hand analogy we started in the last lesson, next to your thumb is your pointer finger. This is also the finger you use to make the #1 sign. In our handy example, your pointer finger symbolizes your husband and should be a reminder to you that your marriage is your #1 earthly relationship.

Titus 2 instructs the older women to train the younger women *"to love their husbands and children, to be self-controlled, pure, working at home, kind, and submissive to their own husbands, that the word of God may not be reviled"* (Titus 2:4-5).

The first thing an older woman is to teach a younger woman is to love her husband.

Every day we are faced with decisions about how to spend our time and where to focus our attention. Being an excellent wife involves being intentional and diligent in loving our husbands on purpose and choosing to make them our first priority.

We might say we are doing this in theory, but based on the divorce rate in the American church and thousands of unhappily married couples in our pews on Sundays, husbands are not being prioritized in practice. We should not assume that because we can intellectually agree that our husbands are to be our priority, that we are actually practicing this priority.

Leaving and Cleaving

Genesis 2:24 tells us that when a couple marries, *"a man shall leave his father and his mother and hold fast to his wife."* The idea here is that both parties leave their families and begin a new one. While we are still called to honor our parents, marriage means our first priority shifts to our husbands. As married women, we are no longer subject to our parents' rule. This priority transfer can be extremely difficult, particularly if a wife's parents don't respect her husband or adhere to biblical roles in marriage themselves. It is imperative that we transfer our loyalty and priority to our new family as soon as we make our vows. Shelly says:

> For the first fifteen years of my marriage, I tried to keep my mother and my husband happy at the same time. It was impossible! Mom was only happy when I defied my husband, and my husband was never okay with that. I was always stuck in the middle. I finally had a wise friend point out my divided heart. She encouraged me to let my mother be upset and to keep my husband as my first priority because that's what the Bible commands. It was messy at first, but Mom finally realized he was first in my life, and she stopped being so demanding. Once he knew he would always be chosen over my mother, my marriage improved.

Check with Your Husband

I remember a friend asking to meet for coffee, and I said something like, "Sounds great. Just let me check with Brent first."

She mockingly said, "You have to ask his *permission*? What is he, your dad?"

I was a little stung by her sarcasm. It struck me that this common act of courtesy is often lacking in a marriage. Yes, I'm a grown-up, and I don't need my husband's "permission" to do things. I'm not his child, I'm his wife.

But he is *my husband.* We are one. What I do with my time affects him, his kids, and his home. He usually checks with me before making plans too. It's one of the ways we stay connected and show one another that our relationship and family come before the other things in our lives.

It is very rare that I check in with Brent and he says he'd rather I not do whatever I'm asking about. Sometimes he needs me to do something else. A few times he has reminded me that I was complaining the day before about having too much to do every day, and he has suggested my plate is too full to add another activity. When he recommends I not do whatever it is, I'm wise to not argue or try to convince him to agree.

Why bother asking if I'm bent on getting my own way? The point is, I should care about his input and apply his counsel. I'm not always as smart and capable as I think I am. Brent knows that. He knows my limits and my needs better than I do at times, and he is often used by God to maintain healthy boundaries with my time.

The simple act of checking with your husband about your schedule communicates to him that he is first, and you are wanting his counsel and direction on how you spend your time. It demonstrates honor toward him to those watching, and it also helps keep your priorities in order.

Make Choices

Carl spends as much free time as possible in his garage restoring whatever old clunker he has in there at the time. Lisa doesn't love cars, but she loves Carl, so she chooses to sit out in the garage and talk with him while he is working. She goes to car shows with him and has even occasionally gotten her own hands dirty when he needed help under the hood. Her husband loves his wife for loving his hobby.

Karen's husband, Justin, travels a lot for work. Since he started his job, she has determined to do everything possible to pick him up from the airport when he gets home. All the other salesmen pay for a stranger to drive them home when they return from a trip, but Karen is always waiting for Justin in baggage claim with a huge smile and a romantic kiss. Sometimes this means she is driving back and forth to the airport several times a month.

She has admitted this is sometimes an inconvenient chore, but she said, "Sometimes our greatest conversations are during that forty-minute drive home from the airport. It's a way for me to intentionally reconnect with him after he's been gone, and he looks forward to coming home to me."

Brent will sometimes call me from work around 7:00 p.m. and announce he has hours of studying ahead of him. I can choose to offer to bring him dinner or to go down to the church to help him. Nearly half the time, he accepts my offer, which means I have to stop whatever I'm doing, pack up food, drive over, and arrive smiling! I'd be lying if I said I always felt like doing that. However, I have determined to make him first in my life, and I am willing to be inconvenienced to show him I love him.

I know women who have taken an interest in fishing, hiking, snorkeling, horse rescuing, panning for gold, antique collecting, woodworking, etc. not because those things interested them, but because they were things their husbands loved, and they chose to love them too.

What choices can you make to invest in the most important earthly relationship you have? A lifetime of choosing your husband over other things will reap rewards in this life and in the life to come.

Date Nights Don't Make Great Marriages

In the majority of marriage books, weekly date nights seem to be a standard prescription for building a healthy marriage. I understand the reasoning behind it: spend intentional time together alone, and your relationship will benefit. While that is true, I've also counseled women who have bought so much into this prescription that in their minds, missing a date night means their marriage is falling apart.

Date nights are great, but they aren't a biblical principle. It is entirely possible to never have an official date and still have a close, intimate, rightly prioritized relationship with your husband.

I can count on one hand the amount of real "dates" I have had with my husband in the last year. He has been out of the country every two weeks for the last five months, and work schedules, kids and grandkids, friendships, health issues, and ministry commitments are all vying for our attention.

Yet I can honestly say we are in one of our best marriage seasons. It's not the formal date nights that have contributed to this, but rather our intentional seeking out of one another's company.

Most of our "dates" end up happening after 9:00 p.m. when we go sit in the backyard (to escape our listening children), or when he is running out to the hardware store and he says, "Want to come with me?"

Even though I have no interest in selecting a new blade for the lawnmower, I say, "Sure!" Our deepest conversations often happen when I choose to let my plans be interrupted because he is feeling chatty at 6:00 a.m., and we end up talking for two hours before we both leave for work.

Lose the Recipe

There isn't a one-size-fits-all recipe for a good marriage. There's no master checklist of ingredients every marriage needs in order to be God-glorifying and personally satisfying. The one thing you "have to" do is to determine your husband is first in your heart and be intentional about staying connected to him.

This will look different for every relationship. Some couples may travel extensively for work, so their connection is maintained through technology and concentrated efforts to spend time together when they are home. In the crazy, exhausting season of having small children, a couple needs to make intentional plans to have time together. The middle years of raising children, with their endless activities and demands, is a season when parents need to make being a couple a priority. An empty nest means time together is easier, but making it meaningful can be more of a challenge. No matter what season you are in, making your husband a priority takes effort and creativity. Pray and ask the Lord for fresh ways that will communicate to your husband that he is first in your life.

You are not always going to *want* to make him the priority. Your husband won't always deserve it, and it will take dying to yourself over and over, often several times in a single day. Sometimes it will feel like you are only feeding his self-centeredness. However, making him your priority honors the Lord, which brings blessings back to your own life. Jesus is always deserving of your obedience.

Second Only to Your Husband

My four-year-old daughter was standing behind me asking a question as I was engrossed in something on my laptop. Apparently she had asked it several times, and I hadn't heard her because my attention was elsewhere. In frustration, she grabbed my face in her chubby little hands, turned my head to face hers, and said, "Momma! Pay attention to me!" I wish that was the only time she has had to do that. Regrettably, my kids have had to ask me to pay attention to them more often than I'd like to admit. I have missed opportunities to minister to them, teach them, cuddle them, and discipline them because I was distracted with other things.

> . . . to love their husbands *and children*, to be self-controlled, pure, working at home, kind, and submissive to their own husbands, that the word of God may not be reviled. (Titus 2:4-5, emphasis added)

The second thing older women are instructed to teach younger women is to love their children. Raising children is often central to our jobs as women, so it is represented by the finger in the center of our hands. Our middle fingers are also the farthest-extending fingers. The things we pour into our children will have the farthest-reaching impact in our world.

Our children are often juggled around the most on our priority list. We are often too tired to serve our spouses, but when our little ones come in with a need, we jump to meet it. Conversely, ministry or social activities can put our kids in last place. Kids will sometimes miss needed naps because their mother wants to have a social life, or they will end up in daycare for long periods of time because their mom works more than she needs to in order to drive an expensive car and eat in nice restaurants. Many children take backseats to their mother's careers, social lives, bank accounts, ministries, and homes.

It is our second priority to make sure young children are getting their proper place in our lives. Their souls, health, social lives, education, and calendar are all entrusted to their mothers when they are small. This is a huge responsibility, and it is one that needs to be saturated with prayer and wisdom.

As children become teenagers, our role shifts from being a caregiver to being a listener, counselor, and helper. They can drive and don't need babysitters, but they are making decisions at this stage that will have lifelong consequences. Their faith is becoming their own, and they are asking hard questions about who God really is. Teenagers need their moms, and we are wise to stay as connected to their hearts as much as we possibly can.

Our role as mothers is not done when our children are grown. It is a privilege to still be able to pour into their adult lives, and we need to make ourselves available to our adult children as a counselor and friend. They are choosing careers and spouses, and are making financial and friendship choices. No matter how old our children get, we are still their moms, and pouring into their lives needs to remain a priority.

This extends to grandchildren as well. Grandmothers can be some of the greatest influences in young people's lives, and we should aim to be available to the little ones God has blessed us with. Pray for your grandkids. Pour as much of your faith into them as you can.

Timothy is an example of how a young life can be greatly influenced by a godly grandmother. As the pastor of the large church in Ephesus, Timothy held a position of great responsibility. In reminding Timothy to stand firm, Paul reminds him of the faith of his mother and his grandmother:

> I am reminded of your sincere faith, a faith that dwelt first in your grandmother Lois and your mother Eunice and now, I am sure, dwells in you as well. (2 Tim. 1:5)

Paul wanted to encourage Timothy to press on in ministry, and he starts off by saying, "Remember your grandma!" Oh, that our children and grandchildren would remember us in times of struggle and find strength to press on because of our example!

Be Real

This isn't a book on raising children, but I will tell you that one of the most important things you can do to prioritize your kids is to be a real Christian. There is likely no one who will influence your children more in their faith than you.

Your sons will likely compare every woman they meet to their mother. Give them a high standard.

Your daughters will likely become wives like their mother. Give them a powerful example.

> She looks well to the ways of her household and does not eat the bread of idleness. Her children rise up and call her blessed. (Prov. 31:27–28)

Do your children see that you really believe what you claim to believe? Do you live out your Christianity before them in a way that makes them want to follow Jesus too? We are foolish if we think we can live however we please and produce kids who will walk with God because we drop them off once a week at church. The old saying, "Do as I say, not as I do" is a great motto to produce kids who rebel against the faith and chase hard after the world as soon as they have the opportunity. Kids who grow up with hypocritical parents do not often see the need to walk with God themselves.

There are no guarantees your kids will grow up and walk with Jesus. They could totally rebel against the faith in spite of your efforts, but be certain it's not because you were a hypocrite.

- Let them see you asking God for wisdom as you make decisions.
- Let them see you applying the Word of God to your everyday life.
- Let them see you making church attendance a priority.
- Let them see or hear about the consequences of sin in other people's lives. Point out the results of decisions that are contrary to the Word of God.
- Let them see you repent when you sin.
- Let them see you choosing to walk in holiness and purity in your own home.
- Let them see that who you are at church is the same person you are at home.

Sometimes it will be easier to act like the world, follow your flesh, obey your emotions, or serve yourself. But the future of the church depends on the obedience of the current generation. Let your children see you choose to truly follow Christ.

When my oldest was six years old, we were walking together through a crowded parking lot when he decided to pick up a rock and throw it up in the air. The rock went super high and came down hard on the back windshield of a brand-new sports car, shattering the window.

We could have walked away. Nobody else had seen him throw the rock. We were in a difficult financial season, and I knew it was going to be crazy expensive to replace the windshield. I honestly thought about just scolding him to be careful about where he threw rocks, and then driving home.

The owner of the car surely had insurance for that kind of thing, right? But what would that teach my son? The only right thing for us to do was to admit the mistake and make it right. So we prayed and asked God to help us to do what we needed to do to honor Him. We walked into the office buildings surrounding the parking lot and asked if anyone knew whose car it was.

It belonged to a smartly dressed businessman in a big office. He came out, and Josh trembled as he told the man he had shattered his windshield. The man slowly blew out a long breath, then said, "Son, I'd like to shake your hand. It takes a big man to admit your mistakes."

Telling Daddy was equally hard, and getting the repair bill was the hardest of all. But Josh never forgot that lesson, and he still talks about it as an adult today.

Kerry also shares an example of telling the truth:

> When we are shopping or eating out with our children or grandchildren and there is something left off the bill accidentally, we always bring it to the attention of the clerk or waitress.
>
> When we buy tickets to something, we always tell the truth about the kids' ages, even if we could save a lot of money by saying the kids are young enough to get the lower-priced ticket. In doing this, we are training our kids and grandkids to honor God by being truthful.

Increase Jesus, Decrease Mom

Our ultimate goal as mothers should be to see our children walk with Jesus for their entire lives. That means it is our responsibility to teach them to increase their dependence upon Jesus and to decrease their dependence upon us. Rather than continually looking to us, it should be our goal to train our children to look to Jesus and to have them depend on Him to lead and direct their lives. One day, they will leave our home and venture out on their own. If they have learned to depend on Jesus, we will send them out with confidence, knowing they will have everything they need to walk in all that God has ordained for their lives.

Honor Your Children's Father

Second to following Jesus, your children need to see you honor their father. Speak highly of your husband, and let your children hear the praise. Let them know that their mom is in love with their dad and that she wants to honor him.

Let them see you doing what your husband asks, even when he's not there to witness it. Our children will honor us the way we have honored our husbands. They will decide by our example whether or not obedience to the rules applies to them, or whether they can manipulate things to do what they want.

Marie needed a dress to wear to a wedding, and she took her teenage daughter along for the shopping trip. Her husband had given her $100 to spend. They found a dress for $175 that fit her beautifully. Marie bought the dress and told her daughter she would just tell her husband there wasn't anything for $100, and he would get over it.

Later that week, she was convicted. She realized she was teaching her daughter to disregard rules and limits and to expect the authorities in her life to "get over it." So she drove back to the store with her daughter, explaining her reasoning, and returned the dress. She prayed with her daughter that God would help her to find a dress within the budget her husband had given her.

Three shops later, they found an equally flattering and stylish dress for $45! But when they got up to the register, the salesperson explained that there was a special sale that day and the grand total for the dress was only $26! Marie then bought a pair of shoes to go with the dress, and a pair of earrings for her daughter—all because she chose to honor her husband and to train her daughter to do the same.

Samantha shares,

> Dad was hardworking and did all he could to take care of us, but he could be harsh and controlling, especially with Mom. When we were teenagers, I remember several times when he made some unreasonable demand or a decision my mom disagreed with, but she wouldn't argue with him or demand her own way.
>
> When she was alone with my sisters and me, she would say to us, "I don't think this is a good idea. I disagree with Dad on this one, but I'm going to do what he wants and smile about it. This is what submission looks like!"
>
> Sometimes we would watch God do a miracle and change Dad's mind, and sometimes we saw that Dad was right after all. More than anything else, those examples prepared us to understand what obeying God and submitting in a marriage means.

When your husband is being unreasonable, when he is wrong, or when he's in the flesh—you don't need to retaliate "so the kids don't think he's right." You don't need to sass back to him or to remind him he needs to love you like Christ loves the church. The Holy Spirit will convict your husband in His time. These flaws in your husband are opportunities for you to honor him, especially in front of your children.

When you fail in this, and you will, allowing you to have a beautiful opportunity to confess your sin to your kids, tell them what you should have done instead, and why. I have had to admit my failures to my kids countless times. They are entirely aware of my selfish, rebellious, and angry tendencies, and they have had ample opportunities to show me grace. At times, I feared it would cause them to lose respect for me. However, when we are real followers of Jesus and we let our kids see our real struggles and our real repentance, they end up having a deeper understanding of how to walk with Jesus as flawed and sinful people themselves.

Priorities Bring Peace

If you hold up your index and middle fingers, it makes the "peace sign." Let that be a reminder that if you put your husband and children on the top of your priority list—and keep them there by your actions—then you will enjoy the peace that doing things according to God's prescription always provides. When we obey God's order, peace is the end result.

LESSON 17 WIFE-CHANGING QUESTIONS

1. Is your husband first in your life? Above your children? Your parents? Your girlfriends? Your church activities? Your job? Your home?

_____

_____

_____

_____

2. What are three practical things you are already doing to keep your husband first?

_____

_____

_____

_____

3. What are three wife-changes you can make to prioritize your husband more effectively?

_____

_____

_____

_____

4. Are your children your second priority? How can you/do you demonstrate this practically?

_____

_____

_____

_____

5. Are you doing all you can to nurture your children's souls? Their health? Their education?

_____

_____

_____

_____

6. What are three wife-changes you can make that will prioritize your children more effectively?

_____

_____

_____

_____

LESSON 18

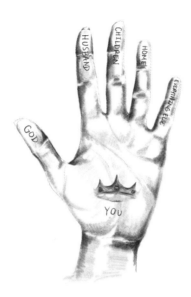

Holy Housework

In our continuing hand analogy, your fourth finger, or your ring finger, is symbolic of your home.

In most societies in the world, the men provide and the women work in the home. In Western culture, the feminist movement caused us to think this was somehow a demeaning indication that women were inferior. However, God is not a misogynist, but a genius Designer, and it is by God's design that wives are nurturing homemakers.

> . . . to love their husbands and children, to be self-controlled, pure, *working at home*, kind, and submissive to their own husbands, that the word of God may not be reviled. (Titus 2:4-5, emphasis added)

Working at home is part of our job description as wives. This does not mean we are not allowed to work outside our homes, nor does it mean a man does not need to lift a finger at home and that women are stuck with all the work. It simply means God has put the wife in the position of overseeing the running of the household. This is a blessing and a privilege.

It is helpful to look at the expression "working at home" in other translations:

- to be keepers at home (KJV)
- to be homemakers (NKJV)

- to be busy at home (NIV)
- to manage their households (ISV)

In every translation, it is clearly part of our calling to keep, manage, and take care of our homes and those living in them. This is no small responsibility, nor is it a curse. Making meals, doing laundry, scrubbing grout, decorating—these are all *holy* tasks in God's eyes. Housework is holy work because God has commanded it to be done, and when we do it with intentional joy, it is received as worship.

Colossians 3:17 tells us, "And whatever you do, in word or deed, do everything in the name of the Lord Jesus, giving thanks to God the Father through Him." This means *all* a Christian does for the Lord—including changing diapers, grocery shopping, sweeping floors, and making meals—*all* of it can be holy work.

In our handy example, your ring finger is your home, and your little finger symbolizes everything outside your home. Look at how this works. Your *home* is represented by the finger between your family (your pointer and middle fingers). Your home acts as the bridge between your family and the outside world. Keeping your home in order makes it a sanctuary for those who are in it, as well as a refuge for those who are outside it.

> The woman was uniquely designed and equipped—physiologically, emotionally, mentally, and spiritually—by her Creator to be a bearer and nurturer of life. In a multitude of ways, she was endowed with the ability to add life, beauty, richness, fullness, grace, and joy to the family unit. There is no greater measure of her worth or success as a woman than the extent to which she serves as the heart of her home.[4] —Nancy Leigh DeMoss

We will discuss the practical aspects of managing our homes in detail in lessons 19 and 20.

Priority Five = Everything Else

Our final priority is everything outside our homes—our ministries, our jobs, our extended family, our friendships, and ourselves.

Ministry Is Last

I once told a woman I couldn't help her with a ministry event because I needed to go grocery shopping and catch up on my laundry. She piously replied with, "You need to let those things go and be busy about the Lord's work!"

Another woman I know ran a large outreach ministry that kept her away from home nearly every day of the week. Standing in her absolute disaster of a house, amid the remains of several fast-food wrappers and piles of dirty laundry, she told me she had just gone and bought new school clothes for her kids because she didn't have time to do laundry. "I just don't care about housework. I'd rather spend my time serving the Lord!" she said.

While both of these dear women sound really spiritual, according to Scripture, their perspectives were entirely out of order.

Managing our homes *is* the Lord's work!

Making sure our families have clean clothes, eat nutritious meals, have soap and toilet paper, and that the trash cans are at the curb on trash day—it is all holy stuff in God's eyes! Jesus can be just as glorified in your sparkling toilet bowl as He is if you serve a bowl of soup to a homeless man.

Each of us is gifted by God to serve the body of Christ in some capacity. This is the way the church works. However, women are often guilty of mistaking *activity for* God as a *relationship with* God, and they neglect their responsibilities to their families and their homes, all in the name of "serving the Lord." When it comes to your priorities, it's important to keep ministry in the right order.

We are not necessarily called to ministry outside our home during every season of our lives. At times, outside ministry is not possible if we are to maintain our other priorities. There are seasons when our husbands and children and our housework require more of our time, and we must pour our gifts into those responsibilities.

There are some women who are at church every time the doors are open and serve in several outside ministries a week. Yet in their homes, the floors you can see are sticky, the laundry is out of control, the trashcan is overflowing with fast-food wrappers, and the dirty dishes are piled high in the sink. And it's not that their homes just happened to be in that state on that particular day—but it's safe to say their homes are in a perpetual state of disaster.

Please don't misunderstand me—it's one thing to wisely choose to leave the laundry for tomorrow because there is someone who needs to be ministered to today, or because you couldn't get to it before you had to leave for your small-group meeting. It's quite another thing to have all four kids sharing the same towel for three days because you've been volunteering at church. We must make sure we are not *neglecting* our homes and our families in the name of ministry.

Ministry and church activities can be a spiritualized excuse for laziness.

The same goes with social events, exercise, involvement with kids' school activities, volunteer work, etc. There are endless distractions that will masquerade as valid excuses for not keeping our homes and our families in order.

Every one of us is going to occasionally leave a sink full of dirty dishes and run off to church, or go visit our parents even though we have nothing to make for dinner. That doesn't mean our homes are out of order. However, if a woman's home is *normally* a disaster—if it's a rare day you can see the top of her kitchen table or can identify the color of her carpeting because you can't see the floor, and yet she has time for outside ministry, church events, or an active social life—her life is out of order.

Elisabeth Elliot said, "Evasion of responsibility is the mark of immaturity."[5] This quote has rung in my ears hundreds of times. If I am avoiding doing what I know I am responsible to do, then I am being immature. James 4:7 tells us, "whoever knows the right thing to do and fails to do it, for him it is sin." The woman who knows the right thing to do at home and does not do it is in sin.

What about Working outside the Home?

In Christian circles, there are many opinions about whether a woman should work outside the home. It is important we don't make doctrines out of opinions, but rather form our opinions based on what the Scriptures say and how God individually leads our own families.

The Bible actually praises some women who worked outside of their homes. The Proverbs 31 woman considers a field and buys it because she is a businesswoman who makes wise financial decisions. She is highly praised for these attributes. Likewise, Lydia, the first Christian convert in Europe, was a seller of purple fabric and was highly esteemed. We see no indication she stopped working when she began to follow Christ.

There may be seasons in your marriage where the most helpful thing you can do for your husband is to get a job and help him provide for your family. In other seasons, helping him effectively may be staying home with your children and running your home. There may be seasons of working full time, working part time, working from home, or not working for a paycheck at all. There are no biblically mandated standards for what a Christian woman is "supposed" to do, other than she is supposed to seek the Lord, help her husband, love her kids, and take care of her home. The way each of us executes this is going to look different because each of us is in a unique situation. Wife-changing is perpetual!

What if My Husband Tells Me I have to Work, but I Don't Think I Should?

This is a common question from young moms. Many times, a baby comes along, and it seems impossible that the mother will be able to stay home. A husband may tell his wife that living on one income is unmanageable, and she needs to continue working.

I would tell that wife God expects her to submit to her husband. I would also remind her God answers prayer, and He may miraculously provide for a woman to stay home with her babies. God may reveal to her it is possible if she is willing to dramatically change her lifestyle. If she is willing to do her own hair and nails, shop at thrift stores and yard sales, forgo eating out and having coffee with friends, drive an older car or not have a car at all, and not take fancy vacations—and *not complain,* then God often gives her the desire of her heart.

Janiene says,

> I worked full time, raised two babies, got dressed by pulling clothes out of the dryer every morning, and fed my family lots of takeout. I made amazing money, but God started showing me I had all my priorities wrong.
>
> However, my husband was not ready to simplify and give up my income. I prayed for three years, until Chad was ready. God moved his heart and gave him a conviction to bring me home to raise our kids. We sold our house and moved to a tiny two-bedroom condo.
>
> Praying and waiting was hard, but watching my husband hear from the Lord, and to still have the conviction that this is how our family should operate, is awesome!

When Brent was called to full-time ministry, we were looking at living on a third of the income we were accustomed to. My oldest was in high school, and my younger two were homeschooled. It seemed impossible that we could live off what the church was offering us. I considered getting a waitressing job in the evenings or working on the weekends. This ended up being impossible, as Brent was traveling for weeks at a time and I could not leave the kids home alone to go to work. I looked at doing work from home, but there wasn't anything that paid enough to justify the time it would take away from schooling my kids and taking care of things at home.

We took a serious look at our budget. We decided that me staying home was the priority for the season of life we were in, so we radically changed our lifestyle. We went down to one car. We moved into a less-expensive home, bought our clothes from the thrift store, and stood in line to get groceries from the food ministry at church. It was humbling and it was hard, but it was also a tremendous blessing for which I am forever grateful.

As our kids got older, I began to work part time, and then full time. However, I would not trade those years we lived on a meager salary. So many incredible lessons were learned because we didn't have money.

Your situation will be different than mine. There is no one-size-fits-all model for motherhood and husband-helping. It may be the Lord's will for you to work outside your home right now. It may be His will for your kids to be in daycare. Trust the Lord with your plans. God leads different families to do different things.

You aren't less of a Christian woman because you work outside your home. Honor your husband and follow the Holy Spirit's leading in your own family.

Extended Family and Friendships

Spending time with parents, siblings, and friends is a huge blessing. It is part of what makes our lives rich and full and rewarding. However, it is very easy to have these relationships take priority over the other things we are called to. There is no set calculation for how much time you should spend with your extended family or friends, but there is a call to keep your own family and your own home the priority over those things.

Ordering your life by these five priorities—God, husband, children, home, and others—allows you to show your children that we do the important things first, and occasionally this leaves us time to do other things we enjoy. It is sometimes easier to take the kids to visit your parents and leave the house a mess for another day. It is more enjoyable to get your nails done with your friend or to serve in a ministry than it is to do another load of laundry while you make dinner. However, those other things are your priority—they come *before* the pleasurable things of life. We don't always get to do what we feel like doing. Sometimes we have to skip playing with our friends and clean our rooms. That's the way real life works. It's what grown-ups do. It's what disciples of Christ do.

That said, there are certainly exceptions. When my mother was put on hospice, Brent and I agreed her care was my priority for that season, and we shifted everything in our lives around helping my parents. When that season ended, I stepped back into my normal priorities. There have been seasons of personal illness and times when we agreed as a family that I would be focusing on some ministry project for a set length of time. There is flexibility within our priorities, but they serve as an essential plumb line for us to order our lives by.

What about You?

Self-love and self-care are very popular concepts in our current culture. While taking care of ourselves is important, there is a foolish, self-centered, ungodly philosophy being promoted even by "Christian" teachers: *Love yourself supremely, be your own hero, don't let anything get in the way of your own dreams, meet all your own needs first and then take care of everyone else* ... This all sounds like a great idea until we factor in that we are naturally selfish creatures who will never exhaust our desire to have more. We will rarely feel like all of our own "needs" are met, and if we follow through with this self-worship philosophy, the people around us will get very little.

While taking care of yourself is certainly necessary, if you are a Christian, you are not the center of your home or your life. Jesus is, and He has actually called you to die to yourself and surrender your right to decide what is best for your life. You have yielded your dreams and goals and rights to yourself. But that's the supernatural way of blessing.

> For whoever would save his life will lose it, but whoever loses his life for My sake will find it. (Matt. 16:25)

It may seem contradictory, but herein is a beautiful paradox. Lose your life for Jesus's sake, and you'll find it. Jesus's philosophy is so shocking in our "love yourself" culture. Do you want to live the most rewarding, fulfilling, satisfying life you possibly can? Then abandon yourself to Jesus entirely. It's Jesus's promised prescription for finding your best life.

That being said, "losing your life" doesn't mean not taking a shower, exercising, or having meaningful friendships. We must take good care of ourselves in order to glorify God and to meet the needs of those around us. Your fingers all connect to *you*, and your priorities work the best when the woman attached to those fingers is physically and emotionally healthy.

Here's the thing: on paper, there probably isn't much time for yourself. A funny thing happens when you choose to order your day according to God's declared priorities. Time for maintaining yourself ends up being there. You can't outgive God. When you choose to walk in obedience and structure your life around what He has called you to do, He blesses you with multiplied time.

That half-hour morning walk you gave up because your husband pulled you back into bed? God gives it back to you in the form of your son's afternoon soccer practice going long so you can walk around the field for those thirty minutes. That coffee date you passed up because you really needed to catch up on laundry? Two weeks later you end up with an unexpected three hours to yourself, allowing you to meet up with that same friend.

There will be seasons where you will need to put your own goals or preferences on hold for the benefit of your family. There will be days when a sick baby will mean you miss your exercise class at the gym, or months will go by where you have little adult conversation. But those seasons pass, and when you get to the end of your life, you will not be sorry you chose to put your own relationships with God, your husband, and your children above yourself and anything else.

Our Biblical Example of Right Priorities

Proverbs 31 beautifully demonstrates how an excellent wife orders her priorities in this same pattern and leaves us a beautiful example to follow:

An excellent wife who can find? She is far more precious than jewels. The
heart of her husband trusts in her, and he will have no lack of gain. (vv. 10-11)

The excellent wife's husband trusts her entirely, and he knows that however
she spends her time, he is going to gain from it. Your husband should be able to
confidently know he is a richer, better man because he married an excellent wife.
Proverbs 31 continues:

She does him good, and not harm, all the days of her life. (v. 12)

The Virtuous Woman has structured her life in such a way that her husband is
benefitted, not harmed, all the days of her life. Every single day she seeks to do him
good. He is her first priority. This should be said of every Christian wife.

She seeks wool and flax, and works with willing hands. She is like the
ships of the merchant; she brings her food from afar. She rises while it
is yet night and provides food for her household and portions for her
maidens. (vv. 13-15)

This woman works hard. She is diligent and *willingly* takes care of her home
and those living in it. She sometimes has to get up extra early to make sure she
cares for everyone in her home. There's nothing selfish or lazy about her work
ethic.

It should be said of us that we are industrious women who don't shy away from
hard work and accomplishing what is expected of us. There is time to rest, but the
bulk of our time is spent working.

She considers a field and buys it; with the fruit of her hands she plants
a vineyard.(v.16)

Our Proverbs friend has interests outside of her home life. She has a strong
business sense, makes a purchase, and turns it into something productive and
enjoyable. While still keeping her priorities in order, being industrious with how
she spends her time outside her home makes her more virtuous.

Likewise, when we are learning and growing in new things, it makes us more
interesting people. We are more refreshed and satisfied personally, more appealing
to our husbands, and have more to give to our children.

She dresses herself with strength and makes her arms strong. (v. 17)

This woman is not wimpy or weak. She is clothed with strength. She also
works to makes herself physically strong.

I love that the verses about how she cares for herself are scattered throughout
this passage. They give the idea that taking care of herself is something she does

in between her care for her husband, her children, her home, her ministry, and her job.

> She perceives that her merchandise is profitable. Her lamp does not go out at night. She puts her hands to the distaff, and her hands hold the spindle. (vv. 18-19)

She is willing to stay up late because there is something to profit from the work she is doing (not because she is binge-watching something!). There is something to be gained from her staying up late.

The distaff and spindle are tools for sewing, and our example is quite skilled at her craft, as she produces profitable merchandise. This does not mean all godly women must sew, but rather, all godly women should be skilled and productive in whatever they are gifted to do. This woman is willing to learn a skill and work hard at it, and we should do likewise.

> She opens her hand to the poor and reaches out her hands to the needy. (v. 20)

Here we see she is involved in ministering to others. Are you a generous, compassionate woman who is willing to reach out?

> She is not afraid of snow for her household, for all her household are clothed in scarlet. (v. 21)

This woman knows storms will come, but she is prepared for them. She has taken care to be ready for the inevitable hard times and has made sure those in her home are prepared. For us, there will be "storms"—sickness, financial strain, aging parents, etc. A wise woman will plan ahead for these seasons and not be taken by surprise when they come.

> She makes bed coverings for herself. (v. 22)

This excellent wife has made her bed attractive. An attractive home is a blessing to her family, and likely adds to her personal enjoyment of her room. Notice she makes this covering herself. She doesn't go out and purchase the most expensive thing someone else made, but labors to make things for herself.

Making our homes attractive and presentable is a praiseworthy endeavor. This doesn't mean our homes must look like something from a decorating website, and we don't have to necessarily make our own stuff, but we can shop around for great prices and work to pull a room together. An excellent wife does what she can to make her home as attractive as possible.

> Her clothing is fine linen and purple. (v. 22)

Fine linen and purple were the most elegant fabric and color choices a woman could wear when Proverbs 31 was written. The Virtuous Woman is well-dressed and takes care of her appearance. This doesn't mean she only shops high-end brands or follows every trend, but she is dressed attractively.

We are wise women if we pay attention to how we present ourselves to the world. Remember that God looks at our hearts, but man looks at the outward appearance (1 Sam. 16:7). We are representatives of Christ to this world. Do we represent a God of order and dignity by our appearance?

A few verses later, Proverbs 31 says "strength and dignity are her clothing." She's not just well-dressed on the outside, but her inward behavior is becoming as well. She is not a wilting, wimpy, or mousy girl. Neither is she an emotionally unstable, PMSing lunatic. Our example is emotionally strong, controlled, balanced, and dignified.

> Her husband is known in the gates when he sits among the elders of the land. She makes linen garments and sells them; she delivers sashes to the merchant. (v. 23-24)

This is a reference to the work she does and the profit she makes because of her work.

> Strength and dignity are her clothing, and she laughs at the time to come. (v. 25)

We continue to see this theme of a dignified, strong woman who is able to smile at the future because she is prepared for it.

> She opens her mouth with wisdom, and the teaching of kindness is on her tongue. (v. 26)

We know wisdom only comes from knowing the Word of God and applying it. The teaching of kindness is on her tongue. Another translation says "the law of kindness is on her tongue." Is it a law—an expected rule that when you open your mouth, kindness will be what comes out? That's the example our Proverbs 31 friend has left us to follow.

> She looks well to the ways of her household and does not eat the bread of idleness. (v. 27)

Her household is well taken care of because she's not idle or lazy. She takes care of her home on purpose, and it shows. How many women have disordered, chaotic homes because they are eating a steady diet of the bread of idleness? Scrolling social media, watching podcasts, etc.

Her children rise up and call her blessed; her husband also, and he
praises her. (v. 28)

Her children know they have a treasure of a mother. So does her husband.
They praise her for who she is.

Ladies, if we keep at this, if we follow her example, our husband and kids will
notice and praise us. We may not hear their praise with our own ears, but they will
praise us, nonetheless.

Many women have done excellently, but you surpass them all. (v. 29)

This is Solomon speaking directly to his wife, sharing that he and his children
think she's the best woman they know. Oh, may this be our life's goal!

Charm is deceitful, and beauty is vain, but a woman who fears the Lord
is to be praised. (v. 30)

The most beautiful thing about this woman is not her good looks and her
charm. Ultimately, she is able to do all the things she is praised for because she is a
woman who fears the Lord.

Give her of the fruit of her hands, and let her works praise her in the
gates. (v. 31)

Solomon ends his praise of this woman by saying she deserves to be blessed
and praised.

It is unlikely our Proverbs 31 friend did all of the things outlined about her in
the same season. The proverb is a depiction of her entire life, not one week! Her
character was one of continual diligence, virtue, and industriousness.

While we can't attain to the fictitious Victoria from the beginning of lesson
16, we are each absolutely able to be versions of the real Proverbs 31 woman. She
had the same twenty-four hours in her day as we do, and her lifetime example of
diligence and industriousness is a legacy we can imitate.

LESSON 18 WIFE-CHANGING QUESTIONS

1. Write the order of priorities God has prescribed for a wife.

   _____

   _____

   _____

   _____

2. In examining this list, what would you say is the current order of your priorities?

   _____

   _____

   _____

   _____

3. What would your husband say is the order of your priorities? (If your husband is the type to honestly answer, go ask him!)

   _____

   _____

   _____

   _____

4. Are there any wife-changes you need to make in your priorities?

_____

_____

_____

_____

5. Go back and read Proverbs 31 and compare yourself to her. Make a list of ways you are like her and ways you need to improve.

_____

_____

_____

_____

6. What is one wife-change you can make this week that will cause you to be more like the Proverbs 31 woman?

_____

_____

_____

_____

CROWN

LESSON 19

Now that we understand what our priorities should be, how do we go about practically implementing them into our lives? The psalmist prayed, "Teach us to number our days that we may get a heart of wisdom" (Ps. 90:12). As you read through this section on order, let this be the cry of your heart.

Budgeting Time

On payday, most of us sit down with a list of bills and decide which ones we will pay right away and which ones we can put off for another paycheck. We know how much we will tithe, what we need that month for housing and utilities, how much we will spend on groceries, gas, tuition, medical expenses, etc. Once we figure out how much we need for all the necessities, we can determine if there is anything left for fun. A wise steward considers what is needed over what is wanted. Only when the needs are funded can the wants be supplied.

If we budget our time using the same principle, we can make sure the priorities that *must* be maintained are met, and that whatever is left over is spent on what we *want* to do with our time.

Time is a currency you get to choose how to spend every day. There is nothing God requires of you that He has not given you the time to accomplish.

There are countless numbers of incredible, detailed, totally amazing organizational systems out there. I've spent hours drooling over expensive planning binders and adorable printable worksheets. I wish there was a perfect system that I could attach in the next few pages and help you put your whole life together. However, each of our lives is different, and there is no one-size-fits-all organizational plan.

We can easily get sidetracked into shopping for the perfect tools and not actually do the work of getting organized. So use the worksheets, the color-coded sticky notes, or the fancy three-ring binder if it really helps increase order to your life.

Just remember that the best organizational plan is the one you actually use. General George Patton said, "A good plan... executed now is better than a perfect plan executed next week."

Order Takes Strategy

We will spend the next two lessons working on a time budget that orders your days according to the priorities that God has called you to in this season of your life. Please understand it is impossible to work through all the material in this chapter in one day. This lesson is intended to be a reference point for you to work through over the next several weeks.

This may be the first time you have ever thought about how much time you spend doing things. If you are truthful in your assessment, you may discover you spend more time on social media than you do reading your Bible, you don't exercise nearly as much as you should, or the bulk of your time is spent at your kids' ball field. Many of us wake up every day in a flurry of activity, rushing from one frantic activity to the next, but at the end of the day we can't really say we accomplished anything. Just because we are busy doesn't mean we are productive.

> God's revealed will for you is that when you get up in the morning, you don't drift aimlessly through the day letting mere circumstances alone dictate what you do, but that you aim at something—that you focus on a certain kind of purpose. I'm talking about children here, and teenagers, and adults—single, married, widowed, moms, and every trade.
>
> Aimlessness is akin to lifelessness. Dead leaves in the backyard may move around more than anything else—more than the dog, more than the children. The wind blows this way, they go this way. The wind blows that way, they go that way. They tumble, they bounce, they skip, they press against a fence, but they have no aim whatsoever. They are full of motion and empty of life.
>
> God did not create humans in his image to be aimless, like lifeless leaves blown around in the backyard of life. He created us to be purposeful—to have a focus and an aim for all our days. What is yours today?[6] —John Piper

Start Your Responsibilities List

- Begin by making a list of your responsibilities. You can download a sample responsibilities list and worksheet under Free Resources at www.nancykaser.com.
- Now evaluate each activity or task and write the frequency it needs to take place. (For example, baby naps need to happen for 2–3 hours every day, while grocery shopping takes 1–2 hours once a week.) When you are finished with each task, you have a general picture of your time budget.

- Put a star by anything on your list that is essential to your life, as opposed to activities that are optional.
- Determine when and how you will spend your time on your required activities. You will then see how much time you have for the "extra" things you'd like to do.

Order Your Husband's Home

As soon as your list is complete, have a conversation with your husband. Show him your initial assessment of your time budget and ask for his counsel. He may think of things you haven't, or he might tell you his goals are different from yours. Listen to his preferences and direction. Decide together what *order* means for your unique home and family.

> When I first started homeschooling, Kevin would often come home to big projects strewn all over the house. I was wanting to show him all we had learned for the day. This led to us having to find a place for all the stuff at dinner time, which was a challenge in our tiny house.
>
> After several weeks of this, he finally said to me, "I know I'm supposed to say the kids' education comes first. I'm supposed to just be happy they are learning so much and not be bothered by the mess. But it's really bugging me. I love what you're teaching them, but I want to come home to a clean house. That matters just as much to me as their education. Is there a way you can have the stuff put away before I get home?"
>
> I was frustrated by this, but I decided to take it as an opportunity to teach my kids to honor their dad. Around 4:00 each day, we have a "get ready for Daddy" time. We put away all our stuff, sweep the floor, and the kids each have a candle they light in anticipation of Daddy's homecoming. This has ended up being a very sweet thing my kids want to do for their father, and I know it blesses him when he comes through the door. —Sophia

> When I lived at home, my dad preferred time with my mom to a clean house. When he came home from work, he couldn't care less if the house was clean, but he expected my mom to be ready to go on a thirty-minute run with him. He valued her time more than anything else, and she always made him the priority. —Aubree

> Mike is passionate about food and cooking, and he loves to grocery shop. Years ago we realized it was just better for the whole family if he did the shopping and cooking. It's not conventional, but it works for our family. He hates dishes, though, so I always clean up. Sometimes he makes huge messes, but I'm so grateful I don't have to cook, I never complain! —Tiffany

Nick travels for weeks at a time for work, and I am left to manage the house while he is gone. I keep a very orderly house and run a small business from home. I struggle more when he is home because he wants my attention and I'm so used to being alone and having my own things to do.

When he is home for a few days, I make sure I am less scheduled and more available for him. He needs my time and attention more than anything else. —Raquel

I didn't grow up in a very orderly home, but my husband's house was always spotless. The state of our home was the biggest challenge in our early marriage. With five young kids, keeping an orderly home just didn't seem possible, but one day I simply asked my husband to help me to get organized.

It was humbling to admit I was in need of his direction, but he was actually amazing at assessing what we needed to do, and he was thrilled I was asking for his help. He worked out a daily routine for me and the kids that was a bit overwhelming at first, but it has proven to be very effective in running our home. It made me realize how good he is in areas where I am weak. —Megan

As long as I have cold water bottles in the fridge at all times for Justin, he thinks I'm the most wonderful wife in the world! —Andrea

Set Up a Housework Routine

My goal is to keep my house in a state where I'm not horrified if someone drops in unexpectedly. When my kids were younger, it generally took me an hour a day to keep up. I would budget for thirty minutes in the morning, fifteen minutes before dinner, and fifteen minutes before bed. Breaking it up through the day allowed me to maintain things without needing a huge chunk of time. Now that my family dynamics have changed, it takes less time, and I've made some wife-changes.

For my morning chore routine, I set a timer on my phone for thirty minutes. It makes it like a game for me. I make a circle through my house and a little circle through each room. If there is nothing to be done in a certain space, I move on to the next. I try to race to get it done faster than I've allowed. If it takes twenty minutes to set my house in order, I then spend ten minutes doing some kind of organization project in a different area every day. Some days I clean out a drawer. Other times I organize bookshelves or sort socks.

Before you think I'm boasting on my stellar homemaking skills, let me remind you I'm a total work in progress. My life and schedule are constantly in transition. I'm always wife-changing! It's taken me over twenty years of working a system to feel like I'm getting it done 80 percent of the time. There are still days I really hope people don't come over unexpectedly, and occasionally my husband announces he's down to his last pair of socks. The goal is to continually give intentional focus to managing my home and to strive to honor Jesus in that effort.

Kids Can Do Housework

If you have kids who are old enough to make a mess, you have kids who are old enough to do chores. As soon as they are old enough to pull toys out of the toy box or books off the shelf, they are old enough to put them away. A toddler can empty trash cans and make their bed. Older kids can do much more.

Your children are future adults. It is your responsibility to train them up to be orderly. Start now. You can ease your own workload by delegating age-appropriate chores to your children.

The Master Schedule

Now that you have a general idea of what you need to do and how long it's going to take you to do it, it's time to put together your master schedule. This schedule allows you to map out your time week by week so you can get the most out of your days.

My master schedule worksheets use thirty-minute time increments. You have forty-eight of these a day, and fourteen or so of them are used for sleeping. That leaves you with thirty-four slots of time for every day. As you view the blank master schedule and sample schedules available under Free Resources at www.nancykaser.com, you will see that some women have lots of blank spaces—these are to be filled in each day. Remember that the master schedule is the skeleton plan, and it is fleshed out differently each week. You will also see in the samples some completely filled-in schedules, as well, so you can see how other women order their days in detail.

Start filling out your master schedule by filling in the tasks you determined were essential in the last lesson. This will make up the general frame of your master schedule. Depending on the size of your family and your season of life, you will need to have varying degrees of detail to your master schedule.

Remember—your schedule is your general plan. It is not your ruler, your leader, or your authority. It is a tool to help you honor God and bless your family. It is meant to bring about peace and beauty and order in your life instead of stress and rigidity because you feel as if it's a law. There are some days when the plan will look nothing like the day you end up having. But at least you had some sort of plan. Try again the next day. By the end of the week, even if you only stick to 50 percent of the plan, you will have added far more order to your life than you would have if you had just let your days happen haphazardly.

Meal Planning

Brent and I were talking with an engaged couple, and I was encouraging the bride-to-be to register for good knives. She replied with, "Oh, I don't need knives or pans or anything. I can't cook." She was totally serious. This twenty-year-old girl was somehow under the impression that cooking is a talent people were either born with or not, like singing or drawing. She had decided they would just eat out for every meal since she didn't have the "cooking talent."

I gently explained to her that cooking was a *life skill* anyone can learn. You find a recipe, buy the food listed on the recipe, follow the directions, and serve the meal. There are even videos online that demonstrate how to perform each step. We are without excuse when it comes to preparing meals for our families.

Feeding your people is a big deal! Meal planning is an essential part of keeping your home. As the manager of your family's menu, you have the responsibility of determining what food comes into your house and what goes into the bodies entrusted to you. You aren't just accountable for filling their bellies, but you are accountable for their health.

Each of us has different convictions about food. Some are adamant about being vegan or vegetarian, some only eat organic, some are very into supplements, and others are more about moderation. Romans 14 tells us these are disputable issues (not under biblical mandate), and each of us will stand before the Lord on our own convictions. I encourage you to pray and ask the Lord if you are doing the best job you possibly can in caring for your family's health, given your personal convictions about food, your budget, and what your husband will actually eat. Look over what you are feeding your family and determine if there are any changes God would have you to make. With a little planning, you can keep them healthy and well fed on the budget you have.

Start by making a list of everything you know how to prepare right now. Really think about this—everything from grilled cheese sandwiches to pot roast to blueberry pancakes. For some of you, making a list of what you know how to cook is very easy because the list is so short. That is okay for now, but I want to challenge you to expand your menu! Make at least one new recipe a week, and before the year is over, you will know how to make so many meals.

I have planned my dinner menu differently during different seasons of my life. When my kids were small and we had dinner together at home at the same time every night, I had a menu system like this:

Monday: Meatless
Tuesday: Mexican or Italian
Wednesday: Pressure Cooker, Crock-Pot, or Casserole
Thursday: Meat and Potatoes
Friday: Fish
Saturday: Soup or Salad
Sunday: Leftovers or Sandwiches

Every Sunday night, since we ate leftovers or sandwiches, I spent some time figuring out what I was going to feed my family for the next week. I began by looking in my refrigerator and pantry and then I made a list of meals I could make for that week based on what we had. This usually took at least half an hour. I then made a grocery list and headed to the store, either on Sunday night after the kids were asleep or early in the morning on Monday. This allowed for my days to run more smoothly through the week and for nutritious meals to be on the table every day.

When my kids got older and our evenings at home became less routine, my menu planning changed significantly. I began to look at our schedule for the week to determine how often there would even be anyone at home at mealtimes. I made more casseroles and Crock-Pot meals that could be served throughout the week whenever people were home. When our kids started moving out and the grandbabies started coming, it became increasingly important to have scheduled times together as a family, so I started making a big Sunday night dinner for our family—giving the girls the night off from cooking for their own families and giving myself the joy of having all my people around my table.

Planning Takes Work

As we have moved into a season that requires less of my time in the kitchen, it is no less important for me to plan for food being in my house and available for whoever is home. When I look at my daily schedule, I can see what I am making for dinner that night and know if I need to pull anything out of the freezer in the morning or if running to the store for a forgotten ingredient is going to be necessary. I actually have an alarm on my phone that goes off every afternoon, reminding me I need to start some kind of dinner. If I don't remind myself, I will have someone telling me at 6:00 that they're hungry, and I will have to put them off for at least another thirty minutes while I get something on the table. That reminder alarm has kept me on track for years.

You will likely have a completely different routine than mine. The key is to have a plan and to intentionally pursue order. You are not going to have this whole master schedule worked out, your meals planned out, your house decluttered, and your kids on a chore schedule by the end of the week. It's a lifelong wife-changing process! Start with one area, get it worked out, and build out from there. A workable, functioning routine typically takes about a month to get fine-tuned. Take small steps. Be more ordered tomorrow than you are today.

*Bonus Material: for tips and encouragement on managing the clutter in your home, see the article titled "Clutter Kills Order" on nancykaser.com and find downloadable samples of:

- Master Schedule
- Mom's Chore List
- Kids' Chores

LESSON 19 WIFE-CHANGING QUESTIONS

Spend the day using the tools on the website. Start your master schedule and begin your meal planning. If you are reading this book as part of a group, plan to have a sample of your master schedule and/or meal plans to share when you meet.

LESSON 20

*You will need your Bible to get the most out of this lesson.

When the Schedule Is Cluttered

> If we really have too much to do, there are some items on the agenda which God did not put there. Let us submit the list to Him and ask Him to indicate which items we must delete. There is always time to do the will of God. If we are too busy to do that, we are too busy.[7]—Elisabeth Elliot

In the last few decades, there has been a gradual glorification of being busy— if we are busy, then we must be productive. If we are busy, then we must be important. If we are busy, it must mean we are living the abundant life. However, being busy with things God has not called us to have in our schedules can be unholy bondage. If we are only doing the things God has called us to do, then we will never be too busy.

Again, God has not given you more to do than He has given you time to accomplish.

In Exodus 18:13–27, Moses got some very wise counsel from his father-in-law regarding his overcommitted schedule. Go read these verses now.

There was a genuine need for God's people to be judged. They needed help with their disputes, and Moses loved them and wanted them to do what was right. He was certainly the most qualified judge in the camp. However, he was one judge overseeing two million people and was wearing himself out! Jethro recognized there was just not enough of Moses to meet all the needs of the people. He advised his son-in-law to select his top priority—representing the people before God and instructing the people about the law and how to live. Jethro advised that trustworthy, God-fearing men should be chosen to judge the people instead. Moses needed to let a good thing go so he could focus on the best things.

Like Moses, when there is not enough time to do all the things you feel you must do, then it is time to re-evaluate your schedule and determine which commitments need to go. Cutting out commitments God has not called you to have is the way to make room for what He has prepared for you. What do you need to let go of in order to make room for God's best?

Every activity, every commitment, every event we agree to attend should be a matter of prayer. We can often assume that because something is associated with ministry or family or service, it is something we should say yes to. However, we must realize that just because something is a *good* thing, it might not be the *best* thing for us to participate in during a particular season. One of Satan's well-laid traps is to keep us in overcommitted schedules full of good things God hasn't called us to do.

In one season in my life, there were simply no blank spaces on my schedule. We were maxed out every single day. If my kids dawdled, I knew it would throw off the entire day, so I barked orders like a sergeant from the front door. There was no opening in the schedule for anything unexpected. We had homeschool co-op functions, Bible study, AWANA, sports practices and games, music lessons, and ministry engagements. That was in addition to our homeschooling, chores, meals, and other needs. I was hurrying them through their days so we could get to the next thing on the schedule. None of the happenings on our schedule were bad. They were all wonderful in themselves, but trying to do all of them at the same time was sucking the peace from our home.

I knew we had to make some changes. But when I looked at each of our activities, I didn't want to give any of them up! I loved all of it! I eventually wrote down every one of our commitments and evaluated the benefits and drawbacks to each of them. I asked the Lord for clear direction. I talked to my husband. I needed some way to know which commitments to cut. None of them seemed easily disposable.

A few days later, I shared my struggle with a friend and asked her to pray for me. In her prayer, she said, "Lord, I ask that you would show Nancy where she can produce the most fruit—that she would be able to see those things that produce fruit one hundredfold and that she wouldn't settle for things that only yield thirty- or sixty-fold—but that her life would only be filled with things that yield the maximum fruit."

She was referring to Matthew 13:8: "Other seeds fell on good soil and produced grain, some a hundredfold, some sixty, some thirty."

In this passage, Jesus was talking about the overall abundance of spiritual fruit in a believer's life as they hear the Word of God. Everyone hears the same Word. Some benefit from it sparingly, some moderately, and some maximize it. Of course, we should all want to yield the maximum; to settle for less would be foolish, right?

The same principle can be applied to how we spend our time. We all have the same twenty-four hours in our days, and we can use those hours to glorify God either sparingly, moderately, or completely. We are wise to seek to yield as much benefit for our families (and ultimately, for the kingdom of God) from our activities as we possibly can.

I eventually chose to step out of women's ministry for that season. It seemed crazy to me at first. I thought, *I'm a pastor's wife! Shouldn't women's ministry be the most important thing to me at church?* However, as I evaluated where the most fruit was being produced in my life, I realized that it wasn't actually in women's ministry at that time. There were also fantastic women in our church who could serve the women more effectively than I could. By stepping down, I allowed more women in our church to use their gifts, and actually, more fruit was produced because I wasn't there. While I missed it, I knew that I was walking in obedience and choosing to devote the best of my time to the things that would yield the most fruit in that season.

This principle of determining how much fruit will eventually be yielded from a certain activity is such a useful measuring tool. I encourage you to use it to evaluate your own activities in light of this concept. When you need to make changes to your over-filled schedule, or when you are deciding whether to take on something new, ask yourself the following:

- Is this activity going to benefit my life (or my child's life) in a positive way?
- Is this activity going to contribute to someone's spiritual growth?
- Is this activity worth the time it will take to be committed to it?
- Will this activity yield thirty-fold, sixty-fold, or a hundredfold in my life? (Or in the life of whomever I am responsible to oversee?)
- If it is not a hundredfold-yielding activity, do I have time to allow for a sixty- or thirty-fold activity in my schedule at this time?

Sometimes our schedules allow us to do things that yield lesser amounts. Other times, they do not. As we seek the Lord about these things, we can be confident that the One who gave us all the time we have will give us the wisdom and direction we need.

> The decisions we make dictate the schedules we keep. The schedules we keep determine the lives we live. The lives we live determine how we spend our souls. So, this isn't just about finding time. This is about honoring God with the time we have.[8] —Lysa Terkeurst

Order Your Heart First

Some days, the plan is just going to fall apart. People get sick. Toilets back up. Things take much longer than they should. It comes back to having your heart right before God. Order starts there. If you are right with God, the messy days will come, but you won't be a mess because of them.

In our efforts to prioritize and order our lives, let us not forget that our ultimate goal is to glorify God in our marriages, in our relationships with our children, in our homes, in our ministries and jobs, and in our bodies. More than a great meal or matched socks, the attitude of our hearts can glorify God and bless our families.

In Numbers 9, the Israelites were daily led by God by a pillar of fire by night and a pillar of cloud by day. Though they had been cleansed, set apart, blessed, and had been given roles within the camp, they still had to be guided by God each step of the way to make it to the Promised Land. God had not done all those previous things to make them able to start toward the Promised Land on their own, but to make them dependent on Him for every step.

As we make our plans and focus on having ordered lives, let's be mindful of the One we ultimately live to please. May we be entirely dependent on His ever-available guidance to lead us to the ordered life He has called us to.

LESSON 20 WIFE-CHANGING QUESTIONS

1. Spend some time praying over your schedule and asking God if there is anything on it He has not called you to do. Is there anything God is leading you to do that you need to add to your schedule? Discuss this with your husband and make any necessary changes while the conviction is fresh.

2. Continue to work on your master schedule and menu plan.

GIFT

LESSON 21

We live in the most sexually informed generation in history. Science, technology, and comfort in discussing the subject have made the last fifty years tremendously sex-saturated. You would think we would be the most sexually fulfilled generation ever. However, with the increase in sexual information and openness has come an increase in perversion, misinformation, and confusion. Christian woman need practical, direct instruction on what the Bible says about sexuality.

In this chapter, we will explore the following specifics concerning marital relations, as well as issues that affect our sexuality outside the bedroom:

- God's opinion of sex
- Common obstacles women face in their intimate lives
- Guarding our emotions, words, mind, and body
- How to repent from sexual sin

When discussing sexuality, every stereotype will be proven false by somebody. No couple is identical. I encourage you to evaluate the counsel given here in light of your unique relationship and to glean what the truth of God's Word has for you specifically.

I also want to encourage you to not assume that because you've been married for decades or because you have lots of previous sexual experience that you can't learn something new. Have a willing, wife-changing mentality. Going back to the foundations of your sexual relationship may lead to a refreshed perspective and a renewed delight in the gift of sex. My hope is that every woman who reads this chapter will have a biblical view of sex and be encouraged to build a dynamic, satisfying, and God-glorifying intimate life with her husband.

God's First Gift

Sex is like a sacrament: it is a spiritual reality demonstrated in a physical symbol. When we have sex, we are renewing our commitment to give ourselves entirely to one another, and we are physically depicting that we are one flesh. This is why the title of this chapter is purposely called "Gift."

gift—*noun*. Something given willingly to someone without payment or earning; a present.

She received a gift on her birthday.

gift—*verb*. The act of giving something as a present, especially formally or as a donation.

He was gifted a trip to Hawaii.

It is insightful to look at sex in relation to both the noun and verb forms of the word "gift". Sex is something we can receive freely as a present from God and our husbands, and it is also something we actively offer and do not expect it to be earned.

Sex is a wedding gift from God. Fortunately, unlike those dishes with blue ducks on them or the chevron-patterned pillows you registered for, you will use this wedding gift for the rest of your marriage!

> Sexual pleasure belongs rightfully only to believers. All others are thieves and robbers. Don't ever let the world deceive you into thinking that we Christians are trying to borrow and purify a limited amount of the world's pleasure.
>
> God created sexual pleasure for his subjects alone, and the world has rebelled against him and stolen his gifts and corrupted them and debased them and turned them into weapons of destruction and laughed at those who remain faithful to the King and use his gifts according to his word. But we will not be deceived.[1]—John Piper

Satan Is a Gift Hater

Satan lies about everything, but he is especially good at lying about sexuality. For generations, he has successfully convinced Christians that sex is wicked, dirty, and sinful. There was a time in church history when it was taught that the Holy Spirit left the room when a couple made love. Some pastors even taught that sex was always a sin, but one God that would overlook if the couple participated in it solely for procreation.

The lies of our enemy must be combatted with the truth of the Word of God. We must remember that sex was all God's idea! The very first command God gave to Adam and Eve was "Be fruitful and multiply." Before the fall, Adam knew God's provision of a wife included the gift of "the two shall become one flesh."

The Bible encourages us to come together. Sex is good for our marriages. It relieves stress, strengthens our commitment to one another, acts as a "reset" button after a disagreement, protects against temptation, burns calories (an average of seventy per session!), and is just plain great entertainment.

Differences in Drives

It is typical for one of you to want sex more frequently than the other. Stereotypically, men have higher sex drives than women. (Though that's not always the case. We will address the opposite scenario next.) A husband's high sex drive is not a burden, but a blessing. It is a God-designed magnet that draws him toward you to pursue closeness. It is also a God-designed opportunity for you to choose to give, whether you are feeling amorous or not.

Make it your goal to cheerfully accept his advances and to satisfy him every time he approaches you. This may not always be possible, but your husband should know his advances will typically be well-received. You are his only outlet for sexual release, and he needs you.

> The husband must fulfill his duty to his wife, and likewise also the wife to her husband. The wife does not have authority over her own body, but the husband does; and likewise also the husband does not have authority over his own body, but the wife does. Stop depriving one another, except by agreement for a time, so that you may devote yourselves to prayer, and come together again so that Satan will not tempt you because of your lack of self-control. (1 Cor. 7:3–5)

Every warning in Scripture is there because we are likely to do what it warns against. We tell our teenagers, "Don't be late" because there is a good chance they will push their curfew. We tell our little ones, "Don't forget to brush your teeth" because they will probably get into bed with green fur on their teeth. In the same way, when the Scripture tells husbands and wives, "Don't deprive one another," it's because that is what we are likely to do.

We see from the verses above that Satan will tempt us if we are not coming together. *Sex is actually a weapon we can use against Satan.* That is not something we should take lightly.

Before you were married, it was the enemy's goal to get you to have sex with your boyfriend. Now that you're married, it is his goal to get you *to not have sex with your husband*. To deprive your spouse of sexual pleasure violates a direct command from God and opens your marriage up to temptation.

There may be times when you are genuinely not feeling well, have an urgent appointment, or have hungry children to feed, and are not able to have sex at a given moment. My counsel to you is to respectfully and romantically tell your husband you'd love to, but you'll both have to wait until later. Give him a time when you plan to satisfy him, and then keep your commitment.

It should go without saying, but there can be absolutely *no* indication to your husband that you are anything less than delighted to make love to him: no eye rolling, deep sighs, or implying you want him to hurry up and get it over with. He should not have to plot to "score" with you or be treated like sex is a reward for being a "good boy."

There will be times in your marriage when you just don't feel like responding to your husband sexually. When those times come and your flesh screams, "No way! Again?" *That, dear sister, is your opportunity to die to yourself and obey God.* Choose to offer your body and your will as a sacrifice to the Lord. Make it a spiritual act of obedience to your Savior.

Excuses, Excuses

Our enemy wants us to have sex as little as possible, so he is quite crafty at giving us excuses for why now is not a good time.

I feel unattractive. Many women don't want to have sex because they feel unattractive. They are embarrassed about their fat rolls or the dimples on their bottoms. My counsel to these women is to work to stay in the best possible shape they can. If you feel sexy, you'll act sexy! However, I've never met a woman who felt absolutely comfortable with her own body. So, die to yourself again. Do all you can to feel pretty, and then surrender yourself to the Lord. Make it about pleasing God. Theresa says,

> As a woman who has struggled with weight issues my whole marriage, I can say no matter a woman's size, it is important to remember that a smiling, happy woman is sexy! Keep yourself clean and made up and dress in a way that makes you feel as attractive as possible. Until you lose the weight, decorate it!

I don't have time. I want to suggest something that will put things in perspective when it comes to having no time for sex. The next time you and your husband make love, time it! Chances are, your encounter will last between seven to twenty minutes. On those marathon nights, it may go longer, but on average, you're looking at around fifteen minutes. If you gift-give three times a week, that's a mere forty-five minutes. Are you willing to give that much time to glorify God in your marriage, keep your husband satisfied, and guard your marriage against temptation?

Some women stay up extra late, waiting for their husbands to fall asleep to avoid having sex. Others get dressed in the closet or get up extra early to shower and get dressed before he wakes up—anything to avoid having him catch a glimpse of their bodies and wanting some attention. What a waste of time! These ladies are spending more time figuring out how to avoid sex than it would take to just love their husbands! Then there's the monthly fight that ensues because he complains he's not getting any; that takes much longer than forty-five minutes!

Sex is not meant to be just for special occasions. It is so much more. Just say yes with a smile. Die to yourself. Choose to give yourself willingly to your husband. You have the time.

I'm too busy. If you are too busy to have sex, then you are too busy. Overcommitment is one of the most detrimental things to Christian marriages today.

I read a great acronym for BUSY: **B**urdened **U**nder **S**atan's **Y**oke.

It is a victory for the enemy to fill your life so full of "good things" that you have no time left to commit to your marriage. It is absolutely vital that you purge anything in your life that is keeping you from fulfilling your role as your husband's lover. Is it your kids' extracurricular activities? Then cut back. You might ask, "Won't my kids miss out if they aren't in soccer, ballet, karate, and piano?" Not as much as they'll miss if their parents' marriage falls apart. Keep your marriage a priority.

Are you overcommitted in your own extra activities? PTA or home-schooling groups, girls' nights, exercise class, even Bible study—these are all good things in themselves, but if they are draining your energy to the point where you are too pooped to whoop, then cut them out of your life and make your marriage a priority.

What about ministry? Are you running to this prayer meeting and to that outreach, or to this fundraiser or on that mission trip? Are you serving the Lord so much that you aren't serving your husband? This is a huge tactic of Satan because he convinces us that serving the Lord is our highest priority—and it is—but we forget that as wives, our first calling in serving the Lord is to love our husbands.

I know most of you schedule out your days—or at least you've started since reading the last chapter. You have an organizer or you at least make a list of things you need to get done that day. So let me encourage you to leave room in your schedule for sex every day. When your husband reaches for you at the end of the day, part of the reason you might roll your eyes sometimes is because you have had in your head since 6:00 p.m. that your evening would include:

- Make dinner
- Wash dishes
- Check homework
- Fold laundry

- Put kids to bed
- Take a shower
- Go to sleep

If you had instead planned: Take a shower, *Make love,* Go to sleep—you wouldn't have such a problem when Romeo makes his move. Plan to make love every day. If it doesn't happen, then you've just added a bonus fifteen minutes in your day. If it does happen every day—you've gotten your heart rate up, you've pleased your husband, you've helped protect him from temptation, and you've honored the Lord. That's being productive! As you are still working on your schedule from the last chapter, I want to encourage you to not delay—*plan* to have sex today!

(Hint: You can write this plan in code to protect young eyes or to prevent your husband from feeling like he's a chore. No one will suspect your scheduled time for "gardening" or "quiet time" means anything else.)

I feel like sex is dirty, and I want to please God. That is a lie of the enemy that you are somehow less holy when you make love to your husband. Many women believe they need to disassociate themselves with anything sensuous in order to be godly. The truth is, when we minister to our husbands sexually and give them our full physical attention, we are being as pure and holy as the grannies working in the soup kitchen. Offering your body freely to your husband with a heart to please the Lord can be an obedient act of worship.

Often when a woman uses this excuse, she is constructing a spiritual screen for her own selfishness. Sex is a gift and a commandment from God. God even devoted a whole book of the Bible to the subject. The Song of Solomon is all about the intimate encounters Solomon had with his wife. Ladies, God is delighted when you give your full physical attention to your husband. If you feel like sex is dirty, then know your feelings are lying to you.

Sometimes a woman feels shame because, in the past, she participated in sex outside of God's design. This is where she must choose to believe that God has truly declared her to be a forgiven, cleansed, and holy new creation. Any feeling contrary to this truth is a lie. God does not hold our confessed sin against us, and our confessed sin has no power to rule our thoughts or our bedrooms. If you are struggling with shame over past sin, a clear conscience can be found in the truth of the Scriptures and in a heart of sincere repentance. Confess your sin, meditate on the truth of what the cross of Jesus has done for you, and be set free.

Women who have experienced the trauma of sexual abuse often struggle to keep their lingering pain out of their bedrooms. Sexual abuse *is* dirty and horrible. Marital sex is not. If your past abuse is causing problems in your intimate life with your husband, I encourage you to not delay in getting Christian counseling. Through the power of God's Word and His Spirit, you can be freed from the grip of whatever happened to you, allowing you to receive full restoration according to God's will.

When the Stereotype Is Off

Vicki married Jeremy, anticipating a fantastic sex life. She was willing and adventurous and expected her husband to think she was the most incredible lover ever. Shortly after the honeymoon, Vicki started to realize Jeremy wasn't as into sex as she was. In fact, he really wasn't interested at all. A year after their wedding, Jeremy made excuses about why he didn't want to make love to her: he was exhausted, he was sick, he had to finish work. Days, and sometimes weeks, went by without their coming together. The few times Vicki said she wanted more sex, it ended in a nasty fight. She feels rejected and disappointed.

Now that she knows her own husband isn't an available outlet, her sex drive seems stronger than ever. Her feeling of frustration carries over into every area of her marriage, and she wonders if she is doomed to a sexless future.

If you can relate to Vicki, I know your heart breaks when you hear of women who have husbands who desire them to the point of being annoying, but your husband just isn't interested. The pain of rejection is devastating, and you wonder if there is something wrong with you or if there is something wrong with your husband. What's worse is you may feel alone in your pain.

Dear Sister, God acknowledges your specific circumstance in His Word. The sin of sexual deprivation can go both ways. 1 Corinthians 7:5 says to not deprive "one another," and Ephesians says that you should render due benevolence to "one another." Not only does the wife's body belong to her husband, but the husband's body belongs to his wife. For a husband to deprive his wife of sexual fulfillment is equally acknowledged as sinful by God.

So what do you do when your husband doesn't pursue sex? Begin with prayer. God sees your unfulfilled needs, and He cares. Remember, God desires that you have a fulfilling sexual relationship with your husband, so ask Him about what to do to get your marriage there. Make a specific list of requests in regard to your intimate life. What do you want God to do?

Ask the Lord to reveal any sin issues that could be affecting your husband's sex drive. Pornography can sometimes be the culprit in this scenario, and this addiction must be addressed if this is the case.

Of course, pornography is certainly not the only reason for a man's lack of sexual connection with his wife. As the Lord leads you, talk about your unfulfilled needs with your husband in a nonconfrontational way. Ask if there is a reason for his lack of interest. Feeling deprived and rejected is a very vulnerable place to speak from, and the timing of this conversation, along with your respectful, gentle spirit, is critically important.

There can be biological reasons for a man's low libido. He has hormones too. Different medications can also decrease sex drive. Respectfully ask your husband to see a doctor, and offer to make the appointment for him. Mr. Macho won't likely want to race right in and say, "Hey, Doc, I don't want to have sex with my wife," but maybe you can persuade him to see the doctor by offering to go with him. Remember, this is about both of you, as well as about your desire for physical intimacy.

There can also be psychological or spiritual issues affecting your sex life. A trained Christian counselor can be highly beneficial. There is no shame in asking for professional help, and it could be the fastest way to fix whatever is causing problems. I caution you to only seek counsel from a therapist who will offer guidance from a biblical perspective.

If there is nothing you can do to pique your husband's desire, if there is no biological reason for his lack of interest, if there is no sin to address, or if he just won't talk about it, then seek the Lord once again. I know that in the midst of your suffering it seems trite for me to tell you to pray, but God knows the issue entirely, and only He can minister to you. You have been given an opportunity to die to yourself. You can honor the Lord by allowing Him to meet your needs as you wait for Him to work in your husband. Just like any sin that is not your own, there is not much you can do about it aside from prayer, but prayer does so much. Consider the story from Ann Marie:

> The enemy keeps people busy, distracted, and tired. That goes for men as well. Combine that with a man who is not an initiator, which leads to problems. I struggled, and still do to some extent because it is so anti-cultural, and the enemy speaks lies into my thoughts.
>
> My husband is not an initiator. I felt like that meant he didn't really love me or care. When I would clearly communicate how that made me feel (probably not always in the most respectful way, I admit), he would see the problem, but nothing would change. In fact, it made him feel like a bad husband.
>
> I finally had to "die to self" in this area and get over feeling rejected or unwanted. When I initiate, my husband always responds. I had to let go of my preconceived notions of my "role" and be willing to be the initiator for the health of our marriage.

Talk to God about Sex!

Make your sex life a matter of prayer. God wants to be invited into your bedroom. He made you. He made your husband. He made sex to be enjoyed by both of you till death do you part. So invite Him into your bedroom. Involve Him in the process. Pray specifically, and expect Him to answer your prayers.

LESSON 21 WIFE-CHANGING QUESTIONS

Have a Wife-Changing Conversation

Your homework assignment for this lesson is to have a conversation with your husband about your intimate life. You may even want to give him a copy of the questions listed below so he can think about his answers for a day and be more prepared for your conversation. You may both write your answers down on a separate sheet of paper. (I recommend having this conversation when you will be able to apply what you have learned immediately after having this discussion.)

1. What lighting does your husband prefer for making love? What is your preference?
2. Does your husband find a particular scent arousing? What about you? Is there a candle scent you both enjoy? What about perfumes/colognes?
3. What turns your husband off? What turns you off?
4. List three things that turn your husband on. What are three things that turn you on?
5. What types of foreplay does your husband prefer? What about you?
6. How does your husband feel about the frequency of your current sex life? How do you feel about it?
7. What is your husband's preferred time of day for sex? What is yours?
8. Does your husband like you to talk during sex? Make noise? What sounds/words can you use to communicate to him better? How would you answer this question?
9. What are your husband's favorite places to be touched? Kissed? What are yours?
10. What position is his favorite? What is yours?
11. What is one sexual thing your husband would really like you to do more of? How would you answer this question yourself?
12. Is there anything specific your husband would like to try intimately? What about you?
13. Is there anything you think is hindering the two of you from having the most fulfilling sex life possible? If so, what can you do to address this situation?

14. Are there some specific things you want to see in your intimate life with your husband? Write out a prayer asking God for these requests.

15. Insert some of your own questions.

_____

_____

_____

_____

**Bonus Material: For encouragement and direction in dealing with a husband's pornography use, see the article "Encouragement for Hurting Wives" under "Free Resources" at nancykaser.com.

LESSON 22

Nearly every book in the New Testament mentions sex. Most verses warn against immorality because the moral environment of the first century was just as bad, and though hard to believe, probably worse than that of our present generation. The apostles lived in a time when sexual depravity was almost universal and practiced without shame or disgrace. Although it seems like a new mentality in our current culture, fornication, adultery, prostitution, and homosexuality were not only condoned, but encouraged and celebrated by most ancient religions. Chastity and sexual purity were relatively unknown virtues. When Jesus came on the scene and His followers began promoting purity and forbidding immorality, it really shook things up. A morally upright, sexually pure, chaste Christian was a total standout in biblical culture.

Today, the Christian who obeys God rather than the prevailing sexual culture should still stand out. We have very clear directions from the Word of God, and these have not changed in over two thousand years. God's standards of a believer's sexual integrity do not change.

Sexual Boundaries

The Scriptures say the marriage bed is undefiled. Therefore, God blesses whatever a husband and wife do with one another sexually, as long as it is not contrary to Scripture. Here is a simple, scripturally based guideline to help you gauge sexual boundaries:

1. The Covenantal Boundary. When you promised to belong only to your husband, and he promised to belong to only you, this included your marriage bed. There can be no one else invited to your marriage bed, whether in person, in mind, in website, in film, etc. That is the covenant that you made on your wedding day between yourselves and with God.

2. The Legal Boundary. We are to live by the law of the land. There are some things that sound exciting, but, well, elevators have cameras and the beach is public. The back of your car in the church parking lot may sound fun, but if you get caught, it's a big ticket, not to mention embarrassing! So build very high walls and have a great time in your own backyard if you fancy the outdoors. The marriage bed is undefiled, but don't break any laws.

This list extends to obeying the biblical laws of sexuality:

- Adultery: when a married person engages in any sexual act with someone who is not their spouse.
- Bestiality: any sexual act committed with an animal.
- Fornication: when an unmarried person engages in any sexual act.
- Homosexuality: engaging in any sexual act with someone of the same gender.
- Incest: any sexual act conducted between family members.
- Orgies: to engage in sex with more than one person at a time; group sex.
- Prostitution: receiving or paying money in exchange for sexual acts.

3. The Harm Boundary. Don't do anything harmful to your mate's body or mind. There is a difference between *hurt* and *harm*. There may be times when sex may be momentarily uncomfortable, but the moment doesn't cause lasting pain or harm. If your husband is hurting you and you want him to stop, then say so. If something is harmful (causing long-term pain, either physically or psychologically), then it should be avoided.

4. The Conscience Boundary. It is fine for couples to experiment with new ways to bring pleasure to one another, but it is never loving to request (and certainly not to insist) a spouse to participate in anything that violates his or her conscience. However, it is important to ask yourself if your aversion to something your husband wants to do is actually violating your conscience or if you are really being selfish. If there is something requested that will truly offend the conscience of either of you, then that boundary should be respected.

If something does not violate any of the limits listed above, then it's likely safe to proceed.

Lock Your Doors

God has given us very clear instructions in His Word that define sexual integrity, and we will look at them closely in the next two lessons.

Most of us drive cars with four doors. Now imagine you are walking alone through a dark parking lot in a rough neighborhood. In order to be safe, what is the first thing you are going to do when you get in your four-door car? You're going to lock the doors. How many doors will you lock? It may sound silly, but would you only lock two doors? No, you would lock all four doors to be safe. The same is true when it comes to sexual integrity.

There are four doors through which Satan typically tries to get a woman to compromise in the area of her sexual integrity.

The Emotional Door

Your heart is not only central to your body physically—pumping blood to the rest of your body—but it is also figurative of you emotionally, where everything you believe, experience, and feel runs through your emotional heart. When the Bible talks about the heart, it is referring to emotions or feelings. Proverbs 4:23 tells us that your heart must be well-guarded:

> Keep your heart with all vigilance, for from it flow the springs of life. (ESV)

> Keep your heart with all diligence, for out of it spring the issues of life. (NKJV)

> Above all else, guard your heart, for it is the wellspring of life. (NASB)

> Watch over your heart with all diligence, for from it flow the springs of life. (AMP)

> Above all else, guard your heart, for everything you do flows from it. (NIV)

> Guard your heart above all else, for it determines the course of your life. (NLT)

In every version, the believer is instructed to guard, watch over, keep his/her heart with all diligence, above all else. What comes from your heart (your emotions) determines the course of your life. The heart is the core of all you are and all you experience in life. When God says to guard it above all else, He is saying "protect the source of your life."

When you married your husband and made that vow to "forsake all others," that didn't just mean you wouldn't have sex with another guy. It also meant your heart would only belong to your husband. Therefore, the only man that a married Christian woman should become emotionally aroused by or attached to is her husband.

Evelyn's hard work as the school board president has taken an enormous amount of her time this year, but she finds it exhilarating. The long hours haven't been so difficult, especially since Pete was elected to the board. Evelyn's husband, Jerry, doesn't have a clue about what she is doing, and when she has tried to tell him what is happening, he answers with a quick, "That's great, Hon." On the other hand, Pete never misses an opportunity to praise Evelyn's work. He supports her ideas at meetings and seems to really get her vision for the school. Lately, Evelyn has started to look for more reasons to contact Pete, not because she really has a legitimate need to discuss school business with him, but because she likes the way he makes her feel.

The enemy will be very deceptive in this area and will make things seem very innocent at the outset. There are subtle ways you can find yourself emotionally attached to a man who is not your husband. This is always dangerous ground. The following is a list of possible ways you could be deceived into leaving your emotional door unlocked:

- Your husband's brilliant friend you can talk to about things your husband just doesn't understand.
- That co-worker who is married to a real toad, and he comes to you and tells you his marriage horror stories. You just want to be a good friend and listen to him.
- The dad you chat with at soccer practice. He's always fun and engaging and is more aware of your kids' activities than your husband.
- The co-volunteer who always shows up to the important meetings. It's so nice to have someone who cares deeply about the cause you are passionate about.
- The old high school friend who found you online and has been sending hilarious private messages about old times.
- The usher at church who gives such godly counsel; you wish you could talk to him all the time.

You can certainly enjoy conversations and activities with men on a safe and social level. My husband's friend, Chris, makes me laugh harder than anyone I've ever met. I love being around him, but I'm not emotionally attached to him. I care for the men on our ministry team, enjoy rousing intellectual conversations with my male coworkers, and I have deep respect for my pastors, but none of these relationships are an unhealthy open door to my heart.

If you're not sure if you are becoming emotionally unguarded with a man who is not your husband, here are some questions that you can ask yourself:

- Do you think of this man several times a day, even though he is not around?
- Do you ever select your clothes based on whether you will see him or not?
- Do you look for excuses to call, text, message, email, or see him?
- Do you wonder if he feels attracted to you?
- Do you wish you could spend time alone with him?

If the answer is yes to any of these questions, guard your heart! Confess your attachment to the Lord, and repent immediately. You may also need to confess this to someone else and be held accountable in order to emotionally distance yourself from him. Yes, it can be embarrassing and humiliating to confess you have emotions for someone other than your husband, but adultery is even more embarrassing and humiliating.

Adultery begins in the heart—and that door must be locked tightly.

Emma's husband was very preoccupied with his work, and Emma felt neglected. Isaac, an attractive young guy at her office, started paying her compliments nearly every day. She knew she should not be so excited by his attention, but she justified it by telling herself she wouldn't feel this way if her husband was more attentive.

Soon, Isaac started sending her private messages, and they met in empty offices at work to talk. Emma felt like she and Isaac connected on a much deeper level than she ever had with her husband. Their secret meetings soon became sexual. The adultery went on for six months before Isaac's wife found out and called Emma's husband. Emma and her husband separated for months. In Emma's own words:

> Rather than turning to God with my loneliness or sharing with my husband how I was feeling, I fell for a well-laid trap of Satan. He attacked at my weak point, and I fell. Not guarding my emotions nearly cost me everything. We barely made it. Sometimes I still don't know if my husband will ever fully trust me again. I can say for certain, though, the momentary thrill was not worth all this pain.

Fire Drill

Just like a fire drill in school is a rehearsal in case a real fire happens, rehearsing how to get out of compromising situations can ensure that you do the right thing when times of temptation come. It is wise to be prepared with responses to possible situations that come up that may jeopardize your emotional door.

When that attractive new neighbor shows up at 11:00 a.m. and wants to just chat: "My husband will be home at six. How about you come back then and we can all talk?"

When a man from your office asks if you can go toss around ideas over lunch: "I make it a rule not to each lunch alone with any man but my husband, so why don't we invite the whole project team for lunch, or you and I can go into the lobby and discuss those ideas right now?"

If a married man comes to you for advice about his marital problems, refer him to your husband or a leader in your church, or ask him if he'd like to invite his wife over to meet with you and your husband. You don't need to be a sounding board for any man but your husband (and maybe your own brother and your sons).

Leave Old Boyfriends in the Past

Are you still emotionally attached to an old boyfriend? Do you think about him when your husband is being a jerk? *Well, Billy never would have treated me like that,* and then you spend the afternoon daydreaming about how great life would have been if only you had married Billy? Remember, there's a reason you didn't marry Billy, and you committed your life before God to your husband. Stop the greener-grass comparisons. Repent of your emotional attachment, and thank God for the husband He has given you.

Guard your heart above all else. In doing so, you are guarding your marriage and protecting your sexual integrity.

The Heart: The Master Panel

One of the coolest features in my minivan is the "magic mom panel" on the driver's door. From my seat, I can control almost the entire vehicle. I can lock every door, open every window, and even prevent my passengers from controlling their own doors and windows.

Guarding your heart is like that panel in my van. Your heart is the master panel for all the rest of your doors. As you guard your heart above all else, the rest of your life will be guarded as well.

LESSON 22 WIFE-CHANGING QUESTIONS

1. Define the meaning of each boundary.
   Covenantal Boundary:

   _____

   _____

   _____

   _____

   Legal Boundary (Governmental and Biblical):

   _____

   _____

   _____

   _____

   Harm Boundary:

   _____

   _____

   _____

   _____

Conscience Boundary:

_____

_____

_____

_____

2. Explain what the Scriptures say about guarding your heart.

_____

_____

_____

_____

3. Do you have any emotional attachment to a man who is not your husband? If so, what is God calling you to do about this?

_____

_____

_____

_____

4. What specific wife-changes can you make to better guard your own heart?

_____

_____

_____

_____

LESSON 23

The Verbal Door

The words that come out of our mouths are directly connected to our hearts. Scripture gives a few examples:

> For out of the abundance of the heart the mouth speaks. (Matt. 12:34)

> For we all stumble in many ways. And if anyone does not stumble in what he says, he is a perfect man, able also to bridle his whole body. If we put bits into the mouths of horses so that they obey us, we guide their whole bodies as well. Look at the ships also: though they are so large and are driven by strong winds, they are guided by a very small rudder wherever the will of the pilot directs. So also the tongue is a small member, yet it boasts of great things. How great a forest is set ablaze by such a small fire! (James 3:2–5)

Our words have the power to control our lives, either to direct us and others in godliness or to direct us and others into destruction. How we use our words directly connects to our sexual integrity.

Verbal Modesty

When we think of modesty, we nearly always think about a woman covering her body so as not to attract attention to herself. While modesty certainly pertains to outward appearances, it also needs to be applied to our words. The word "modesty" is defined as "behavior, manner, or appearance intended to avoid impropriety or indecency."

Modesty, for the Christian, entails a sense of humility before God.

Between my mother and my grandmother, I grew up with constant lessons on what was "ladylike." I can still clearly hear their voices saying things like, "Ladies don't burp out loud," "Ladies cross their ankles when they sit," or "Ladies don't wipe their mouths on their arms." However, the phrase I heard the most from my matriarchs was, "Ladies don't talk like that."

"Ladylike" speech was of utmost importance in my upbringing. Profanity, slang, tart comebacks, boasting, and gossip were major offenses. "Ladies don't talk like that." It was just assumed every female should want to be a lady.

The Bible promotes the idea of verbal modesty as well:

> But now you must put them all away: anger, wrath, malice, slander, and obscene talk from your mouth. (Col. 3:8)

Let no corrupting talk come out of your mouths, but only such as is good for building up, as fits the occasion, that it may give grace to those who hear. (Eph. 4:29)

She opens her mouth with wisdom, and the teaching of kindness is on her tongue. (Prov. 31:26)

Put away from you crooked speech, and put devious talk far from you. (Prov. 4:24)

Let the words of my mouth and the meditation of my heart be acceptable in Your sight, O Lord, my rock and my redeemer. (Ps. 19:14)

The fear of the Lord is hatred of evil. Pride and arrogance and the way of evil and perverted speech I hate. (Prov. 8:13)

It is not what goes into the mouth that defiles a person, but what comes out of the mouth; this defiles a person. (Matt. 15:11)

This is just a small sampling of the scriptural instruction regarding our words. Verbal modesty is a huge issue to God, and therefore, it should be important to us.

Verbal Faithfulness

Be faithful to your husband not only physically, but verbally as well. Verbally bonding in any way with someone other than your husband is dangerous and destructive. You might say, "Well, my husband is Mr. Silent! He doesn't talk to me!" Dear Sister, find a girlfriend to talk to. You have no business verbally bonding with any man other than your very own Mr. Silent. If you need a man to listen to you, get on your knees and pour out your heart to God, who is not only willing, but is waiting for you to do so.

Flirting Is Verbal Immodesty

Olivia is training for a half marathon and runs in her neighborhood every morning. Jack lives two streets over and often waves to her as she's running by. A few weeks ago, he called out, "Is someone chasing you every morning? You're so fast!"

She huffed back, "Ha! No!"

To which he replied, "I'd like to chase you!"

The compliment gave her an instant rush. Rather than let it go, Olivia called behind her, "You should try!"

The whole rest of the day, she thought about Jack and how her own husband would never say something like that to her. The next morning, she put on a little makeup and her cutest running outfit before she headed out the door.

Flirting is often seen as harmless fun. It gives us an ego boost when someone pays us a compliment or lets us know they find us attractive. You can't help someone saying something to you, but you can certainly control your own responses.

There is a difference between giving and receiving compliments and flirting. If a man says, "You did a great job on that presentation," or you tell a co-worker, "I like the color of your shirt," that's not necessarily flirting. It's fine to give and receive verbal praise.

However, we are wise to guard against giving praise to a man in a way that communicates attraction, such as "You have a really great jawline," or, "I wish my husband's voice sounded more like yours." It is never appropriate to engage in flirting with anyone other than your husband. Flirting or sexual talk in any form is opening the door to an inappropriate relationship that could destroy your marriage. Save your sassy, cute, or suggestive comments for your own husband. A great response to a flirtatious comment is, "I'll tell my husband you think so!"

Cyberspace Counts

Typed or texted words to another man are still unguarded words. There is an epidemic in the church today with people carrying on emotional affairs via email, social media, texting, and various other avenues using technology. There are even sites dedicated to helping people cheat on each other. In fact, several surveys show many people don't think internet relationships are actually cheating because couples aren't meeting in person. There is less guilt involved, and people justify it as a "safe" alternative to actually cheating on their spouse. The fact that they are looking for an "alternative" at all should be deeply concerning.

> My high school boyfriend, Ben, started sending me private messages on social media. At first, it was just reminiscing about old times, but that quickly led to him telling me he still had feelings for me even though he was married too. The feeling of being wanted was exhilarating. We started messaging and sending photos to one another every day. I felt justified in talking to Ben because I felt ignored and unappreciated by my husband. After a few weeks, we started planning a secret meeting. I think we would have started a physical affair if Ben's wife hadn't found our messages and called my husband. I was angry and defensive at first. That quickly turned to shame. I almost lost my family and ruined

another marriage because I didn't protect myself against an emotional attachment to another man. —Sydney

An online relationship is just a gateway to a physically adulterous one, just like an emotional affair leads to a physical one. Christian ladies don't talk, type, or text like that. Be a Christian lady. In every possible form, be a woman who keeps her verbal door locked.

A Sacred Circle

I remember that when I got back from my honeymoon, I was really embarrassed to go to church because I knew everyone would know I had been having sex for the last ten days. People kept asking me, "How was your honeymoon?" I couldn't stop blushing, because even though we did occasionally leave our hotel room to enjoy the scenery and food, we spent much of our time enjoying one another's bodies. It's not like I could look at the church ladies and casually say, "Well, the sex was fantastic! I just couldn't get enough!"

Your intimate life with your husband is absolutely sacred. It is a gift meant to be shared by only the two of you and kept entirely between you for your whole lives.

Sadly, I have heard girls talking with their friends so casually about their sex lives:

"Oh, Billy wants sex every morning before he goes to work."

"Tom can only last three minutes before he finishes. I'm sick of it."

"If I never had sex with Josh again, I wouldn't miss it one bit."

"Rick is so good at oral sex, I beg him for it all the time."

So guess what happens when these friends see Billy and Tom and Josh and Rick? They think Billy is a sex addict, Tom is selfish and immature, Josh is a terrible lover, and they'd like to experience what Rick can do.

Mrs. Billy, Mrs. Tom, Mrs. Josh, and Mrs. Rick have dishonored their husbands by casually inviting their friends into their own sacred circles. These wives have made their husbands to be seen in negative ways or have possibly caused their friends to stumble.

How would you feel if your husband told his friends he'd be happier with his sex life if you had bigger breasts? What if he told his Bible study group to pray for you because you are never in the mood, or what if he shared with his buddies that you are really good at some particular sex act? You'd be horrified, angry, and embarrassed, right?

Do not share any specific details with anyone about what goes on in your intimate life. It is sometimes appropriate to make generalized references to being intimate, but it is not necessary to offer any detailed information about what goes on in your sacred circle.

Your husband should be absolutely certain you will protect his reputation, guard his shortcomings, and safeguard his secrets.

There are exceptions to this of course. In counseling other women, I have occasionally shared a personal experience that may help a bride in her own marriage. I usually ask Brent's permission to share whatever might be beneficial for someone to hear. However, even in those situations, I will attempt to generalize things as much as possible.

If there is something going on in your intimate life you need counsel about, then sharing details with a counselor might be necessary. There are a few guidelines to asking for counsel on sexual matters:

- Only seek advice from a trusted friend or counselor who can counsel wisely and biblically.
- Speak with your doctor, but make sure the counsel he/she gives you is in line with the Scriptures.
- Avoid asking for counsel on sexual matters from someone who is newly married, as the voice of experience is usually much wiser than the voice of youth.
- Make sure if you do ask for counsel, you are doing so in order to benefit your marriage and out of love for your husband.
- Let your husband know of your plans to ask for counsel before you seek it.

Any form of verbal immodesty is sin. If you are guilty, then repent. Determine before the Lord to have no form of verbal immodesty on your lips. Be a woman who safely guards her verbal door.

Some of the most wonderful times, hilarious moments, and deepest struggles of our marriage have taken place in my sacred circle with my beloved. We have some great stories—but they're our secrets. Make your own sacred-circle stories and keep them secret.

The Physical Door

If you ever watch cooking shows, they'll tell you "presentation is everything." Celebrity cooks will then prove their point as they bring out a magnificent castle made out of kale and goat cheese—it's all about the presentation!

The same goes with garage sales. Most people look forward to sleeping in on Saturday morning, but I get up before the sun to go looking through other people's junk with my friend. We follow the signs and slow down in front of the sale. If there's a few boxes with junk spilling out of them and clothes thrown on a plastic tarp on the lawn, we're not stopping. We say that sale is "not stop-worthy." However, if the people have taken the time to make a neat little store in their driveway, we park and get out. Presentation is everything.

Likewise, how we present our bodies to the world around us matters far more than food or sales presentations. The two sides of the physical door are the way we dress and our bodily contact with others.

Modest in Dress

Can people tell that you are a godly woman by the clothes you wear? Or do they think you are *not* a godly woman by the clothes you wear?

Here is the rule when it comes to getting dressed: love your neighbor. Yes, love your neighbor.

Consider this. Most men are visually stimulated, and your Christian brothers are in a desperate battle to honor the Lord and their wives by not looking lustfully at women. In light of this, if you insist on wearing seductive clothes with the intention of making men desire you sexually, are you behaving lovingly or selfishly?

I have heard girls argue, "Well, this is what I'm comfortable wearing, and if men have lust problems, then that's their problem! They need to learn to control themselves." It is sin for you to knowingly cause your brothers to stumble. You are having your ego stroked by someone else's sin, and you need to repent.

> Likewise, I want women to adorn themselves with proper clothing, modestly and discreetly. (1 Tim. 2:9)

Rules regarding length and style can be helpful, but they can also be blurry lines that depend on culture, occasion, and body type. Style boundaries don't necessarily deal with a woman's heart to love those around her. You can wear a tent and be immodest in it. Modesty is a really a matter of the heart.

Sisters, love your neighbor. *Choose to die to yourself* and find stylish clothes that honor the Lord. Wear clothes that are proper, modest, and discreet.

Modest in Photos

I am shocked by some of the social-media photos I see of church ladies. Provocative bikini shots, sexy workout pictures, and images taken in the bathtub have been posted by the same girls sitting in women's Bible study. These ladies took spicy photos of themselves on their cell phones (usually dozens at a time because a good selfie takes work!), cropped and filtered the best shot, thought of a cute caption, and then put it out there for all the world to see. For what purpose? Was there any consideration of loving their neighbor or glorifying God in their provocative selfie posting? Perhaps it is done in ignorance and innocence, but it is likely an effort to get likes and comments about how sexy they are.

Men in our churches don't have to go looking for internet porn. They can get an eyeful of their Christian sisters' almost-naked bodies by scrolling through social media. Oh, foolish women! Let's love our neighbors by striving for modesty, both in person and in photos.

Let It Go? No!

My husband has counseled several men who married women who did their hair, wore makeup, dressed nicely, and took care of themselves, and now she's um . . . different. Modesty does not equal sloppy, frumpy, or out of style. You can stay with current styles and take care of your appearance, no matter your age or how long you've been married.

Ladies, just as we need to dress modestly, we also need to maintain our appearance as much as we can. There is only one man in the world you need to please with your clothes and your hair and your underwear—the one you married. Some of you may be married to a guy who wouldn't notice if you wore a lime-green muumuu every day and shaved your head bald.

Some of you, like me, are married to a guy with very specific tastes and preferences. Brent likes my hair long and he dislikes ponytails. He prefers me in dresses and skirts, so that's the look I go for. Your husband may prefer you to not wear makeup and thinks you're stunning in yoga pants and a messy bun.

Cater to your husband's preferences as much as you can. Your heart should be to please your husband with your appearance. He is likely surrounded by women in the world who look good, smell good, and take care of themselves. Let him come home to one of them.

Are you continually working toward looking your best? Have you let things slide in the area of your appearance? Don't surrender. Your naked body is the only one your husband gets to see. Your clothed body is how you present yourself to the world, and it reflects on your husband (and your Savior). Keep it up!

Wear makeup if you need it, invest in a good hairstyle, and update your wardrobe occasionally. Spend as much time getting ready to see your husband as you do when you're going out with your friends. Don't surrender to the temptation to give up on your body. Keep exercising. Be careful with what you eat. Do the best with what you have. Don't let it go.

Physical Contact with Other Men

Keeping the physical door locked isn't just about what we wear or how we look. There are appropriate ways we can physically touch people, and there are inappropriate ways of touching as well.

Let's talk about hugging. Hugs are great. Be generous with them. But when it comes to men who aren't your husband, daddy, biological brothers, sons, or grandsons, full-body hugs are not appropriate. If a hug is in order, use a "Christian brother side hug." You can easily turn your body to the side and put your arm around his shoulder. This still counts as a hug, but is clearly platonic.

Now I know there are exceptions to this. I know you might come from a "kiss on the lips" family, or Uncle Ernie has given you a bear hug since you were born, but the idea is you need to reserve any type of real physical affection for your immediate family only.

Avoid Appearances of Evil

First Thessalonians 5:22 tells us to *"abstain from all appearance of evil."* This simply means we need to protect our reputations. If you can help it, be careful not to give people a perception that you are doing something sinful.

It is wise to have a standing rule that you are never alone with a member of the opposite sex unless he is part of your immediate family. The pastors of our church do not counsel women alone in their offices with the door shut. They either bring another person into their office before they shut the door, or the door stays wide open.

If you work in a school or office, you can adopt this same policy: do not close the door unless there is another person in the room, or, if the office has windows, make sure the blinds are up so everyone can see there is nothing but business going on in there.

This can also go with being alone in a car with a man. In our house, this has been tricky with driving teenagers home. But what would you think if you saw Pastor Brent driving in his truck at midnight alone with a seventeen-year-old girl? He may just be taking my daughter's friend home, but you don't know that, so that's why he will always have another kid in the car with him. It protects his reputation and also guards the kids.

> Whenever we had a teenage girl babysit for us, my husband never picked her up or took her home. I did both. When my own daughter started babysitting, we adopted the same guidelines. Some people were offended at first, but when we explained it protected them as well as our daughter, they were appreciative. —Tiffany

This does not mean that we need to constantly be worried about what everyone else is thinking. That could make us crazy. Misunderstandings will happen; however, there are certain things we can do to lock our doors and protect ourselves and others against misperceptions. This is not only a gift to our husbands, but an offering to the Lord.

LESSON 23 WIFE-CHANGING QUESTIONS

1. What is verbal modesty?

   _____

   _____

   _____

   _____

2. Are you guilty of flirting or any other kind of verbal immodesty? If so, what wife-changes is God calling you to make?

   _____

   _____

   _____

   _____

3. What does it mean to guard your sacred circle?

   _____

   _____

   _____

   _____

4. How should a woman who professes Christ dress?

_____

_____

_____

_____

5. Is there anything you need to change about the way you dress or present yourself to the world?

_____

_____

_____

_____

6. Is there anything you need to work on to improve your appearance?

_____

_____

_____

_____

7. Was there anything else in this chapter that challenged or ministered to you?

_____

_____

_____

_____

LESSON 24

The Mental Door

Have you ever thrown something in the wash that had Velcro on it? If the scratchy side of the Velcro isn't stuck to the soft side when it goes into the dryer, then it gets stuck to every piece of clothing as it spins around. It really sticks, and it's very hard to pull that stuff off!

Our minds are a lot like Velcro because we just grab on to stuff, whether we want to or not, and once something is stuck in our minds, it's very hard to remove it.

As a married woman, your only sexual thoughts should be about your husband. There is no room for entertaining sexual thoughts about anything or anyone else. Finding any source of mental sexual excitement apart from your husband is a breach of your sexual integrity.

Pornography Is Sin

Most of the time when we think of porn, we think of men who browse the internet, watch movies, or leaf through magazines. Sadly, there is an increasing number of women who are getting themselves into the bondage of pornography. Statistically, it is not the image-type of pornography that is ensnaring women. Women tend to be less visually stimulated and are typically more aroused by racy story lines.

However, there is plenty of female-friendly pornography all around us. You can go into any retail store in America and pick up a "romance" novel. These steamy stories are pornography for women because the sexually charged story lines cause women to fantasize. Women can be addicted to these erotic story lines as strongly as men can be addicted to internet porn.

The same can be said about nighttime TV or daytime soap operas. These hour-long dramas are usually full of fornication and adultery. One study showed that 75% of the sexual situations shown on television are between unmarried people! Sex in today's society is only sexy if it is somehow rebellious or forbidden. What can be less forbidden or rebellious than sex between a married couple who are committed to only be with each other for the rest of their lives? Married sex just doesn't increase ratings.

Women won't always browse internet porn, but they will visit blogs or websites or read articles that offer sexual "advice" and spell out erotic story lines.

Sexually charged magazine articles are often all there is for reading material at the hair salon. This is all a sneaky form of pornography.

Do not think you can read or watch these things and not have them affect you. It's like Velcro—it sticks. Filling your mind with racy movies, songs, romance novels, TV, and sexually charged articles will leave you in a state of being constantly unsatisfied and frustrated with your own reality. When you are having sex with your husband, your mind will likely think back to that steamy scene in the show you watched an hour ago, and you may find that far more exciting than the guy whose dirty socks you just picked up off the floor.

> *Turn my eyes from looking at worthless things*; and give me life in Your ways. (Ps. 119:37, emphasis added)

We can't escape every sexual thing in this culture, because it's everywhere, and it's not going to get better. However, we can choose not to participate. We do have control over what we allow to stick in our minds. We can choose to raise the standard of holiness and not make versions of pornography our form of entertainment.

Every word you read, every conversation you have, every show you watch, every book or article you read, and every image you look at has the potential to stick in your mind. Therefore, guard your mental door against anything that is not holy or wholesome, and you will be able to walk in the light, knowing your integrity is secure.

> Do not be conformed to this world, but be transformed by the renewal of your mind, that by testing you may discern what is the will of God, what is good and acceptable and perfect. (Rom. 12:2)

Perhaps some of you may have husbands who have been into some type of pornography during your marriage. I have also heard of couples watching pornography together as a type of foreplay. Any type of pornography in your marriage is offensive to God and is detrimental to your marriage. It is not something you should participate in or tolerate. Pornography is a type of adultery and can destroy your marriage.

If your husband is involved in this practice, you need to first cover the matter in prayer and then talk to him about it. Begin by explaining to your husband that using pornography is not a victimless act. Tell him you are deeply hurt by his actions.

Then prayerfully seek to get help for him and for yourself. Accountability is often essential in having victory over this area of bondage. Go to your pastor or a trusted, biblically solid friend. If you are in the midst of this trial in your life, there is help for you, and there is tremendous hope for your husband to live in the light of purity and holiness through the process of repentance and restoration.

There is more encouragement for you on this subject on the Free Resources page at nancykaser.com.

Mental Adultery

Many women imagine sexual situations with other men in order to become more aroused with their husbands. Sexual fantasizing is a trap and a lie from the enemy. When you think about something or someone other than your husband when you are intimate with him, you are mentally bringing someone or something else into your marriage bed. If you are in the habit of fantasizing, confess this sin to the Lord and begin to retrain your mind to focus on only what is happening in your own bed with your own husband.

Flying Solo

Because the marriage bed is undefiled, if you are enjoying an intimate encounter with your husband and either of you stimulates yourselves while you are together, doing so is not sinful. Your pleasure is being mutually enjoyed and can be encouraged. This is not selfish sex.

However, if your husband has left for work and you suddenly have a sexual inclination, you are in sin if you decide to give yourself an orgasm instead of exercising self-control until he gets home and can be intimate with you. As a married woman, your only outlet for sexual release is your husband. *If he is not available, then you need to exercise self-control.*

Masturbation is an issue we don't often talk about in church. The Bible does not expressly forbid masturbation; therefore, we can't dogmatically state the practice itself is sinful. However, when a woman or a man masturbates, the thoughts that accompany the act are generally not pure, noble, or praiseworthy—and the Bible is very clear about our thoughts being accountable to God (Phil. 4:8). Masturbation and fantasy are usually inseparable, and some unholy fantasy, scenario, or ritual is played out in the mind in order to reach orgasm. This is why masturbation is done in secret and is typically followed by guilt.

Choose to be sanctified—set apart entirely for holiness—when it comes to your sexuality.

> This is the will of God, your sanctification: that you abstain from sexual immorality; that each one of you know how to control his own body in holiness and honor, not in the passion of lust like the Gentiles who do not know God. (1 Thess. 4:3–5)

For every orgasm a woman gives herself, she robs herself of an intimate encounter with her husband. Women who have habitually masturbated are often unable to reach orgasm with their husbands because they have trained their bodies to respond to the fantasy in their minds rather than the reality in their beds.

Self-stimulation can be addictive and very difficult to stop. The only way to kill a bad habit is to starve it to death. If you are trying to break free from this habit, remove anything sexual from your life that is not your husband. He is to be your only source of excitement. Resolve to not have an orgasm without him.

> Your body is the temple of the Holy Spirit who is in you, whom you have from God, and you are not your own. (1 Cor. 6:19)

Unforeseen Mental Attacks

Mental attacks can come in many disguises, and if you aren't being careful to lock your mental door, you can suddenly find yourself in dangerous situations, such as:

- When the handsome guy in the grocery store flirts with you in the produce aisle and your thoughts turn to wishing maybe you had met him before you got married.
- The newly divorced neighbor who is extra attentive while your husband is on a business trip. The ego boost is exhilarating, and suddenly you're thinking, *What if my husband died? Would my neighbor be interested in me? Or, He really needs a friend. Maybe I'll bake him a batch of cookies. I'm sure he is starved for home cooking.* And poof! The mental door is unlocked and open.
- What about fantasizing about your next husband? You know, after the tragic accident that will take your current inconsiderate husband out of the picture. After you mourn for a year or so, maybe that really hot usher at church will finally make his move, and he'll treat you better than your late husband ever did, and he will be a great father to your kids, and the sex will be incredible . . .

Thinking about old boyfriends, coworkers or neighbors, fantasy men, or our next husbands causes us to mentally violate our marriage vows and undermines God's plan to grant us sexual and emotional fulfillment with our own husbands. We need to make a covenant with our mind not to look at other people (real or imagined) to fulfill our emotional needs and desires in ways that compromise our sexual integrity. Those thoughts *must* be taken captive.

We destroy arguments and every lofty opinion raised against the knowledge of God, and take every thought captive to obey Christ. (2 Cor. 10:5)

While riding down the road, if some billboard or marquee puts a desire into my mind for some illegitimate sexual pleasure, I take that desire and say, "Jesus, you are my Lord and my God, and my greatest desire is to know and love and obey you, so this desire is really for you. I take it from your competitor, I purge it, and I direct it to you. Thank you for freeing me from the bondage of sin." It is remarkable what control we can gain over the direction our desires take, if we really long to please Christ.[1] —John Piper

Above all else, your motivation is to please God with your sexuality. Put all your attention into one relationship—the one you have with your own husband. Focus on your marriage wholeheartedly. Assume your husband is the man you will grow old with. Make no allowances for mental attachments to other men. Lock your mental door.

Locked Doors Create Open Doors

So there we have our four doors that consist of:

- Our heart that we are "to guard above all else, because it is the wellspring of life." (Prov. 4:23)
- Our words that flow "out of the abundance of the heart." (Matt. 12:34)
- Our bodies that are to be modestly dressed and treated as a "temple of the Holy Spirit" that belongs only to our husbands. (1 Cor. 6:19)
- Our minds, where we are to "take every thought captive to obey of Christ." (2 Cor. 10:5)

I realize a section like this can seem like a long list of rules about what Christian women should and shouldn't do. I suppose it is. However, it's not the rules that motivate us to guard our lives. It is the love of Christ that compels us to love the world around us and to glorify God as much as possible so we have no hindrances in our marriages or our witness. When we guard the doors of sexuality, we ensure that every possible door to a God-glorifying marriage and a Christ-representing witness to the world remain open. Locked doors create open doors.

LESSON 24 WIFE-CHANGING QUESTIONS

1. Are you guilty of looking to anything besides your husband to meet or enhance your sexual desires?

_____

_____

_____

_____

2. What can you do to better guard your mental door?

_____

_____

_____

_____

3. What is your specific plan of action when you realize a door has become unlocked?

_____

_____

_____

_____

LESSON 25

Acknowledge, Ask, Alleluia!

Perhaps as you have read this chapter, you have recognized that you are guilty of some form of sin. As we finish this section, we'll look at the story of how one man recognized his own sexual sin and got back into a right standing with God.

Psalm 51 was written by King David as a song of repentance after he had been confronted with his sin.

David had hundreds of wives and concubines. One day he was walking on the roof of his house and saw Bathsheba taking a bath on her rooftop. Bathsheba was married to Uriah, a soldier who was off fighting a war for David. David found Bathsheba irresistible, sent for her, and she came to the palace. They committed adultery, and Bathsheba got pregnant.

When Bathsheba told David she was expecting, David realized he had to cover up his sin because her husband hadn't been around to get her pregnant. He sent for Uriah and told him, "You've been working hard in the fight. Go home and enjoy your wife for a while."

However, Uriah's devotion to the king was so great that he refused to go home to his wife. Eventually, David sent a letter to the captain of the army and had Uriah put in the front of the line of battle to ensure Uriah's death so that the adulterous affair wouldn't be discovered.

David thought he'd gotten away with this whole thing, sent for Bathsheba, and made her his wife. On the outside, the whole mess was all cleaned up and David appeared to be a hero for taking in this widow. The prophet Nathan came in and let David know that God had seen everything and that David hadn't gotten away with anything. David was busted.

It is at this moment that David wrote Psalm 51, which gives us a model of how to approach God with our sin and shame, and how to walk away knowing we are clean and restored.

> *Have mercy on me, O God,* according to Your steadfast love; according to Your abundant mercy blot out my transgressions. Wash me thoroughly from my iniquity, and cleanse me from my sin! For I know my transgressions, and my sin is ever before me. Against You, You only, have I sinned and done what is evil in Your sight, so that you may be justified in Your words and blameless in Your judgment. Behold, I was brought forth in iniquity, and in sin did my mother conceive me. (Ps. 51:1–5)

David acknowledges he has sinned, and he asks for God's mercy. He doesn't minimize his actions, blame someone else, or make excuses.

The light of truth is bright. If it has revealed any areas of sexual sin in your heart or life, your next step is to present yourself to the Lord and acknowledge your sin. Come before Him and hold your sin up to the light and confess it to Him.

In verses 6–12, David continues:

> Behold, You delight in truth in the inward being, and You teach me wisdom in the secret heart. Purge me with hyssop, and I shall be clean; wash me, and I shall be whiter than snow. Let me hear joy and gladness; let the bones that You have broken rejoice. Hide Your face from my sins, and blot out all my iniquities. Create in me a clean heart, O God, and renew a right spirit within me. Cast me not away from Your presence, and take not Your Holy Spirit from me. Restore to me the joy of Your salvation, and uphold me with a willing spirit.

David asks for what he knows God wants to give him:

- truth in the inward parts,
- wisdom in the hidden parts of his heart,
- to be washed and made clean, and
- to have a clean heart and a steadfast spirit.

Ladies, it is God's will for you to have these things, for you to be delivered from your sin and to walk before Him with a pure, clean heart. After you acknowledge your sin to God, ask Him to make you clean.

After his acknowledgment and asking for forgiveness, David worships God in verses 13–17:

> Then I will teach transgressors Your ways, and sinners will return to You. Deliver me from bloodguiltiness, O God, O God of my salvation, and my tongue will sing aloud of Your righteousness. O Lord, open my lips, and my mouth will declare Your praise. For You will not delight in sacrifice, or I would give it; You will not be pleased with a burnt offering. The sacrifices of God are a broken spirit; a broken and contrite heart, O God, You will not despise.

Knowing God has heard his prayer and granted his requests, David starts praising the Lord because he knows God has forgiven him; therefore, he can stand before the Lord clean again.

In effect, David says, "God, I know I don't have to go to the temple and make sacrifices and burnt offerings to You to make up for this horrible sin. I can't pay for this myself. If I could, I would. But I know You delight in my broken and contrite heart, and You take that as my sacrifice." Finally, in the rest of the Psalm, David says he's going to make a burnt offering anyway, just to worship the Lord.

"*When we confess our sins, God* "*is faithful and just to forgive us our sins and to cleanse us from all unrighteousness*" (1 John 1:9). When you acknowledge your sin before the Lord and you ask to be forgiven and cleansed, you can walk away praising the Lord, knowing your request has been received and granted.

God has made it so simple. Sometimes we think we have to stay really guilt-ridden and sorry to punish ourselves for our sin, that God will only really forgive us if we sufficiently beat ourselves up to show Him we really mean it. Friends, God knows your heart, and He is faithful to His Word. Once you have acknowledged your sin and asked for His forgiveness, you can say, "Alleluia!" because you know you are forgiven!

"Acknowledge, ask, alleluia" is the recipe for repentance and restoration.

LESSON 25 WIFE-CHANGING QUESTIONS

As you have read this chapter, are there any sin issues you recognize you need to repent from? If so, don't wait! Repent, and write out prayers right here, following David's example of repentance.

Acknowledge:

_____

_____

_____

_____

Ask:

_____

_____

_____

_____

Alleluia:

_____

_____

_____

_____

INCREASE

LESSON 26

In chapter one, we paralleled marriage to a house. We began by laying a foundation in the Word of God, yielding to the authority of Scripture. Then we moved through four different chapters focusing on different principles of being a godly wife. These principles of Help, Smile, Order, and Gift are the pillars of your marriage.

Get ready to raise the roof!

Increase

> increase—*verb.* To make something greater or grow in size or value.
> *She wants to increase her taco consumption.*
> increase—*noun.* An instance of making greater or growing.
> *Taco consumption will result in an increase in her dress size.*

When you *increase* Jesus in your life, there will be an *increase* in His glory, and as a result, you will gain an *increase* of blessings. When you make much of Jesus, you consequently decrease yourself. The process of sanctification—being conformed into the image of Christ—is a lifelong process of decreasing self and increasing Jesus.

Reflecting the Gospel in Your Marriage

Christian marriages should be declaring to the world, "Look! We are different because we have obeyed God's design for marriage, and it's glorious!" The world should look at our marriages and see the power of the gospel displayed in them. Think about the Christian couples you know. How many of them fit this description of marriage? Sadly, we are often hard-pressed to find a handful of gospel-declaring marriages even in our own churches.

> For this cause shall a man leave his father and mother, and shall be joined unto his wife, and they two shall be one flesh. This is a great mystery: but I speak concerning Christ and the church.
>
> (Eph. 5:31–32)

The joining of a husband and wife contains a meaning far deeper than what we see on the surface. God created man and woman with an illustration in mind. Marriage is intentionally patterned after the relationship between His Son and the church. Saying marriage is a "mystery" doesn't mean it is difficult to figure out; rather, it means it was formerly unclear, but now it has been explained. Marriage began as a shadow of what was to come, and now it is clear through the example of Christ and the church.

As married women, the thought that we are granted the privilege to display divine realities should fill us with wonder and reverence. How humbling to think we are chosen by God to reflect something so marvelous to the world!

Every marriage doesn't automatically display this mystery. Ephesians 5 gives us clear directions about how a husband and wife can consciously aim to illustrate this mystery to the world:

> Wives, be subject to your husbands, as to the Lord. For the husband is the head of the wife as Christ is the head of the church, his body, and is himself its Savior. As the church is subject to Christ, so let wives also be subject in everything to their husbands. (Eph. 5:22–24)

According to the divine pattern, wives are to take their unique role from the example of the church, as "the husband is the head of the wife as Christ is the head of the church." The church submits to Christ as her head. Jesus loves the church supremely, and (if choosing obedience) the church submits to and obeys Christ. As the church submits to Christ, so wives are to submit to their husbands.

Headship, in God's design, is not tyranny, but Christlike sacrificial giving. A Christian husband is directed to pour himself out for his family the way Jesus pours Himself out for the church. If the husband is the head of the wife as verse 23 says, this means he is to lead with a selfless love that is willing to die to give her life. John Piper says,

> "Christ bound Himself with a towel and washed the apostles' feet. If you want to be a Christian husband, copy Jesus, not Jabba the Hutt."[1]

Of course, none of us model this illustration perfectly. We are still flawed, selfish, sinful creatures, and we habitually lose sight of this illustration. Even so, we must regain our focus on the divine picture and intentionally aim to reflect it more clearly.

A Temporary Illustration

As important as earthly marriages are, they are temporary institutions. When we get to heaven, this illustration will no longer be necessary. The picture will be complete. The groom will have His bride, and that union will be entirely perfect. In his book *Heaven*, Randy Alcorn says,

> In heaven there will be one marriage, not many. That marriage will be what earthly marriage symbolized and pointed to, the marriage of Christ to His bride. So we will all be married—but to Christ. The one-flesh marital union we know on Earth is a signpost pointing to our relationship with Christ as our Bridegroom. Once we reach the destination, the signpost becomes unnecessary. That one marriage, our marriage to Christ, will be so completely satisfying that even the most wonderful earthly marriage couldn't be as fulfilling. Earthly marriage is a shadow, a copy, an echo of the true and ultimate marriage. Once that ultimate marriage begins, at the Lamb's Wedding Feast, all the human marriages that pointed to it will have served their noble purpose and will be assimilated into the one great marriage they foreshadowed. The purpose of marriage is not to replace heaven, but to prepare us for it.[2]

Marriage Is a Gospel Tract

> People need to see God in you, as you love your spouse. The world desperately needs to see an accurate reflection of Christ and the church in our marriages, because this is about God's glory! We need a fundamental

shift in our thinking about what is at stake in the way we live our lives and the way we live out our marriages.[3] —Lisa Chan

My friend Trisha is an amazing evangelist. She has devoted her entire life to sharing the gospel with anyone she meets. She has equipped thousands with tools to effectively share the gospel with the lost. One of the things I have learned from Trisha is to always have gospel tracts with me and to look for opportunities to pass them out to people. We pass them out in the fast-food window, to people in line at the grocery store, to the package delivery people, and we sneak them into office waiting rooms. Those little folded papers have been used countless times to clearly spell out the good news of salvation through the cross of Christ to anyone who chooses to read them. My grandfather was actually born again because of a gospel tract.

Your marriage should be a living gospel tract, advertising the redeeming power of the cross to people who are looking on. What message is your marriage sending to those who are "reading" your life? People are watching to see if being a Christian makes a difference. If your marriage follows the biblical pattern, the gospel will be seen by the world. Conversely, if your marriage is a mess, then it's not just your marriage that is messy, but you are tarnishing the beauty of the gospel.

When Rob and Heidi lived as missionaries in a Sudanese refugee camp, they found evangelism difficult. The people were firmly set in their cultural belief system and resisted anything that had to do with Jesus. As the months passed, Rob and Heidi prayed for a way to unlock the doors keeping so many Sudanese from the truth.

One day, Heidi had spent the entire morning at the river washing her family's clothes. (If you've never had to wash your clothes in a river, trust me—it's a lot of work!) She had just finished hanging their clothes on a line in front of their hut when it started to rain. The unexpected torrential downpour would surely knock all the clothes off the line and onto the muddy ground below. Heidi ran out with a basket, as did all the Sudanese women who had done laundry that morning, and started frantically pulling the clothes off the line. Rob helped her, and even ran to help other women in the camp to salvage what they could.

The next day, a group of women were standing outside Heidi's hut. "Why does your husband help you with the laundry? Our husbands would never help us. Laundry is women's work. What can we do to make our husbands help us?"

Heidi had the open door she and her husband had prayed for. She shared with them that Rob acts like her God. The Christian God sacrificed Himself for others and demonstrated it on the cross, and people who follow the Christian God end up becoming more like Him. That began an incredible work of God in the refugee camp. Because of the picture their marriage displayed among those people, thousands have come to Christ in that region.

Diane and Jay have their own construction business. She runs the office, and he oversees the jobs. Their company is presented as a "Christian Family Business" to their customers in their advertising.

However, their employees see a very different side of this "Christian family." There are almost daily fights in the office between them, and when they are away from each other, disrespectful, unkind remarks about the other are made in front of their employees.

The bitterness and contention between the bosses makes for a very tense work environment. The staff views them as complete hypocrites, and roll their eyes whenever Diane and Jay start talking about their faith, because obviously it isn't working for them, except maybe to fool a few customers into thinking they are good people.

Your Part of the Picture

Is your marriage an accurate reflection of the relationship between Christ and the church? You might say, "Well, it would be, except that my husband doesn't _____!" While it's true that a complete picture of the gospel requires both a husband and a wife living to glorify God, *you* are still responsible to glorify God in your marriage, independent of what your husband does.

Like I mentioned in chapter two, you can only be responsible for your own part in the illustration (your side of the sandwich). Be faithful to be the most accurate reflection of the church in the way you submit to and honor your husband.

The fact is, you have Jesus as your example of how to live in a one-sided marriage. Consider this: Jesus has chosen a very sinful, flawed church as His bride. He is disobeyed, disrespected, undermined, ignored, and rejected on a regular basis. The sacrificial love is often one-sided in the relationship Jesus has with His church. And what does Jesus do? He loves His bride, gives to her abundantly, serves her, sanctifies her, washes her, forgives her repeatedly, delights in her, and lavishes her with affection.

So if you're in a one-sided marriage, be like Jesus. Love your spouse unconditionally. Model for the world how Jesus, your bridegroom, has loved you in the way you love your husband.

> Let your light shine before others, so that they may see your good works and
> give glory to your Father who is in heaven. (Matt. 5:16)

Within your marriage—yes, the one you have today—you have an opportunity to display the gospel.

How is your own light shining in this world? Are people able to look at you and your marriage and decide that following Christ makes a difference?

If you are a true believer in Jesus, then you should absolutely stand out as being different from nonbelievers. Ephesians 2:1–7 tells us that, before we were saved, we were dead in our trespasses and sins, but once we put our faith in Christ, we were made alive:

> And you were dead in the trespasses and sins in which you once walked,
> following the course of this world, following the prince of the power of
> the air, the spirit that is now at work in the sons of disobedience— among
> whom we all once lived in the passions of our flesh, carrying out the desires
> of the body and the mind, and were by nature children of wrath, like the rest
> of mankind. But God, being rich in mercy, because of the great love with
> which He loved us, even when we were dead in our trespasses, made us alive
> together with Christ—by grace you have been saved— and raised us up
> with Him and seated us with Him in the heavenly places in Christ Jesus, so
> that in the coming ages He might show the immeasurable riches of His grace
> in kindness toward us in Christ Jesus.

Becoming a Christian doesn't just make us nicer than nonbelievers. It makes us living among the dead! Are you acting like someone who is living among the dead?

The Strategy to Possibly Win a Husband to Christ

Culturally speaking, when the New Testament was written, a woman was essentially seen as property. When these instructions were written to Christian wives, the culture was very different than American culture is today. If a woman came to faith in Christ, independent of her husband, the potential for conflict was huge. That is why nearly all of the Scriptures dealing with unequally yoked marriages address a believing wife's perspective— because the degree of difficulty was much greater for a Christian wife.

Though our culture is far different, there are still very real challenges and temptations that can come to a woman who becomes a believer or begins to take her walk with God seriously when her husband does not. Whether a wife becomes a Christian after she is already married, whether her husband claimed to be a Christian before they married and then denied his claim later, or whether the wife married him knowing he wasn't a follower of Jesus and hoped to convert him after the wedding, being married to a nonbelieving husband is a challenge that Christian women across the globe face.

A woman in this situation may face several obstacles. She may encounter intense persecution from her husband. He may challenge her intellectually, ridicule her emotionally, or physically forbid her from attending church. There may be challenges regarding how to raise the children or how to spend holidays, particularly if her husband wants to observe non-Christian religious holidays.

Conversely, a believing wife may feel superior to her husband. She can easily start condescending to her spiritually inferior husband and become attracted to other men who follow Jesus. These situations can lead to serious problems, and they are why the Scriptures warn against interfaith marriages.

The Bible warns that a believer should not be "yoked" to a nonbeliever. Being "unequally yoked" is a farming term. A yoke is a piece of wood that sits across the neck and shoulders of oxen while they plow a field or pull a cart. It is important to yoke two oxen that are the same size. Otherwise, the burden will be uneven on the animals, the yoke will rub raw spots on one of the animals, and the cart or plow will not be pulled straight. In connection with a marriage, being unequally yoked will result in tremendous burdens, raw spots, and crooked paths. If you have ever heard a woman married to an unbeliever share her heart, she will share that her husband's lack of faith permeates her entire life and causes her great grief.

So is it possible for a wife to live out God's design for marriage when her circumstances don't align with God's plan to begin with? *Yes.* God knew that women in this common situation would be tempted to flip out, flesh out, or move out. So in His kindness, He told us precisely what to do if we are married to an unbeliever:

> If any woman has a husband who is an unbeliever, and he consents to live with her, she should not divorce him. For the unbelieving husband is made holy because of his wife, and the unbelieving wife is made holy because of her husband. Otherwise your children would be unclean, but as it is, they are holy. (1 Cor. 7:13–14)

Saying her husband is "made holy" by his believing wife does not mean he is automatically saved simply because his wife is a Christian. We know each individual soul stands before God alone, and no one will be admitted into heaven on the basis of association. Remember, the word "holy" means "set apart." An unbelieving husband who lives with a Christian wife is set apart by his wife's influence. His home, his children, and his marriage are directly influenced by the godly conduct of his wife, and therefore, he is set apart and more likely to believe the gospel himself. Likewise, the children in an unequally yoked home are set apart—they are greatly influenced by their mother's faith.

Without a Word

There has likely never been an unbeliever who was nagged into the kingdom of God. Yet many a Christian wife fires a relentless verbal assault on her unbelieving husband, thinking if she just says the right thing, leaves the right Scripture on the mirror, or sighs heavily at the right time, then surely her husband will fall on his knees in repentance and start loving her as Christ loves the church.

But instead, the husband rebels against anything to do with his wife's faith, resents her church and what it has done to his wife, and he may even be pushed further toward the world.

The Bible does not tell a wife to preach at her unsaved husband. It doesn't tell her to argue with him, nor does it suggest a wife tape a Bible verse to every one of his beer cans, slip gospel tracts into his lunch every day, or go into his car and preset every station on the radio to the local Christian broadcast. There is not one scripturally endorsed or spiritualized form of manipulation that will be effective in winning a husband's soul.

So what's an unequally yoked wife to do?

She becomes a unique missionary:

> Likewise, wives, be subject to your own husbands, so that even if some do not obey the word, they may be won without a word by the conduct of their wives, when they see your respectful and pure conduct. (1 Peter 3:1-2)

A believing wife's mission field is to shine for Jesus in her marriage to her unbelieving husband. But this shining is not obnoxious or manipulative. The strategy the Bible provides is for that wife to conduct herself in a very specific way:

- Be subject (submissive) to her husband.
- Win him without words.
- Treat him respectfully.
- Conduct herself in purity.

The gentle submission and respectful, pure conduct of a born-again wife is the most powerful evangelistic tool she has. It's not what she says, but it is who she is that has the most influence on her husband. Without conversation and without harassment from the wife, but by her behavior—*this* is the God-given plan of reaching an unsaved husband. What an incredibly simple strategy! Simple, but certainly not easy.

If you are married to a nonbeliever, there is so much *hope* for you and for your husband. You are a missionary. God has uniquely placed you in the position to reach that unsaved man. Your marriage is evidence of God's hand on his life. Notice that the verse says, "Even if some do not obey the word, they *may* be won" (emphasis added). It may take years. It may take decades. Your husband may never actually come to Christ. This verse is not a promise, but a prescription.

Take courage, Missionary, because there are countless missionaries all over the world who live among unsaved people. These missionaries love the unbelievers they live among, live out the gospel before them, and pray for them faithfully— and it can take years or decades till they see someone come to Christ. Sometimes no one is converted, but those missionaries are still pleasing the Lord because they are devoting their lives to living in their mission field. Be faithful. Be consistent. Be diligent in prayer. Joyfully serve the Lord where He has called you, leaving the results to Him.

LESSON 26 WIFE-CHANGING QUESTIONS

1. When you considered Christian couples you know who reflect a gospel-centered marriage, who did you think of? (Consider writing them a letter thanking them for their example.)

_____

_____

_____

_____

2. Explain what it means that marriage is a picture of Christ and the church.

_____

_____

_____

_____

3. How is a wife to be like the church?

_____

_____

_____

_____

4. What can you do in your role as a wife to improve your illustration to the world of how the church relates to Christ?

_____

_____

_____

_____

5. How is a husband to be like Jesus?

_____

_____

_____

_____

6. Write a prayer for your husband to be made more and more into Christ's image, and to be able to reflect Jesus in his role as a husband.

_____

_____

_____

_____

7. What is the strategy the Christian wife is given to win her unbelieving husband to Christ?

_____

_____

_____

_____

LESSON 27

Jesus Must Increase

Out in the desert, John the Baptist had gathered quite a following while baptizing people. When Jesus began His public ministry, many of John's followers left him and began following Jesus. Some of John's disciples saw this and quickly informed John that the people were leaving his group to join Jesus. They likely expected John to be upset or to tell them some kind of strategy to get his followers back.

But that's not what John did at all. In fact, he encouraged this departure from his own following and rejoiced because it was happening. John understood that true joy comes when we magnify Jesus and delight in His exaltation.

John describes himself as the friend of the bridegroom who rejoices that He has come to take His bride. John then says the fact that people are no longer following him, but are following Jesus instead, has brought him nothing but joy. John said, *"Therefore, this joy of mine is now complete. He must increase, but I must decrease"* (John 3:29–30).

John understood that the only way to experience true joy is for Jesus to increase. This principle is true in every area of life, but particularly within a marriage.

What Are You Living For?

Most couples spend their entire lives with their families as the primary focus. About fifty years are spent building their lives around their own relationship and their children, grandchildren, homes, churches, and friendships—the whole focus of their lives is centered around the short time they have together on earth. This "family first" mentality is often proclaimed as a sort of "second gospel" and preached from many pulpits in America. It's a nice idea: focus your life on the people closest to you; get as much happiness and fun out of this life as you possibly can. I smile just thinking about it.

However, happiness is not God's ultimate plan for the Christian family.

When a man asked Jesus what the greatest commandment was, Jesus answered with, "You shall love the Lord your God with all you heart and with all your soul and with all your mind" (Matt. 22:37). In theory, we all can agree that loving God is supreme over all our other loves. But is that our reality? Is loving God the greatest goal in our families? As followers of Jesus, we are called to live a life focused on God's glory, on seeing the lost world around us come to know Him, and to be women who live in a way that both glorifies God and draws others to Him. Are we really, truly living for that?

If all the prayers you prayed over the last year were published in a little book, what would most of those prayers be about? Think about that. Are your prayers mainly geared toward asking God to change people and circumstances so that you and your people can be happier and more comfortable?

What your prayers are centered on reveals what your priorities are.

Honestly, my prayers often reveal that it's not God who is on the throne of my life. I often focus my prayers on my own happiness and my own comfort. I ask for material things for myself so I can be comfortable. Now that's not to say I shouldn't ask God to touch and heal my sick body or provide for my material needs. The Scriptures encourage me to pray about everything. However, I must ask myself: do my prayers stop after I've asked God for what I want for myself?

How often are my prayers being lifted up for the lost world or for the spiritual apathy I see in believers around me? What about my own apathy? How often do I pray for missionaries, for the salvation of my unsaved friends and family, or for my pastors and children's ministry workers? How many times have I asked God to show me how much more I can give of my time and my resources for the furthering of His kingdom? The truth is, I often pray far more for the things that make me comfortable. Oh, how shallow and idolatrous? In reality, I'm often asking God to join me in the worship of myself.

As we move into this final chapter, I want to shift your eyes *off* your marriage and *off* yourself, *because it's really not about your marriage or yourself.*

It's Not about Your Marriage

Many Christian couples put their marriages and families on the thrones of their lives. Their mission in life is to have a happy family. If they can have that, then nothing else really matters. Husbands and wives often give very little attention to the fact they will spend eternity (billions upon billions of years!) with Jesus. While we may believe in eternity, most of us are guilty of living for the temporal. Something is terribly off in our perspective.

> We often hear the phrase "God first, family second" in church circles. While we say it a lot, I don't see how this phrase is actually impacting anyone. Think about it. What if you were to switch to a "family first" mentality? What actions would you really have to change?[3] —Francis Chan

If a "family first" mentality wouldn't change how we live, then we aren't truly putting God first.

Whether or not God is really first in our lives stems from our motivation. Are we seeking to be fulfilled in the temporary human relationships we are blessed with, or are we aiming to be ultimately satisfied in Christ alone?

> The power and impulse to carry through the self-denial—the daily, monthly, yearly, decades-long dying that will be required in loving an imperfect wife and loving an imperfect husband to the glory of God— must come from a hope-giving, soul-sustaining, superior satisfaction in God. Our love for our wives, and theirs for us, will not glorify God until it flows from a heart that delights in God more than marriage. Marriage will be preserved for the glory of God, and shaped for the glory of God, and sweetened for the glory of God when the glory of God is more precious to us than marriage.[4] —John Piper

What Is Your Motivation?

If a woman is seeking to be a godly wife because she wants to glorify God so others might be drawn to Him, then she's truly putting Him first. However, more often than not, women follow the biblical formula for marriage not because they are wanting to please God, but because they are wanting to please themselves. They are banking on the blessings that often come as the paycheck for the work, and their hearts are disappointed when the check is absent or late.

Do you see the difference?

The fighting in Darla's home was only broken by long periods of silence. She decided to attend a marriage class at a local church to see what she could do to make things better. For the three months she attended the class, she diligently applied everything she was taught. She acted submissive, she smiled, she had more sex, and she even started praying.

However, after the class was over, her husband hadn't changed a bit. Darla thought she had done enough to make him change in twelve weeks, but it hadn't worked. She decided all the "Bible stuff" wasn't applicable to her because it hadn't served to make her marriage what she expected it to be.

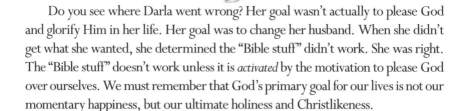

Do you see where Darla went wrong? Her goal wasn't actually to please God and glorify Him in her life. Her goal was to change her husband. When she didn't get what she wanted, she determined the "Bible stuff" didn't work. She was right. The "Bible stuff" doesn't work unless it is *activated* by the motivation to please God over ourselves. We must remember that God's primary goal for our lives is not our momentary happiness, but our ultimate holiness and Christlikeness.

Could You Be Happy without Jesus?

John Piper asks a question that is very sobering:

> The critical question for our generation—and for every generation—is this: If you could have heaven, with no sickness, and with all the friends you ever had on earth, and all the food you ever liked, and all the leisure activities you ever enjoyed, and all the natural beauties you ever saw, all the physical pleasures you ever tasted, and no human conflict or any natural disasters, could you be satisfied with heaven, if Christ were not there?[5]

I want to say I couldn't be satisfied without Jesus, but in reality, my own lack of intimacy with Christ, my own apathy about prayer and sharing the gospel with the lost, and my focus on my own comfort and happiness reveal that I am often quite satisfied without Him.

When faced with this reality, there is nothing for me to do but confess it as sin, repent, and pursue my relationship with Jesus. I long for a renewed zeal and focus to live my life in light of the awesome fact that I will spend eternity with the One who died to save my soul.

Broaden the Focus

On social media, women proudly post photos of their adorable families with captions like, "My whole world" or "The reason I live." While I can appreciate their public declaration of love, according to Scripture, their worlds and reasons for living are in error.

When we look at the entire Bible and see how it all points to the glory of God, we realize structuring our entire lives around our marriages and families is quite shallow.

Look at the bigger picture. Your marriage is only one aspect of your life, and it's not the main aspect. You are not only a wife, or only a mother, or only an employee, or only a church member. You are perhaps all of those things. But they are overwhelmingly eclipsed by the fact that you are a child of God, a follower of Jesus, created for His purposes, and you are designed to bring Him glory.

I am absolutely crazy about my family. I enjoy them immensely, and they are my favorite humans on the planet. However, their happiness is not the supreme goal of my life, nor does their happiness make my life fulfilling. If my kids and my husband were all in a tragic accident and died, I would be devastated. I would grieve and be terribly lonely, but my reason for living would not be gone.

My mission in life would not be thwarted, because I'm not living for my family. My life is about Jesus, and I will never lose Him. Therefore, I will always have a reason to go on. Second Corinthians 5:15 says, *"And He died for all, that those who live might no longer live for themselves but for Him who for their sake died and was raised."*

For You, My King

Remember that Jesus wore a crown. It wasn't a mark of royalty or a crown of honor. Jesus wore a crown of thorns—a crown made to cause Him pain, intended to make Him look ridiculous and to mock who He claimed to be. As Jesus wore that crown, He was beaten, mocked, spit upon, and crucified. For me. For you.

When you are challenged to die to yourself, to give up your rights, to serve your husband when you'd rather serve yourself—whether it be picking up a mess, packing a lunch, or forgiving a horrendous offense, you can look to your Savior—the One who wore the crown of thorns for you—and you can say, "For You, my King!"

When your husband wakes you up at 1:00 a.m. because he can't sleep and wants some "help," you say, "For You, my King!"

When his sister shows up unannounced at dinner time with her four kids, you pull out extra plates, and say, "For You, my King!"

Your husband left the oven on again. Turn it off and don't say anything except, "For You, my King!"

Every opportunity you have to glorify God, no matter how small, is a privilege! Your life is not actually about you, and it's not about your husband. It is not about your marriage or your family. As a Christian, your life is all about Jesus. And the One who wore a crown of thorns and laid down His life to save your soul is entirely worthy of every sacrifice you can make.

LESSON 27 WIFE-CHANGING QUESTIONS

1. In your own words, explain the meaning of the verse, *"He must increase, but I must decrease"* (John 3:30).

   _____

   _____

   _____

   _____

2. How can you specifically be increasing Jesus in your own life right now?

   _____

   _____

   _____

   _____

3. Would you say that loving God with all your heart, soul, and mind is the supreme goal of your family? How is this actually shown in your life?

   _____

   _____

   _____

   _____

4. What other goals are competing with God's goals for your family?

_____

_____

_____

_____

5. What does your current prayer life reveal about the focus of your life?

_____

_____

_____

_____

6. Could you be satisfied with heaven if Christ were not there? If so, write a prayer of confession and repentance, and ask for a renewed passion for knowing Jesus.

_____

_____

_____

_____

7. In what specific circumstances can you incorporate the idea of "For You, my King"?

_____

_____

_____

_____

LESSON 28

The Hero of the Story

Do you remember the Greek mythology story of Narcissus? As the son of a god, Narcissus was extraordinarily handsome and was desired by many. One day, Narcissus came to a pond and bent down to take a drink. Upon seeing his reflection, he fell instantly in love with his own image. He was infatuated with the handsome face looking back at him, and he couldn't bear to take his eyes off himself. Narcissus stayed at the edge of the pond, gazing longingly into his own eyes until he died.

Today when someone is self-absorbed, they are said to be narcissistic. I'm sure you know someone who is entirely in love with themselves, so much that they generally have no thoughts of others, except for how others might be a benefit to them.

Tragically, much of the modern church is promoting a Christian form of narcissism. From pulpits all over the world, churchgoers are being told God is all about them, God exists for their happiness, and that God wants them comfortable, wealthy, and healthy. Christians are taught to use the Bible to comfort themselves, to bring about power and healing to themselves, and to guarantee themselves the best life they can have on this earth.

Many people adopt this form of "Christianity" because it falls right in line with their own thinking that *God is all about me! That's awesome! Cause I'm all about me too! The Bible is all about me? Wow! How can I use it to love myself even more?*

This is *not* the message of the Bible. The Bible is *for* you, but it is not *about* you. It is not a glorified self-help book where you can go for tips on how to have a more satisfying existence. I have been to more than one Bible study where the first question asked after reading a passage of Scripture isn't "What do you learn about God in this passage?" but rather, "How does this apply to you?" While the Scriptures do provide us with clear instruction for ourselves that we desperately need to know and apply, we often miss the bigger picture and focus entirely on ourselves. *The Bible is about God.*

> You search the Scriptures because you think that in them you have eternal life; and it is they that bear witness about Me (John 5:39).

Some children sit in Sunday school classes coloring pictures of biblical figures who are examples of either "the faithfuls" or "the failures." The constant message is "Be like this guy and your life will be better," or "Don't be like this guy and your life will be better," or even "Work harder, make good decisions, and stay out of trouble, and God will bless you."

We have generations of "believers" who have been spoon-fed this "gospel" that says God is all about their happiness and that good boys and girls get to have happy lives. Scores of churchgoers have passed hundreds of Sunday mornings listening to sermons that are all about themselves instead of Jesus. They drive away from their church service enlightened about themselves, while God remains in the shadows. If you don't attend a church where Jesus is glorified above man and where the Word of God is exalted above a typical self-help book, I encourage you to pray about finding a new church. Even Charles Spurgeon gently admonishes:

> Leave Christ out? O my brethren, better leave the pulpit out altogether. If a man can preach one sermon without mentioning Christ's name in it, it ought to be his last, certainly the last that any Christian ought to go to hear him preach. . . . A sermon without Christ in it is like a loaf of bread without any flour in it. No Christ in your sermon, sir? Then go home, and never preach again until you have something worth preaching.[6]

The Bible is a long narrative that all connects and points to Jesus, and it climaxes on His life, death, resurrection, and return. From Genesis to Revelation, we read the glorious truth of one Hero who ultimately wins in the end. The Bible is for you—every promise and truth is yours to claim—but it's not about you. Friends, you are not the hero in the Bible. Jesus is.

Count the Cost

Salvation is absolutely free, and yet it will cost you your life.

That seems like a contradiction, but think about it. The salvation of your soul is offered at no expense. It is a free offer. But taking the offer means you surrender your life to your Savior. You have been bought with a price, and now you belong to the purchaser.

Following Jesus is costly. It will cost you your pride, your rights, your popularity, your wealth, and your comfort. Maybe it won't cost you all of these, but it will cost you something for sure. If it doesn't cost you anything, then you're following the wrong Jesus.

Jesus Himself said we need to count the cost of being His disciple:

> Now great crowds accompanied Him, and He turned and said to them, "If anyone comes to Me and does not hate his own father and mother and wife and children and brothers and sisters, yes, and even his own life, he cannot be My disciple. Whoever does not bear his own cross and come after Me

cannot be My disciple. For which of you, desiring to build a tower, does not first sit down and count the cost, whether he has enough to complete it? Otherwise, when he has laid a foundation and is not able to finish, all who see it begin to mock him, saying, 'This man began to build and was not able to finish.' Or what king, going out to encounter another king in war, will not sit down first and deliberate whether he is able with ten thousand to meet him who comes against him with twenty thousand? And if not, while the other is yet a great way off, he sends a delegation and asks for terms of peace. So therefore, any one of you who does not renounce all that he has cannot be My disciple." (Luke 14:25–33)

Is this the Jesus you are following? Is this what being a disciple of Christ has cost you? Have you renounced all you have and chosen to love your Savior more than you love your family—so much so, that in comparison, your love for Jesus makes your love for your family look like hate?

When the angel came to Mary and told her she was going to be pregnant with the Messiah, it wasn't all good news for Mary. Showing up pregnant when she was supposed to be a virgin wasn't going to earn her any respect from her family or her in-laws. Mary would be unjustly ostracized by her community and labeled as an ungodly woman. Her reputation was at stake, her relationship with Joseph was in jeopardy, and her own goals and plans for her life were canceled by the angel's announcement. Mary could have cried out, "Now wait a minute, God! My family will kill me if I show up pregnant! I have a wedding coming up. Joseph and I have decided to wait two years to have kids. I have my own plans!"

Yet Mary didn't protest at all. She embraced this call on her life by saying, *"Behold, I am the servant of the Lord; let it be to me according to your word"* (Luke 1:38). Obeying God's calling on her life cost Mary everything, but she was willing to pay that price.

Sisters, are you willing to echo Mary's declaration? Can you respond to God's calling on your life to be a helper to your husband by saying, "Behold, I am the servant of the Lord. Let it be to me according to your word"? May this be the heart cry of every wife!

Take Up Your Cross

If anyone would to come after Me, he must deny himself and take up his cross daily and follow Me. (Luke 9:23)

This verse is cited six different times in the gospels.

> For whoever would save his life will lose it, but whoever loses his life for My
> sake and the gospel's will save it. (Mark 8:35)

This verse appears in three of the gospels.

Again and again the gospel informs us that following Jesus means denying yourself, taking up your cross, and losing your life.

Jesus told His disciples that anyone who wanted to follow Him would have to take up his or her cross. Today we wear crosses around our necks and display them on our walls as beautiful decorations that remind us of Christ's sacrifice. However, in Jesus's day, crosses were not decorative items. Neither were they sources of minor irritation or inconvenience. A cross was an instrument of execution that caused a slow, torturous death. When Jesus told His disciples to take up their cross, He was essentially saying that being His followers means we willingly sign up for our own slow executions.

Dietrich Bonhoeffer said, "When Christ calls a man, he bids him come and die."[7] What cross are you bearing for the gospel in your life right now? If there is no death to yourself, no sacrifice of personal ambition, and no struggle to lay down your rights, then you should question whether you are really a disciple.

> But whatever things were gain to me, those things I have counted as loss for
> the sake of Christ. More than that, I count all things to be loss in view of the
> surpassing value of knowing Christ Jesus my Lord, for whom I have suffered
> the loss of all things, and count them but rubbish so that I may gain Christ.
> (Phil. 3:7–8)

Superficial or Sacrificial?

Many churches today are filled with superficial followers of Christ. They fill stadiums on Sundays to listen to brilliant speeches on the love of God and the power available to them to live better lives. They leave excited to "follow Jesus" in order to fulfill their own dreams.

There were crowds who superficially followed Jesus when He walked the earth too. Large crowds chased after His miracles, hoping they could get one for themselves. Consider the following verses:

> And a large crowd was following Him, because they saw the signs that He
> was doing on the sick. When the people saw the sign that He had done,
> they said, "This is indeed the Prophet who is to come into the world!" (John
> 6:2,14)

Jesus was a popular celebrity who had a huge following, but He wasn't fooled by the fan club.

> Now when He was in Jerusalem at the Passover Feast, many believed in His name when they saw the signs that He was doing. But Jesus on His part did not entrust Himself to them, because He knew all people and needed no one to bear witness about man, for He Himself knew what was in man. (John 2:23–25)

The crucifixion weeded out the superficial followers from the sacrificial ones. The enormous crowds who superficially worshipped Jesus as a celebrity when they could get something from Him were not big fans when He was brutally murdered. After the resurrection, those who chose to follow Jesus abandoned their previous occupations and positions and sacrificially lived for Him through intense persecution. Their discipleship was costly.

So what about you? Are you superficially or sacrificially living for Jesus?

In our current American culture, we don't yet face radical persecution for our faith, so we might be tempted to think this cost of discipleship mentality is overemphasized. While you may not have a grand opportunity to die to yourself, your everyday life presents plenty of little opportunities to lay down your life. That is especially true in marriage.

When you have a chance to die and you take it, successfully killing your flesh, then you reflect Christ. Dying to self actually causes your life to bring Christ glory. Even if it's something as small as picking up your husband's socks, not answering back sarcastically, or making love to him when you'd rather sleep—all of these "small deaths" are opportunities to be a true disciple who daily picks up her cross and follows her Savior.

My demanding of my rights, living for my own comfort, and seeking my own glory—these all need to die. For Jesus to continually increase in my life and my marriage, I must choose to die more and more. As John 3:30 reminds us, *"He must increase, but I must decrease."*

> If you are ever going to have a marriage of unity, understanding, and love, you have to be willing to fight daily, but not with your spouse. You need to be committed to fighting with your self. You need to be committed to fighting against the powerful draw of your self focus. You need to fight the instinct to indulge those boiling emotions and powerful cravings. You need to exegete your desires, corral your motives, critique your thoughts, and edit your words. You need to battle until your litany of "I want" becomes a joyful list of "I would be glad to's."[8] —Paul David Tripp

LESSON 28 WIFE-CHANGING QUESTIONS

1. Can you think of any examples of narcissistic Christianity?

   _____

   _____

   _____

   _____

2. Since becoming a follower of Jesus, in what ways have you been called to "pick up your cross?" What have you sacrificed for the sake of the gospel?

   _____

   _____

   _____

   _____

3. Prayerfully consider whether you can identify yourself as a superficial or sacrificial follower of Jesus. Give the reasons for your answer.

   _____

   _____

   _____

   _____

4. What "small deaths" are you currently being called to in this season of your life?

_____

_____

_____

_____

5. How are these "small deaths" transforming you more into Christ's image?

_____

_____

_____

_____

6. Was there anything particularly impacting or insightful for you in this lesson?

_____

_____

_____

_____

CROWN

LESSON 29

Is There Oil in Your Lamp?

Most people do not get engaged and married on the same day. There are some who elope, but the majority of couples have a period between the engagement and the wedding when they plan for their wedding day and prepare to live together as husband and wife. In Jesus's day, there was a similar period of waiting. However, it was the groom who went off and prepared the wedding feast for his bride. The bride would not know the exact day or time the groom would commence the celebration. She would make herself ready and wait with her friends in excited anticipation for the groom to come and take her to the celebration.

Similarly, as the church, we are living in the period between the engagement and the wedding. Jesus spoke a parable about this period of time in Matthew 25:1–13:

> Then the kingdom of heaven will be like ten virgins who took their lamps and went to meet the bridegroom. Five of them were foolish, and five were wise. For when the foolish took their lamps, they took no oil with them, but the wise took flasks of oil with their lamps. As the bridegroom was delayed, they all became drowsy and slept. But at midnight there was a cry, "Here is the bridegroom! Come out to meet him." Then all those virgins rose and trimmed their lamps. And the foolish said to the wise, "Give us some of your oil, for our lamps are going out." But the wise answered, saying, "Since there will not be enough for us and for you, go rather to the dealers and buy for yourselves." And while they were going to buy, the bridegroom came, and those who were ready went in with him to the marriage feast, and the door was shut. Afterward the other virgins came also, saying, "Lord, lord, open to us." But he answered, "Truly, I say to you, I do not know you." Watch therefore, for you know neither the day nor the hour.

There are ten virgins, five wise and five foolish. They are expected to be ready to meet the groom when he comes with brightly shining lamps to provide light for all who come to the feast. However, half the virgins brought lamps with no oil (think of it like lamps with no light bulbs or candles with no wicks).

The oil in the lamps of the virgins is symbolic of the Holy Spirit dwelling inside of the believer. It is only a truly born-again believer who has the Holy Spirit. These ten women all together represent the church. Some people within the church are brightly shining lights, and they have a source of fuel, or power to keep their lamps burning. There are others who might physically be in church with the appearance of looking to meet their groom, but have no way to produce the light that the wedding feast requires. These have outward religion, but no internal power.

As they are all sleeping, an announcement is made that the bridegroom has come! The virgins start bustling to get ready to meet him, and *all* of the waiting women trim their lamps,

Consider this. The five unprepared virgins outwardly pretend they are ready— they trim empty lamps, symbolically going through the motions but having no real power. Seeing their folly, they ask the impossible. They ask the wise women to share some of their oil. The fact that the five wise virgins won't give them any oil is not meant to teach selfishness, but to teach the impossibility of borrowing faith. The foolish virgins thought they could perhaps borrow the power they needed at the last minute, but borrowing oil from someone else is not possible. Each person is responsible to have their own. John Piper explains the account of the ten virgins is meant to teach the impossibility of borrowing the power of the Holy Spirit—the impossibility of borrowing obedience and faithfulness.

> It's too late. That is what we will see. What the wise virgins mean when they say in verse 9, "There won't be enough for both of us, go buy your own oil," is this: We can't have faith for you and for us. We can't have inner spiritual life for you and for us. We can't give you obedience and the faithful use of God-appointed means. If you neglect them, in this life, we can't create them for you. Each one bears his own load. So in desperation the foolish virgins, who wasted their lives, ran for the impossible: instant end-time obedience. Instant end-time faith.[9]

These foolish virgins hear terrifying words from the bridegroom when they try to enter the wedding feast: "Truly, I say to you, I do not know you." Outwardly, they could convince people they had everything they needed to meet the groom; however, when the groom came, the truth about what was really in their lamps was revealed. All their outward performance could not cover up the fact that there was no real power—no lifesaving faith—in their lamps.

Jesus ends His parable by saying to the hearers, "Watch therefore, for you know neither the day nor the hour." This is an exhortation to those in the church to be ready! This parable was given by Jesus to cause people to take careful spiritual inventory and to be absolutely sure they were not merely practicing outward religion, but, that they were walking in genuine faith.

It is impossible to live in obedience to God's Word apart from the power of the Holy Spirit. We simply can't do it in our own strength. We are entirely dependent on Him to be the wives He is calling us to be.

The Bridegroom *Will* Come!

I hope every woman reading this book is an oil-toting believer; however, we all know people who are falsely assured they are going to meet the bridegroom based on their owning a lamp. Perhaps if some of the wise virgins had pointed out to the foolish virgins that their lamps were actually empty, the foolish virgins would have been able to get their own oil before the groom came!

If you know someone like the five foolish virgins, I encourage you to pray for them faithfully and to seek opportunities to earnestly warn them of their lack of saving faith. Be a light that burns so brightly for Jesus, your Groom, that others become keenly aware of their own lack of oil. You are the light of the world. Let your light shine for your Groom.

Happily Ever After

When we plan a wedding, we don't just throw it together and hope for the best. We spend hours making decisions about every detail. We want our wedding day to reflect ourselves—our tastes, our style, and our love. It typically takes months to plan a wedding. Then the big day finally comes, the celebration commences, and the party is all over in about four hours. All that planning and preparation goes into one four-hour party.

One of the perks of being married to a pastor is getting to go to a lot of weddings. I am so amazed at the creativity and variety. In the last few years, I have been to several weddings: a bohemian-themed wedding where the bride and bridesmaids were barefoot, a country wedding where everyone wore boots, a fairy-tale style wedding, and a super-formal wedding with a harpist and elegant ice sculptures. I have also attended several traditional-style weddings that were all entirely lovely.

Weddings today are diverse, and there are endless possibilities! Unlike the unlimited wedding-planning tools of today, when I got married, the only resources were bridal magazines and some local wedding expos. I seriously think women who got married before the internet should get a do-over wedding!

But guess what? I *am* going to have another wedding! And my next wedding will be more stunning and amazing than my first one or anyone else's wedding has ever been. My Groom, Jesus, is planning the whole thing, and it will be a fantastic, marvelous surprise to see it on that day. What I do know is I will be entirely radiant, spotlessly clean, free of wrinkles and blemishes, and clothed in pure, bright white linen. I will see my Groom, and I will be united to Him forever. The thought of this is thrilling to me and my heart aches for that day to come.

If you are a follower of Jesus, then you'll be there too. You'll also be the bride wearing white. Every believer will be attending the marriage supper of the Lamb—the greatest wedding ceremony and reception ever orchestrated—and *we* will be the bride.

The wedding to come will not be all about the bride like our weddings on earth. This wedding will be all about the Groom:

> Then I [John] heard what seemed to be the voice of a great multitude, like the roar of many waters and like the sound of mighty peals of thunder, crying out,
>
> "Hallelujah! For the Lord our God the Almighty reigns. Let us rejoice and exult and give Him the glory, for the marriage of the Lamb has come, and his Bride has made herself ready; it was granted her to clothe herself with fine linen, bright and pure"—for the fine linen is the righteous deeds of the saints.
>
> And the angel said to me, "Write this: Blessed are those who are invited to the marriage supper of the Lamb." And he said to me, "These are the true words of God." (Rev. 19:6–9)

This is the wedding God has been preparing for you. Are you getting yourself ready? Your life on earth is pointing to whether you are looking forward to your eternal marriage or whether you are living your earthly one. Are you living your life for your earthly groom or your heavenly Groom?

> So before the end of human history when the Savior and Judge will return to save and to judge, you were born. You are now called by God to showcase the power of His Holy Spirit by the way you live. Your mission is to do this until He calls you home or returns to end human history, and you will then be rewarded—by the God who created you, the Son who died for you, and the Spirit who empowered you—for giving the world an accurate picture of His love. All of this culminates in the marriage of the Lamb, where you will join every believer throughout all time as the bride and be married to the only true King, with whom you will live and reign throughout all eternity.[3] —Francis Chan

Jesus is engaged to His bride—the people who follow Him from every tribe and race and nation. He came the first time to die for His bride, to pay a sort of dowry with His own blood. He will come a second time to marry her, the church.

This should fill us with intense longing! Oh, to see our heavenly Groom! We will *behold* Him! Just think of it! Our real "happily ever after" is coming! It is really, really going to happen! Are you ready?

Fellow bride of Christ, I want to assure you that whatever you endure in this life, will all be *worth it* when you behold your Groom. He will fulfill every dream you have ever had. He will be the perfect husband. You will live in absolute bliss for all eternity. This life will seem shorter than a four-hour wedding reception in light of eternity. Fix your eyes on your heavenly Groom. Live this life entirely for Him and for His glory. Your own "happily ever after" is promised by God Himself.

LESSON 29 WIFE-CHANGING QUESTIONS

1. In examining your own life, is it possible you are like one of the foolish virgins who is outwardly living like a Christian but lacking genuine, saving faith?

_____

_____

_____

_____

2. Do you know someone who is like one of the foolish virgins? Write out a prayer for that person.

_____

_____

_____

_____

3. Take a few moments to think about what it will be like when you behold Jesus—your bridegroom—for the first time. What are you most excited about when you think of this?

_____

_____

_____

_____

4. Are there any wife-changes you need to make to be more ready for your Groom when He comes?

_____

_____

_____

_____

LESSON 30

Don't Just Be Convicted—Do Something!

Acts is the book of the Bible that tells us what happened immediately after Jesus's ascension. This title is significant. The early disciples of Jesus had seen His miracles, they had witnessed the crucifixion, and they were confronted with their risen Savior. Did they then all sit in church pews and discuss what this all meant, attend seminars about these issues, and break into different schools of thought on them?

No! They *acted* on these things! They moved! They responded by *doing* something!

You will have wasted the last few weeks reading this book if you only feel convicted and then stay exactly where you are.

> But be doers of the word, and not hearers only, deceiving yourselves. (James 1:22)

The church is full of believers who are filled with conviction but no doing. Don't allow yourself to hear the truths of the Scriptures and not be moved into action.

Be a Frog, Not a Tadpole

A few years ago, I was on vacation with my family, and I took a hike along a stream with my youngest son. We came to an area of still water and discovered dozens of giant bullfrog tadpoles. Like any normal ten-year-old boy, Seth begged me to let him catch some and take them home. And like any good homeschool mom, I jumped at the chance to do a free science project. So we caught eight tadpoles and brought them home in a jar.

We put them in an old fish tank we had in the garage and figured that over the next few weeks we would watch them grow legs and turn into frogs, and we would send them out into the world to catch flies and make more tadpoles. Because that's what frogs are supposed to do, right?

After a month of feeding those little slimy things, not one of them had grown legs. After two months, still no change. Three, four, five months—no change. Six, seven, eight months—still no change. I daily fed them tadpole pellets and changed the water in their tank, and after eight whole months, they were still just bigger, slimy black fish, knocking into each other with their fat heads in that tank.

We left on a mission trip, and while we were gone, their caregiver was not diligent, and all the tadpoles died. I flushed their fat, slimy bodies and as I cleaned out their empty tank, I started thinking about how their whole lives were such a waste. Those silly tadpoles never grew up and they never got out of the tank. They never went and made more tadpoles, and they missed the whole point of being bullfrogs.

I thought about how that parallels the lives of many believers in the church today. How many churches are filled with tadpole Christians?—people who sit in the pews month after month. They go to conferences and retreats and attend small-group Bible studies for decades. They know the Bible inside and out, but they never act on what they know. They don't get out of the church and make disciples. They just hang around the church, bumping into each other with their fat heads full of knowledge, and they lose their whole purpose for being Christians in the first place.

Christian Sister, you now have a head full of knowledge about how to have a marriage that glorifies God. But that knowledge is absolutely useless if you don't put it into action.

Now it's time to do something with what you know.

Move into the Promised Land

After the children of Israel had been brought out of bondage and then were organized, given roles, and provided with the tools they needed to accomplish those roles, it would have been natural for them to think they were then totally ready to enter into the Promised Land.

> One would be tempted to think that after such extensive preparation—a virtual transformation from slave people to Promised Land people—the actual entering into the Promised Land would be easy. This was not the case. The preparation was exactly that—preparation. Ahead of them are the greatest challenges, challenges that can only be met by faith. A soldier might think boot camp finishes something—but it doesn't. It only prepares for a greater challenge: The actual battle itself.[10] —David Guzik

What you actually end up *doing* with what God has shown you on this journey will be different than what your girlfriend does. However, you are both called to action. If you have been convicted by things you have read in these pages, don't be resistant to what the Holy Spirit wants to do in you. He only brings your faults to light because He loves you and doesn't want your growth to be stunted like my son's poor tadpoles.

You've been instructed by God so you can do something with that instruction. Begin walking in obedience to the things God has revealed to you. You might not do everything exactly right; in fact, I can guarantee you'll stumble along the way. But to do nothing after you've been instructed to do something will be a gross failure. Better to do something feebly than to do nothing at all.

It's Not Going to Be Easy

In the book of Numbers, when the Israelites sent spies in to check out the Promised Land, they came back and announced that the land was indeed flowing with milk and honey—all God had said about it was true—*but* there were mighty people in the land. Ten of the twelve spies convinced the people the giants were proof that they would be better off going back into slavery in Egypt. The Israelites mourned that they had ever been delivered from slavery because they saw things were not going to be easy. They expected to just have the good life God had promised, but not have to do any work or fight any battles to get it.

We can be tempted to be just like those Israelites, looking at the promised land of a God-glorifying marriage, but when we realize there are giants to face— that it's going to be a long battle and a lot of hard work—we end up thinking we would have been better off never seeing the possibilities in the first place.

Those Israelites ended up wandering in the desert till they all died. What a tragedy! God had wanted to give them everything, but they only wanted it if it was going to be easy. They missed out on living in the land flowing with milk and honey, and they moved from place to place for the rest of their lives. The same can happen to us if we are unwilling to engage in the battle and put in the work it will take to obtain the life God has called us to live.

When you get to heaven, you will get to rest. Until then, work hard. Labor for what God has for you. Fight your many battles with the right weapons against the right enemy. Arrive in heaven exhausted because you lived your whole life working to please God. It won't be easy, but it will be absolutely worth every effort.

More than Fried Chicken

I once went to a memorial for a friend's mother. In the span of ninety minutes, several family members got up to speak about the deceased woman. The most anyone had to say about her was she was a fantastic cook—she made incredible fried chicken—and her house was always spotless. It was one of the most depressing services I've ever attended, and it made me wonder what my friends would actually say about me if I died. Would there be more to mention than fried chicken and a clean kitchen floor?

You get one life. Just one span of around eighty years to live out a life intended to glorify God. Depending on how old you are, you either have a few years or a few decades left. What is God calling you to use those years for? I guarantee it's not just to enjoy yourself, make fried chicken, and clean your house. What are you going to do with the years you have left that will leave a lasting legacy that glorifies God and causes others to want to know Jesus?

You Won't Be Sorry

When you get to heaven and the wedding feast commences, you won't be at all sorry that you chose to die to yourself on earth. You won't be wishing you had won those arguments, you had trained your husband to pick up after himself, or that you convinced your husband the thermostat should be set at a certain temperature. You won't be wishing that you would have demanded your rights, hung on to bitterness, withheld sex, or any other thing that might be tripping you up today.

Things might not get better on your husband's side. He could possibly remain exactly as he is till death do you part. However, if you do all these things with the goal to please and honor your Groom, Jesus, then it will be worth it in eternity.

When you see your Groom, when you look into Jesus's eyes, you will realize that a thousand lives would not be enough to give to Him. You will see Him in His glory, and you will realize that any hint of pride, or unforgiveness, or jealousy, or selfishness was absurd. Let us be women who begin to adopt this heavenly perspective now.

Jesus must increase; I must decrease.

LESSON 30 WIFE-CHANGING QUESTIONS

1. What specifically have you been called to do in response to what you have learned in this book?

_____

_____

_____

_____

2. How are you going to walk in obedience to this calling?

_____

_____

_____

_____

3. Have you asked to be filled with the Holy Spirit so you can be empowered to live out all that God has called you to be as a Christian woman? If not, then write a prayer asking for this guaranteed gift.

_____

_____

_____

_____

4. Are you in need of a fresh filling of the Holy Spirit? (Your answer should always be an emphatic Yes! to this question.) Write out a prayer asking for the Holy Spirit to give you the power you need to walk in obedience and be a bold witness for Christ in the world.

_____

_____

_____

_____

Crown

What man wears a crown? Only one of great importance or royalty. Without the symbol of authority on his head, he would be seen as just an ordinary man. It is his crown that displays the truth about his position.

You are called by God to be a crown to your husband, to tell the world you are married to a man of honor. By your behavior, you announce whether he is just an ordinary man or an extraordinary one. We began our study by looking at Proverbs 12:4: "The excellent wife is a crown to her husband." As we have gone through the Scriptures together, I hope you have come to realize that being an excellent wife is all about seeking to honor and obey God. If you make being a wife all about your relationship with God, then you will naturally be a crown to your husband.

A wife who is a crown to her husband is rare, and "an excellent wife who can find? She is far more precious than jewels" (Prov. 31:10).

Be an excellent wife. Be a crown to your husband.

Your Own Crown Awaits

Do you realize that when you choose to honor God this way, you will actually be gaining a crown of your own? It's absolutely amazing that God not only gives us salvation from hell, His guidance in this life, and the sure hope of an eternal heaven—but wait . . . there's more—you also get your own crown in heaven!

> Henceforth there is laid up for me the *crown of righteousness,* which the Lord, the righteous judge, will award to me on that Day, and not only to me but also to all who have loved His appearing. (2 Tim. 4:8, emphasis added)

> Blessed is the man who remains steadfast under trial, for when he has stood the test he will receive the *crown of life,* which God has promised to those who love Him. (James 1:12, emphasis added)

> And when the chief Shepherd appears, you will receive the unfading *crown of glory.* (1 Peter 5:4, emphasis added)

There are crowns waiting for you in heaven! Whether these are literal headpieces, or figurative crowns, the idea is there is real reward waiting for you in eternity. As you aim to be an excellent wife who crowns her husband, remember you are simultaneously attaining your crown in heaven. Jesus told us to store up for ourselves treasures in heaven. Keep working on that crown!

> Do you not know that those who run in a race all run, but one receives the prize? Run in such a way that you may obtain it. And everyone who

competes for the prize is temperate in all things. Now they do it to obtain
a perishable crown, but we for an imperishable crown. (1 Cor. 9:24–25)

Here's the thing about that heavenly crown: We read in Revelation 4:10 that
there are twenty-four elders gathered around the throne of God, and they take
their crowns off and cast them before the throne of God and worship Him, saying,
"Worthy are You, our Lord and God, to receive glory and honor and power."

There is no verse stating every believer will cast their crown before God's
throne in heaven. But I sure hope I get to cast my crown at His feet, because
everything I have in heaven is because of Jesus anyway.

I know a woman who went on a mission trip and met a poor young widow
who had no means of supporting herself. The woman was barely able to feed her
two small daughters and was entirely dependent on charity from the church,
because in her culture, she could not go get a job to support herself.

When she got home, the missionary went to a jeweler and sold her wedding
ring (with her husband's full support) and sent the money to the young widow so
she could buy a house and land and support herself. The missionary said, "What
good are thousands of dollars doing on my finger when it could be helping a widow
to live? I honestly wish I had a hundred wedding rings to sell so I could help a
hundred widows. Giving up my own little treasure is nothing compared to what
Jesus has done for me!"

May this be the heart we all have in heaven when it comes to any crowns we
might receive. Do it for the crown, if only because it will be one more thing you
can give back to Jesus. I hope we each have hundreds of crowns so we can cast
them at the feet of Jesus and worship Him. He alone is worthy.

Crown Notes
Yield

1. Charles H. Spurgeon, *Morning and Evening* (Crossway: Wheaton IL, 2003).
2. Charles H. Spurgeon, *Morning and Evening* (Crossway: Wheaton IL, 2003).
3. Paul David Tripp, *What Did You Expect?* (Crossway: Wheaton, IL, 2010).
4. Paul David Tripp, *What Did You Expect?* (Crossway: Wheaton, IL, 2010).
5. Elisabeth Elliot, *Let Me Be a Woman* (Tyndale Momentum: Carol Stream, IL, 1999).
6. Nancy Leigh DeMoss, *Lies Women Believe* (Moody Press: Chicago, IL, 2001).
7. Paul David Tripp, *What Did You Expect?* (Crossway: Wheaton, IL, 2010).
8. Charles H. Spurgeon, *Morning and Evening* (Crossway: Wheaton, IL, 2003).

Help

1. David Guzik, *Study Guide for Ephesians* 6, blueletterbible.org.
2. John MacArthur, "What Is the Helmet of Salvation?," July 6, 2018, gty.org.
3. Paul David Tripp, *What Did You Expect?* (Crossway: Wheaton, IL, 2010).
4. David Guzik, *Study Guide for Ephesians* 5, blueletterbible.org.
5. Martin Lloyd-Jones, David Guzik's *Study Guide for Ephesians* 5, blueletterbible.org.
6. Elisabeth Elliot, *Let Me Be a Woman* (Tyndale Momentum: Carol Stream, IL, 1999).

Smile

1. Charles H. Spurgeon, "The Swiftly Running Word," a sermon, July 3, 1881.
2. Paul David Tripp, *What Did You Expect?* (Crossway: Wheaton, IL, 2010).
3. Vermon Pierre, *"Forgiveness Is a Marathon,"* August 12, 2015, thegospelcoalition.org.
4. Matt Walsh, "Your Husband Doesn't Have to Earn Your Respect," themattwalshblog.com.
5. Elisabeth Elliot, *Let Me Be a Woman* (Tyndale Momentum: Carol Stream, IL, 1999).
6. Nancy Leigh DeMoss, *Lies Women Believe* (Moody Press: Chicago, IL, 2001).

Order

1. Elisabeth Elliot, *Let Me Be a Woman* (Tyndale Momentum: Carol Stream, IL, 1999).
2. David Guzik, *Study Guide for Numbers* 2, blueletterbible.org.
3. Wendy Speake, "Pray First—Ask Questions Later," wendyspeake.com.
4. Nancy Leigh DeMoss, *Lies Women Believe* (Moody Press: Chicago, IL, 2001).
5. Elisabeth Elliot, *Let Me Be a Woman* (Tyndale Momentum: Carol Stream, IL, 1999).
6. John Piper, "What Is Your Aim?," desiringgod.org.
7. Elisabeth Elliot, *Secure in the Everlasting Arms* (Vine Books, 2002).
8. Lysa Terkeurst, *The Best Yes: Making Wise Decisions in the Midst of Endless Demands* (Thomas Nelson: Nashville, TN, 2014).

Gift

1. John Piper, "Sex and the Single Person," Feb. 1, 1981, desiringgod.org.

Increase

1. John Piper, "Marriage: A Matrix of Christian Hedonism," Oct. 16, 1983, desiringgod.org.

2. Randy Alcorn, *Heaven* (Tyndale House: Carol Stream, IL, 2004).

3. Francis and Lisa Chan, *You and Me Forever* (Claire Love Publishing: San Francisco, CA, 2014).

4. John Piper, "Love Her More, Love Her Less," April 11, 2016, desiringgod.org.

5. John Piper, *God Is the Gospel: Meditations on God's Love as the Gift of Himself* (Crossway: Wheaton, IL, 2005), 15.

6. Charles H. Spurgeon, "Sermon #768," undated.

7. Dietrich Bonhoeffer, *The Cost of Discipleship* (Touchstone, 1937).

8. Paul David Tripp, *What Did You Expect?* (Crossway: Wheaton, IL, 2010).

9. John Piper, "Jesus Christ, the Bridegroom, Past and Future," April 4, 2004, desiringgod.org.

10. David Guzik, *Study Guide for Numbers 10*, blueletterbible.org.

Order Information

To order additional copies of this book, please visit:

www.nancykaser.com

www.redemption-press.com

Also available on www.Amazon.com and www.BarnesandNoble.com
Or by calling toll free 1-844-2REDEEM